MW01618612

JEWISH
LIVING
SIMPLY EXPLAINED

## OTHER BOOKS BY RABBI ZALMAN GOLDSTEIN

Going Kosher In 30 Days!
The Brit Milah Companion
The Friday Evening Synagogue Companion
The High Holiday Synagogue Companion
The Jewish Mourner's Companion
The Jewish Wedding Companion
The Junior Congregation Synagogue Companion
The Kotel Siddur
The Passover Seder Table Companion
The Rabbi's Companion
The Shabbat Synagogue Companion
The Shabbat Table Companion
The Sultan's Trap and Other Miraculous Tales

## OTHER BOOKS BY RABBI MICHOEL A. SELIGSON

Annotated Hayom Yom (Hebrew)
Chassidic Insights and Directives for the Holidays (Hebrew)
Collection on Grace After Meals (Hebrew)
Collection on the Celebration of 19 Kislev (Hebrew)
Collection on the Mystical Chain of Creation (Hebrew)
Complete Index to the Rebbe's Journals (Hebrew)
Complete Index to the Rebbe's Talks (Hebrew)
Customs of the Chabad Rebbes on Shabbat (Hebrew)
The Life of Reb Avrohom, the Doctor, Seligson (Hebrew)

## PRAISE FOR
# JEWISH LIVING
## SIMPLY EXPLAINED

"FINALLY! RABBIS GOLDSTEIN AND SELIGSON have created an amazingly clear and comprehensive work that introduces people from all walks of life to the wisdom of Chabad Chassidut, one that can serve as a wonderful resource for every home, school, and Chabad House worldwide." — ***Rabbi Manis Friedman, world-renowned Chassidic scholar, author, and lecturer, and dean of the Bais Chana Institute of Jewish Studies***

"THERE'S A LOT OF WISDOM packed into this well-written and clearly organized book. One can read it straight-through or use it as a reference book. Regardless of one's beliefs or current level of religious observance, *"Jewish Living Simply Explained"* relates a pure and unique perspective on mankind's relationship with the Almighty and the world, offering moral and spiritual insights that will inspire and uplift anyone who reads it." —***Rabbi Simon Jacobson, Chassidic scholar, author of "Toward a Meaningful Life," and dean of The Meaningful Life Center***

"Einstein is reputed to have said, 'Everything should be made as simple as possible, but not simpler.' In clear precise language, Rabbis Goldstein and Seligson, two ardent and profound students of Chassidut, convey a great deal of valuable information about Judaism—and do so on page after page. The reader will learn a lot, and no less important, have a wonderful time while doing so." ***—Rabbi Joseph Telushkin, author of "Rebbe" and "Jewish Literacy"***

"JEWISH LIVING SIMPLY EXPLAINED is the most concise, eloquent, and broad guide about Jewish life and belief through the lens of Chabad teachings ever produced in English. It is beautifully and clearly presented, and represents a priceless resource for anyone interested in the basics of Chabad philosophy." —***Rabbi Lawrence Kelemen, author of "Permission to Believe" and "Permission to Receive"***

"MANY PEOPLE KNOW what Chabad Chassidim look like; not many know about their about their approach to Jewish life and belief. In this volume, Rabbis Zalman Goldstein and Michael A. Seligson set forth the essence of Jewish Living from a Chabad perspective. The result is an easy-to-read guide that curious folks of every kind may learn from and appreciate." ***—Professor Jonathan D. Sarna, University Professor and Joseph H. & Belle R. Braun Professor of American Jewish History, Brandeis University***

"THIS BEAUTIFULLY WRITTEN BOOK is a description of the history, ideas and practices of traditional Judaism as seen from the perspective of Chabad Chassidism. It shows how Chabad teachings infuse spiritual significance into the life of a Jew and can therefore serve as a guide to those seeking a Jewish life of meaning and true religious connection." ***—Professor Lawrence H. Schiffman, Ph.D., NYU professor of Hebrew and Judaic Studies, prolific author, and expert on the history of Jewish law and Talmudic literature***

"AS BEFITTING ITS NAME, Chabad [*Chochma*, *Binah*, *Daat*] Chassidut is a deep and profound source of Jewish wisdom. Rooted in the depths of Kabbalah, it also strives to bring the esoteric down to earth and to translate the ethereal into practical guidance for living as a Jew and indeed as a human being. *"Jewish Living Simply Explained"* brilliantly encapsulates both the essential theoretical teachings and their practical applications in a manner that is accessible and helpful to people at all levels of Jewish learning. It also provides detailed sources for further study. A wonderful work that I recommend highly." ***—Rabbi Dr. Yitzchak Breitowitz, rabbinic scholar, prolific author, and renowned lecturer on Jewish law and ethics***

"THERE IS NO JEWISH ORGANIZATION in our time that is touching Jews—and non-Jews—as effectively as Chabad. If you want to know what Chabad believes about almost any issue—religious or secular, Rabbis Goldstein and Seligson have done you great service. They have distilled Chabad teachings on myriad subjects into over 150 single-page descriptions. It's like a concise 'Encyclopedia Chabadiana.'" ***—Dennis Prager, bestselling author, columnist, and nationally syndicated radio talk show host.***

"JEWISH LIVING SIMPLY EXPLAINED is a veritable 'Wikipedia' of Chabad thought—the first 'go-to' source for understanding an aspect of Jewish living or learning through the wisdom of Chassidic thinking. It will give the beginner a starting point for further discussion with a Rabbi or Rebbetzin. And it will prove just as useful to a Rabbi or Rebbetzin looking for a practical and simple way to introduce a new concept to a student. Each topic is explained in a way that allows it to be easily applied to daily life. For the instructor, the collection of references alone justifies the cost of the book." ***—Chana Silberstein, Ph.D., Director of Education at the Roitman Chabad Center, Cornell University, and educational consultant for the Rohr Jewish Learning Institute (JLI)***

"A WONDERFUL RESOURCE for every Jewish home. The breadth of subjects treated in this deceptively small, yet masterful work is simply staggering!" ***—Rabbi Shais Taub, acclaimed Chassidic mentor, author, and teacher of Jewish mysticism***

# JEWISH LIVING
## SIMPLY EXPLAINED

BASED ON TEACHINGS
OF THE REBBES OF CHABAD

RABBI ZALMAN GOLDSTEIN
RABBI MICHOEL A. SELIGSON

# JEWISH LIVING SIMPLY EXPLAINED

Based on the Teachings of the Rebbes of Chabad

Rabbi Zalman Goldstein • Rabbi Michoel A. Seligson

FIRST PRINTING

The Jewish Learning Group
1-(888)-56-LEARN
www.JewishLearningGroup.com

ISBN 978-1-891293-29-0

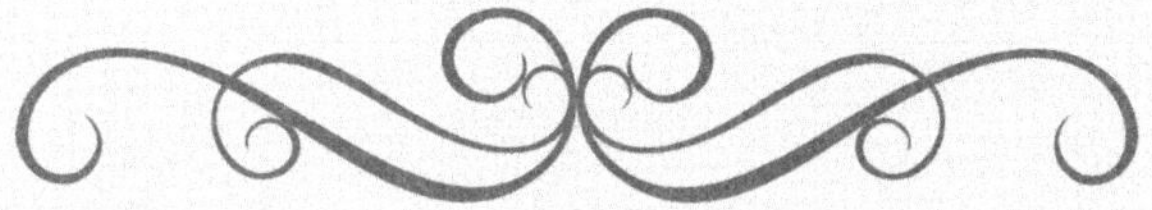

*Dedicated in Memory of*

**Rabbi Yosef and Chana Goldstein**

of blessed memory

---

*This project was generously supported by*

**Mr. & Mrs. Golan and Yocheved Leah Ben-Oni**

In Honor of R' Moshe Shuchat, Rabbi Shaya Gansbourg, and Rabbi Gedalia Shaffer, of blessed memory

# Table of Contents

Introduction ..... 15
How to Use this Book ..... 19

## CREATION

Creation ..... 22
The World ..... 23
Creation in Six Days ..... 24
Age of the Universe ..... 25
Time ..... 26
Stars and Planets ..... 27
Worldly Upheavals ..... 28

## JEWISH HISTORY

Jewish History ..... 30
Our Patriarchs ..... 31
The Giving of the Torah ..... 32
The Land of Israel ..... 33
The Holy Temple ..... 34
Kohen, Levi, Yisrael ..... 35
Sacrifices ..... 36
Exile ..... 37

Dispersion ..... 38
Moshiach ..... 39

## TORAH & MITZVOT

The Torah ..... 42
The Oral Torah ..... 43
Mitzvot ..... 44
Jewish Customs ..... 45
Free Choice ..... 46
Reward & Punishment ..... 47
Repentance ..... 48
Prayer ..... 49
The Synagogue ..... 50
Tefillin ..... 51
Honoring Parents ..... 52
Tzedakah ..... 53
Love of a Fellow Jew ..... 54
The Nations of the World ..... 55
The Noachide Laws ..... 56
Conversion ..... 57

## TORAH STUDY

Sacred Books ..... 60
Spiritual Intuition ..... 61
Kabbalah ..... 62
Practical Kabbalah ..... 63
The Talmud ..... 64
Rishonim & Acharonim ..... 65
The Study of Talmud ..... 66
The Daily Study of Chitat ..... 67
The Daily Study of Rambam ..... 68

## CHABAD CHASSIDUT

Chassidut ..... 70
Chabad Chassidut ..... 72
The Role of a Rebbe ..... 74
The Role of a Chassid ..... 75
The Soul's Purpose ..... 76
The Purpose of the Jew ..... 77
Serving the Almighty ..... 78
Harnessing the Physical ..... 79
Integrating Form & Material ..... 80
There is None Beside Him ..... 81
Divine Providence ..... 82
Inward Simplicity ..... 83
Self-Awareness ..... 84
Character Refinement ..... 85
Mind Over Emotions ..... 86
Serving God with Joy ..... 87
Every Jew Matters ..... 88
The Simple Jew ..... 89
Outreach ..... 90
The Mitzvah Campaigns ..... 91

## LIFECYCLES

Pregnancy & Birth ..... 94
Circumcision ..... 95
Naming a Child ..... 96
Pidyon Haben ..... 97
Upshernish ..... 98
Birthdays ..... 99
Bat Mitzvah ..... 100
Bar Mitzvah ..... 101
Dating ..... 102

Marriage ........ 103
Livelihood ........ 104
Applying Talents ........ 105
Illness ........ 106
Old Age ........ 107
Death & Afterlife ........ 108
Funeral ........ 109
Mourning ........ 110
Tombstone ........ 111
Resurrection ........ 112
Reincarnation ........ 113
A Tzaddik's Resting Place ........ 114
A Tzaddik's Yahrtzeit ........ 115

## THE JEWISH HOME

The Jewish Home ........ 118
Choosing a Community ........ 119
Mezuzah ........ 120
Kosher Dietary Laws ........ 121
The Jewish Woman ........ 122
Modesty ........ 123
Mikvah ........ 124
Marital Harmony ........ 125
Having Children ........ 126
Education ........ 127
Yeshiva ........ 128
Setting an Example ........ 129
Hospitality ........ 130
Challenges ........ 131
Drifting Children ........ 132
Disabilities ........ 133

## HEALTH & CULTURE

Eating ... 136
Sleep ... 137
Health Maintenance ... 138
Self-Improvement ... 139
Doctors ... 140
Medicine ... 141
Psychology ... 142
Meditation ... 143
Art ... 144
Music ... 145
Secular Knowledge ... 146
Science ... 147
Technology ... 148

## AROUND THE YEAR

Shabbat ... 150
Rosh Chodesh ... 151
Rosh Hashana ... 152
The Fast of Gedaliah ... 153
Yom Kippur ... 154
Sukkot ... 155
Simchat Torah ... 156
Chanukah ... 157
The Fast of the 10th of Tevet ... 158
Tu B'Shvat ... 159
The Fast of Esther ... 160
Purim ... 161
Passover ... 162
Sefirat HaOmer ... 163
Pesach Sheini ... 164
Lag BaOmer ... 165

Shavuot ........ 166
The Fast of the 17th of Tammuz ........ 167
The Fast of Tisha B'av ........ 168
Notable Days in Chabad ........ 169

## RESOURCES

Glossary ........ 172
The Rebbes ........ 174
Recommended Reading ........ 176
Study Guide ........ 178
Listing of Works Cited ........ 182

# Introduction

The life-long adventure of learning entails absorbing knowledge directly from expert scholars and teachers, as well as assimilating wisdom through self-study. Each method has its place on the journey of creating a life of meaning for ourselves, our family, and our community.

***Jewish Living Simply Explained*** attempts to consolidate both. It furnishes summaries of the teachings of the seven Rebbes of Chabad, addressing such questions as the purpose of our existence and our role in the completion and perfection of the world, and provides practical application for day-to-day Jewish living in easy-to-understand language.

The teachings of the Rebbes embody a magnificent inheritance of profound faith-affirming literature that spans the vast sea of Jewish writing and scholarship. These include the prime corpus of the Torah and its myriad commentaries, the Talmud and its various offshoots, the Midrash and highly mystical Kabbalistic works, and the endless collections of rabbinic responsa and Jewish philosophical treatises.

Many esoteric teachings have become accessible to all due in large part to the rise of the Chassidic movement in the eighteenth century. The Baal Shem Tov, founder of Chassidism, unified the seemingly disparate areas of Jewish scholarship by combining practical Jewish law and observance with the mystical infinitude of the Kabbalah. In doing so, he provided both the simple Jew and the scholar a means to access an internal spiritual experience and deeper understanding of God, the world, and their own purpose and meaning.

The work and worldview of the Baal Shem Tov was furthered and expanded by his disciple, Rabbi DovBer, the "Maggid of Mezeritch" (1704–1772) and his "spiritual" grandson, Rabbi Schneur Zalman of Liadi (1745–1812), who is known as the Alter Rebbe and is the founder of Chabad.

Building on the wisdom of his predecessors, the Alter Rebbe developed a structured and systematic elucidation of the mystical-spiritual aspects of Jewish faith and Torah observance, providing greater understanding of the esoteric foundations of Judaism.

The Alter Rebbe's emphasis on the intellectual understanding of spiritual concepts deepened and enriched the roots of faith of the thousands of his followers, nourishing their souls by enabling them to comprehend and embrace the Divine in everyday life. He showed how the heart can be reached through the mind by learning, questioning, and contemplating in order to reframe our perspectives of God and the world. (Hence the name Chabad, a Hebrew acronym for *chochmah*, *binah*, and *da'at*—wisdom, understanding, and knowledge).

His successors, the Rebbes of Chabad (see "***The Rebbes,***" p. 174), expanded on his teachings to elevate religious understanding, fervor, and observance of world Jewry to this day.

Studying *Chabad Chassidut*—Chassidic philosophy, teachings, and interpretations as articulated by the Rebbes and their disciples—is a richly inspiring and rewarding endeavor. Its ideas are very approachable and applicable. Though studying Chassidut with a skilled Chassidic teacher is ideal, anyone can comprehend this wisdom on his or her own. However, given the sheer number of works developed by the Rebbes over the past two-and-one-half centuries—enough to fill an entire library—it can be daunting to know where to begin.

This brings us to the purpose of this book:

***Jewish Living Simply Explained*** is an introductory overview of core ideas of Chabad thought applied to a wide range of topics surrounding Jewish life. Each topic is crafted to provide a "glimpse through the Chabad lens" of the world around us, benefiting readers while requiring little previous background.

The material presented is a very brief distillation from the vast body of Chabad Chassidic works. As such, it is by no means exhaustive; rather, it is meant for serve as a springboard to further study.

The book is divided into sections based upon a progression which follows threads from one topic into the next. Nonetheless, each topic can still serve as an independent capsule of information. (To get the most out of the book, read "***HOW TO USE THIS BOOK,***" on p. 19.)

Individual teachings are generally attributed to the Rebbe who taught them. When a topic references "The Rebbe," without specifying a particular individual, this generally refers to the seventh Rebbe of Chabad, Rabbi Menachem Mendel Schneerson, whose teachings effectively synthesize the material developed by the Rebbes who preceded him, and is also why many of the sources provided point to the Rebbe's talks, letters, and works.

• • • •

The research, treatment and outline for each topic was prepared by Rabbi Michoel A. Seligson. As a leading educator and lecturer on Chabad Chassidut, his contributions greatly shaped the comprehensive scope of this work. Developing and expanding upon his seed material was both a delightful and educational experience. I am profoundly grateful for his exceptional dedication, guidance, and generous advice throughout the writing process. Quite simply, without him there would be no book.

Tremendous thanks to Chana Silberstein, Ph.D., Director of Education at the Roitman Chabad Center, Cornell University, for reviewing the work in progress and sharing many excellent insights and suggestions; and to the team at Kehot Publication Society, for giving of their time to critically review, enhance, and further refine the material.

Thank you Rabbis Yitzchak Breitowitz, Manis Friedman, Simon Jacobson, Lawrence Kelemen, Shais Taub, and Joseph Telushkin; as well as professors Jonathan D. Sarna and Lawrence H. Schiffman; and Dennis Prager, for perusing the manuscript and sharing your kind words, encouragement, and endorsements.

Thank you Fred Casden, Leibel and Fraida Estrin, Mrs. C. Miller, and my children Manya, Chana, and Hindy, for assistance with editing and proofreading.

Suzanne Brandt, Chaim Fogelman, Aryeh Friedman, Melissa Grover, Hershel Lazaroff, and Hershel Rosenbluh, were all generous with excellent feedback and suggestions, for which I am forever thankful.

I thank my parents, Rabbi Yosef and Chana Goldstein, of blessed memory, for being wonderful role models of heartfelt Jewish outreach and education. In addition to raising a family of rabbis and Chabad *Shluchim* (Hebrew for "emissaries") who today serve Jewish communities around the world, the care they personally showed in reaching out to Jewish people from all backgrounds and at all levels of observance was exemplary.

I grew up watching my father teach Chassidut to people around our home table, at the shul down the block, on the radio, and wherever else he could. His gentle and clear manner of explaining complex ideas still influences me and the many who became his lifelong students. My mother, of blessed memory, nurtured countless Jewish souls in her own modest way. I pray that the fruit of their earnest toil and steadfast dedication to the ideals of the Torah and the teachings of Chassidut continue to bring them blessing and honor for generations to come.

I thank the Lubavitcher Rebbe, for all that he has given to the world—and to our family in particular—through his loving guidance and care. His unparalleled scholarship, piety, deep devotion, and unceasing dedication to nurturing Jewish faith continue to affect and inspire millions of people around the world.

Last, but certainly not least, I thank God for all the good He continues to bestow upon me and my family. I am especially grateful for the opportunity to bring His wisdom into your home and heart, hopefully inspiring your life a little—maybe even a lot—along the way.

***Rabbi Zalman Goldstein***
Zalman@JewishLearningGroup.com

# How to Use This Book

We encourage you to read ***Jewish Living Simply Explained*** from beginning to end, as each section builds on information from the preceding sections. While you can also learn much by skipping around, proceeding in order will aid with overall comprehension. It may also be helpful to head over to the section ***The Rebbes*** (p. 174) so that when a particular rebbe is cited, you will be able to understand his contribution in historical context.

While each topic contains a valuable summary of key teachings, it is understandably not an exhaustive treatment. To encourage further study, we have included extensive references under the heading ***More to Explore*** at the bottom of each page. Most refer to Hebrew works, including Chassidic discourses (*"Maamorim,"* in Hebrew) and public talks (*"Sichot,"* in Hebrew) of the Rebbes, many of which have been translated into several languages over the past several decades. There are also references to Biblical and Kabbalistic texts, as well as works composed by various authors (a complete list is found on page 182).

To make reading ***Jewish Living Simply Explained*** comfortable for all readers, we often use English terminology, such as "Mount Sinai," instead of *"Har Sinai,"* or "Book of Psalms" instead of *"Tehillim."* In some instances we've included the Hebrew word in parentheses right after the English word. Other times, the opposite is true: The Hebrew term is followed by the English equivalent in parentheses. Should you encounter terms or names that may be unfamiliar, visit the ***Glossary*** (p. 172).

The sidebars titled ***Bottom Line*** provide a quick summary of the material presented on the page, and the ***Ponder/Action*** sections give a thoughtful take-away and practical suggestions for implementing these concepts in day-to-day life.

We have also provided a ***Recommended Reading*** list of works in English (p. 176) and a ***Study Guide*** (p. 178) for those wishing to further their study of Chabad Chassidut.

# *Creation*

### Bottom Line

This world is the focal point of creation because, as the Alter Rebbe notes, "the Almighty desired to have a dwelling place in the lower realms."

### Ponder/Action

▸ Do a mitzvah and learn Torah for the express purpose of making your space a fitting dwelling place for God.

# בריאת העולם

# Creation

The Torah's opening verses establish that the world was created through the word of God and from absolute nothingness. Over a period of six days, the entire cosmos took shape, including the beginning of time and space; creation of the seas and oceans, sun, moon and all heavenly galaxies; the formation of all plant and animal life; and finally, the creation of mankind. By the seventh day, everything was complete.

God continues to give life to creation by the means of creating "something from nothing." Were He to withdraw His constant involvement, all reality would cease to be as if it never existed. Presently, God's continual presence is hidden, allowing creation to function seemingly independently.

Our Sages taught that the Almighty created the universe because He wanted to share His kindness with others and to be known. The Alter Rebbe summarized this idea by stating, the Almighty "desired to have a dwelling place in the lower worlds."

In a spiritual sense, "higher" and "lower" reflect the amount and nature of Godly revelation and energy. The more evident the revelation, the "higher" the world. Given the concealed spiritual energy animating our world, the earth and its inhabitants are considered the "lowest" form of creation, but certainly not the least important. In fact, it is only on earth that the ultimate purpose of creation can be expressed. It is through the study of Torah and performance of its mitzvot that the material world is elevated and more openly connected to God. This elevation enables the physical world to reveal its spiritual essence, thereby creating a "dwelling place" on earth where God feels at home.

Chassidut explains that all of creation, including our world, is inherently good because it was made by a perfectly good and benevolent Creator. True, nature's concealment of its Godly roots belies its supernal life-source, which gives room for doubt, apathy, darkness, and even evil to exist and flourish. However, through the study of Torah and careful observance of its mitzvot, our surroundings are illuminated with Godliness. This leads to the ultimate revelation of the world's true positive essence. Just as a little light banishes a lot of darkness, spiritual "light" transforms the world's natural concealment of Godliness into a conduit for revelation.

### More to Explore

Torah, Bereishit 1:1-31; Tanya, chap. 36; ibid. Iggeret Hakodesh, chap. 20; Sefer HaMaamorim, 5643, pp. 39-42; ibid. 5652, p. 7; ibid. 5663, pp. 82 and 112; ibid. 5666, pp. 3 and 7 (bottom); Likkutei Sichot, vol. 6, p. 19, footnote no. 55, and ibid. p. 21, footnote 69; Sichot Kodesh, Simchat Beit Hashoeva 5715, chap. 23 and on; ibid. Balak 5724; ibid. Shmos 5726.

# העולם

# The World

According to the teachings of our Sages, God's precious love for the world, and the Jewish people in particular, is comparable to the bond between husband and wife. In King Solomon's Song of Songs (*Shir Hashirim*), we find the phrase *Bosi L'Gani Achoti Kallah* ("I have come into My garden, My sister, My bride"), which refers to the revelation of God's Divine presence in the Holy Temple. The metaphor chosen by King Solomon reflects this idea, and our Sages tell us the relationship between God and the Jewish people is described by this allegorical reference.

A flower garden doesn't produce food or other necessities; rather, it exists to provide joy and delight to others. In the same sense, God created the physical world to bring joy and delight. The service of the Jewish nation beautifies and enhances God's "garden," allowing the Almighty to derive great satisfaction and happiness from His creation.

Often, however, mankind cannot sense the "garden's" true beauty, or the desire of God to delight in it. Chassidut addresses this paradox, noting that the Hebrew *Olam* ("world") is related to the Hebrew *He'elem*, ("hidden"). Indeed, though the Godly origin of the world is currently hidden, through the study of Torah and performance of its mitzvot, we can still bring the Almighty joy and satisfaction.

Chassidut also notes that the Hebrew word *Gani* ("my garden") is related to *Genuni* ("my bridal chamber"), the place where people feel most comfortable and free to reveal their essence. This reflects the close relationship between God and the Jewish people and also refers to the era of *Moshiach* (the Messiah), when the concealment of Godliness will be completely abolished.

Learning Torah and performing mitzvot hasten the transformation of the *Gani* ("my garden") into *Genuni* ("my bridal chamber"), when all of creation will experience the delight God derives from this world—His "garden."

**Bottom Line**

This world, in contrast to all other heavenly spheres, has the potential to generate the most sublime satisfaction and joy for the Almighty.

**Ponder/Action**

▸ Ponder the kindnesses of the Creator, that such seemingly insignificant beings as we, mere mortals, can bring great delight to the "Greatest of all great" of Whom it is written, "There is no delving into His greatness." This should inspire us to serve God with an eager heart and joyous spirit.

**More to Explore**

Shir HaShirim 5:1; Sefer HaMaamorim, 5738, V'shavti B'sholom, chap. 16; ibid. 5746, Ki Tovou (near end); Sichot Kodesh, Beshalach 5733, chap. 1; ibid. 10 Shevat 5735, chap. 2; Hayom Yom, 8 Kislev.

**Bottom Line**

The Torah's measurements are precise and absolutely true, thus there is no need for apologetics.

**Ponder/Action**

▸ Observe Shabbat and Jewish holidays at their proper times.

# ששת ימי בראשית

# *Creation in Six Days*

According to the account of creation in the Torah, God created the world in its complete and functioning state over a period of six days, followed by a seventh day of rest. Through the ages, the Jewish people have commemorated this seventh day with the observance of Shabbat.

Modern apologists have attempted to align prevailing scientific theory about the age and origin of the world with the Torah's account of creation, suggesting that the six days mentioned in the Torah refer, perhaps, to some other dimension of time — maybe "God's time."

The Rebbe staunchly opposed this explanation on the basis that it fundamentally undermines the concept of Shabbat as a day that follows a six-day week as we have always known it to be. He promoted the literal interpretation of the Torah's six days, each being a regular 24-hour period.

The Torah itself restates: "For in six days God made the heaven and the earth, the seas and all that is in them, and He rested on the seventh day. Therefore, God blessed the Shabbat day and sanctified it." The day of Shabbat is expressly specified as the seventh day following the six days of creation.

The Rebbe reminded correspondents that it is, in fact, impossible for modern science to conflict with the Torah, for the Torah addresses absolute truth, while science deals with what is possible to ascertain with our limited human knowledge (see *"Science,"* p. 147).

Anyone familiar with the development of scientific thought knows that science has undergone a fundamental change since medieval times. Previously, it was held that scientific observations describe categorical reality. Today, science is expressed in terms of probability and hypotheses instead of absolute certainty. Thus, trying to reconcile the words of Torah with ever-evolving scientific theory is unnecessary, careless, and even intellectually dishonest.

**More to Explore**

Torah, Shemot 20:11; Pirkei D'Rebbe Eliezer, chap. 3 and on; Midrash Rabbah, Bereishit; Talmud, Sanhedrin 38b; Igrot Kodesh of the Rebbe, vol. 6, p. 296; ibid. vol. 7, p. 133; ibid. vol. 13, pp. 137 and 405.

# גילו של היקום

# Age of the Universe

According to Jewish law and tradition, we are just over 5,778 years from creation (at the time of the printing of this book). Concerning modern popular scientific theories that conflict with this time line, the Rebbe explained it is necessary to bear in mind that science uses available observations to formulate theories and hypotheses, while the Torah deals with absolute truths. Forced alignment of these two radically different disciplines is entirely out of place.

Regarding science, we must first distinguish between empirical evidence, i.e., that which is based on observation or experience, and speculation, which attempts to explain phenomena that cannot be duplicated in the laboratory. "Scientific speculation" is actually a conflict in terms, as "science," strictly speaking, means "knowledge," while speculation cannot be honestly called knowledge. At best, science speaks in terms of theories inferred from certain known facts (see *"Science,"* p. 147).

Extrapolation from known and observable science to inexplicable experiences drawn from history is categorically uncertain, and the level of unreliability increases with distance from what has been proven empirically. Scientific speculation regarding the age of the universe is an example of such uncertain extrapolation.

As the Rebbe has often written, the entire structure of science is based on the observation of reactions and processes as they exist in nature at the time of observation. The inadequacy of scientific theory regarding the origin of the universe is evident when one considers they are based on data that has only been observable over a relatively short period of time— ranging from decades, to certainly no more than a few centuries. Building on this limited range of data, itself imperfect, scientists purport to explain phenomena occurring thousands, and according to many, millions and billions of years ago.

With data being utilized from a time period so minuscule compared to the length of time passed since the events being considered, it is small wonder that various scientific theories about the age of the universe not only contradict each other, but in certain cases mutually exclude one another. In light of the fundamental inherent weakness of the scientific method, Jews can maintain confidence in the absolute truth of the Torah's account of creation and the Jewish counting of years since then.

**Bottom Line**

The Jewish tradition regarding the age of the universe is based on the Torah, which is absolute Truth, whereas scientific theory speaks in terms of theories and probabilities.

**Ponder/Action**

▸ Scientific speculation on the age of buried fossils or other ancient artifacts is a fool's-errand, since no honest scientist can say with certainty what atmospheric conditions for decay were like 200 years ago, much less 1,000 or 5,000 years ago—how much more so millions of years ago!

**More to Explore**

Igrot Kodesh of the Rebbe, vol. 12, p. 61; ibid. vol. 13, pp. 137, 143, and 403; Letters from the Rebbe (English), 11 Tishrei, 5712; ibid. 10 Cheshvan, 5716; ibid. 1 Sivan, 5716; ibid. 18 Tevet, 5722; ibid. 17 Cheshvan, 5723; see also "Mind Over Matter," edited and translated by Dr. A. Gotfryd. Ph.D. (Jersualem 2000).

# Time

The concept of time, including the idea of sequence/before and after, is also part of creation. Its source is the spiritual attribute *malchut* of *atzilut*, where time and place receive their limiting dimension. Even though time enforces limits, it is of significant value in Torah. In fact, the first commandment given to the Jewish people is to align the Jewish holidays with the seasons and formulate a calendar.

Everything created, from the vastest celestial system to the smallest cell, has a noble role—and so does time. Frittering time away is a waste of its potential and an obstacle to the realization of its ultimate purpose. Every moment with which we are blessed is filled with intention and accomplishment. It is up to us to safeguard time and ensure that even the most fleeting second is elevated and used to God's best purpose.

According to our Sages, creation is being renewed and re-energized every second, and every minute is orchestrated by Divine providence and is presented to us intentionally. Therefore, we are taught not to postpone a good activity for the next moment, for the next moment is a totally new creation.

When looking at a large body of water, we can see the entire sun's reflection in it. Yet if we were to remove a few drops of water, the entire sun would still be reflected in each drop. This analogy teaches that every unit of time is one part of the complete picture of the entire creation. We actualize time by drawing spiritual light into our environment through living life according to the Torah and influencing others in positive ways.

Rabbi Levi Yitzchak Schneerson, the Rebbe's father said, "Hours must be 'counted hours;' then the days will be 'counted days.' When a day passes, one should know what he has accomplished and what remains yet to be done, and in general, one should always see to it that tomorrow should be much better than today."

Success with time occurs when we are focused on the activity at hand, giving it our total attention such that all other matters cease to exist. This is using time to its fullest potential. We should especially take advantage of the beginning of the day, when we are most energized. This is an excellent period to dedicate to the Almighty with studying and meditating on Chassidic texts and meaningful prayer.

### Bottom Line

Every bit of time, every day that passes, is not just a day but a life's concern.

### Ponder/Action

▸ The Rebbe was quoted saying, "The world says that time is money, and I say that time is life." Every minute that passes "empty" is a loss that cannot be returned. Therefore, we need to be quick and alert in utilizing the time available for the best possible purpose.

### More to Explore

Tanya, part 4, chap. 7; Sefer HaMaamorim, 5712, Vayikach; Torat Menachem, vol. 12, p. 55; ibid. vol. 14, p. 315; ibid. vol. 21, p. 96; ibid. vol. 53, p. 429; ibid. 5748, vol. 1, pp. 572-573; ibid. 5749, vol. 2, p. 205; Sichot Kodesh, Erev Simchat Torah 5718, chap. 11; ibid. 19 Kislev 5733, chap. 4; ibid. 12 Tammuz 5737, chap. 8; ibid. 15 Shevat 5741, chap. 1; Hayom Yom, 1 Iyar.

# מערכת השמש והכוכבים
# Stars and Planets

The colossal and intricate solar system is a part of creation that expresses the greatness of the Almighty. In the words of King David, "The heavens recount the glory of God, and the sky tells of the work of His hands." The prophet Isaiah tells us that the Almighty knows every star and calls them by name, with each star having its own unique qualities.

In Jewish thought, our people have often been compared with the stars. For example, in the Torah, God promised our patriarch Abraham that his descendants would be as numerous as the stars. Also, the commentator Rashi compares God's counting of the Jewish people after they left Egypt, to the way He counts the heavenly stars. Besides the analogy's expression of how plentiful the Jewish people will be over history, there is another lesson in this comparison to stars.

There is great variety among stars, with some appearing large and easily visible, and others so tiny and distant they can only be seen through a powerful telescope, if at all. Astronomers explain, however, that the size, distance, and visibility of a star offer very little information about its true nature. Stars that look small can, in fact, be quite immense and powerful, and all stars contain great quantities of heat and light.

The same is true for every Jew. Each is unique and has a divinely ordained individual contribution to make in this world. At times when we might feel small and unimportant amid the vast multitudes of people, some of whom may even seem much "brighter" and more "powerful," we should remember that every Jew possesses limitless spiritual power and God-given capacities perfectly suited to his or her unique life mission and challenges. These capabilities are realized through the study of Torah and performance of its mitzvot, which not only elevates each person spiritually, but affects his well-being and that of everyone around him.

Regarding the ancient belief that personal and global events are caused or controlled by the stars and constellations, Chassidut explains that the Jewish nation receives their vitality from God directly from "above the stars," and therefore have nothing to fear from planetary movements or cosmic events. Indeed, the Hebrew term *Mazal* ("constellation") is related to the word *nozal*, meaning "flow" or "drip," indicating that the constellations are merely instruments and conduits through which God bestows His energy and blessing to the other nations of the world.

### More to Explore

Torah, Rashi on Shemot 1:1; Tehillim 19:2; Yeshayahu 40:26; Talmud, Shabbos 156a; Kuntres U'Mayon; Likkutei Sichot, vol. 6, p. 7; ibid. vol. 15, pp. 7-12; ibid. vol. 20, p. 288; Torat Menachem, vol. 55, pp. 116 and 123; Igrot Kodesh of the Rebbe, vol. 27, p. 223.

### Bottom Line

Torah allows us to delve and research the solar system and thereby see the greatness of the Almighty, but we should remember that the stars and constellations cannot determine or influence the life of a Jew.

### Ponder/Action

▸ Remember that the nation of Israel is rooted in Hashem. The Talmud states, *Ain mazel l'Yisrael*, "the Nation of Israel is not ruled by any constellation." On a deeper level, the Baal Shem Tov taught that the *Ain Sof*—unknowable God—is the true source of *mazal* for the nation of Israel!

## Bottom Line

Beyond above nature, the Jewish people, through the study of Torah and performance of its mitzvot, can influence worldly events in positive ways.

## Ponder/Action

▸ All that God does is ultimately for the good.

# תהפוכות העולם

# *Worldly Upheavals*

Worldly upheavals, global instability, and terrorism are some of the things that make us doubt if we are safe and can cause us to feel bewildered, scared, and lost. Some events may even lead to questions whether God is even still there or cares about the world. Feelings of pain and confusion when faced with adversity is a common reaction, yet with a deep awareness of human emotions, God has provided a comforting assurance. God is aware of everything that transpires in His universe and protects this world as His most precious possession.

Uncertainty is nothing new, yet when we harness its potential for positive action, we can turn despair into hope and darkness into light. The Torah relates that during the giving of the Ten Commandments, Mount Sinai trembled violently. The commentaries explain that the world seemed to teeter on its edge and only regained equilibrium once the Torah was given and accepted by the Jewish people. These events, our Sages tell us, provide a metaphor for dealing with adversity. When the world trembles and appears be on the brink of falling into chaos, it is Torah and mitzvot that are the antidote. Maintaining our faith in the face of extreme challenges, rectifying our personal shortcomings, and rededicating ourselves to sincere Torah observance starves evil of its power and restores peace, tranquility, and spiritual sustenance to the world.

The Torah, which originated from above and beyond this world, has the ability to convert negative energy into energy useful in serving the Creator. As such, its core is never affected by external changes in the world. Instead, the Torah remains a steady anchor for those who hold firm to it. Thus, when worldly upheavals occur, the ideal Jewish approach is to tap into the Jews' innate ability to rise above doubt and despair, and remember that nothing happens in the world by chance. Everything occurs for an ultimate good, often known only by God. As inheritors of this faith, we have the ability—even responsibility—to convert sorrow into growth, destruction into rebirth, and pain into healing.

Our contribution to stabilizing our environment is accomplished by strengthening our observance of the Torah's teachings. Our Sages also note in this regard that children can be an especially powerful influence on parents to increase their religious observance, resulting in greater religious consistency and stability in the home.

**More to Explore**

Torah, Shemot 19:18; Likkutei Sichot, vol. 3, pp. 819-820; ibid. vol. 22, pp. 218, 220, and 321; Sichot Kodesh, Emor 5734, chap. 1, ibid. Vov Tishrei 5738, chap. 6; ibid. Rosh Chodesh Iyar 5741, chap. 41; ibid. Bechukosai 5741, chap. 90; ibid. 2nd day of Shavuot 5741, chap. 23 and 38; Hayom Yom, 5 Shevat.

Section Two

# *Jewish History*

**Bottom Line**

Jewish history is more than a record of the past — it is a guidepost for the present and future.

**Ponder/Action**

▸ We should study Jewish history from reliable sources to attain knowledge, guidance and religious inspiration.

# היסטוריה יהודית

# Jewish History

The libraries of the world are full of history books detailing the mighty empires of old, including those of Greece, Rome, and Persia. Though admired and revered as pinnacles of human achievement during their turn on the world stage, they all eventually fell and disappeared. Meanwhile, the Jewish people, a tiny minority among the vast nations of the world, exiled from their homeland for nearly 2,000 years, continues to exist and thrive.

This incredible feat has been possible partly because the Jewish people are inherently one entity, having served as guarantors for one another throughout history. So although we may be few in number at a particular time, our population is actually quite large compared to all the other nations. In addition, our innate ability to elevate the spiritual over the physical and quality over quantity enables us to transcend the limitations of space and time.

In spite of our having suffered terribly—often horrifically—at the hands of the gentile nations throughout history, we have always risen and rebuilt, remaining steadfast in our faith in the Almighty. This has been made possible, of course, by virtue of God's mercies but also due to the great spiritual heritage we carry: which is the Torah and its mitzvot.

History has also taught us several important lessons, as at times, deceitful individuals have attempted to reinterpret the Torah at variance with the authentic tradition carefully handed down from generation to generation. Their rationale was the supposed necessity to "get with the times," or to "throw out the old and adopt the new," and behave such that we'd receive "acceptance by the nations of the world." Every time, however, one of two things resulted: the provocateurs eventually went their own way and cut themselves off from the Jewish people, or they (or their descendants) ultimately returned to Torah and its age-old tradition. This is further demonstration that those who devoutly follow the letter and spirit of the eternal Torah are bound to the Infinite God, and will thus always endure.

In addition, our consistent identification as Jewish—both at home and in public—fosters pride in our Jewish heritage, aligns us with God's desire, and invites the ultimate respect and support from the nations of the world.

**More to Explore**

Sichot Kodesh, Bereishit (2) 5731, chap. 11; ibid. 10 Shevat 5733, chap. 11; ibid. 19 Kislev 5734, chap. 3; ibid. 10 Shevat 5736, chap. 3; ibid. 12 Tammuz 5733, chap. 1; Kfar Chabad (weekly), no. 1051, p. 53; ibid. no. 1071, p. 36; ibid. no. 1373, p. 39.

# האבות

# Our Patriarchs

The *Avot* ("Patriarchs") Abraham, Isaac, and Jacob, lived about 3,500 years ago and are the founding fathers of the Jewish nation. They also epitomize various concepts in Jewish thought and tradition. For example, they are likened to the three holidays of *Pesach*, *Shavuot,* and *Sukkot;* the three Holy Temples with the third to be revealed through *Moshiach* (the Messiah) in the final redemption; and the "Three Pillars," consisting of Torah study, service of God, and deeds of kindness. Our Sages taught that each of the Patriarchs endowed their Jewish descendants with distinct attributes that characterized their Divine service. Abraham served God with love, as reflected in the verse, "Abraham, who loved Me." Similarly, he was a paradigm of kindness to his fellow man, both materially and spiritually. For all these reasons, Abraham is associated with the attribute of *chesed* (kindness; giving to others).

Isaac was characterized by *gevurah* (severity or judgment; also translated as might or fear), as expressed in the phrase, "the awe of Isaac." Isaac served God through perfect fear and awe. At this level of purity, he could not tolerate even a trace of evil. For this reason, God told him to remain in the Land of Israel and forbade him from traveling to Egypt during the famine.

Jacob's service combined the characteristics of the other two, kindness and might. As Jacob said, "The God of Avraham and the fear of Isaac were with me." This middle path is called *tiferet* (beauty; harmony). It is also identified as *rachamim* (mercy). This synergistic approach enabled Jacob to manifest perfection in his personal life and affairs. In the same way, Divine service that fuses opposing emotional attributes will empower a person to overcome the difficulties and challenges of life. This is one reason why Jews are generally called *Beit Yaakov* ("House of Jacob") or *B'nei Yisrael* ("The Children of Israel," which is another of Jacob's names).

Our Patriarchs have also been likened to a chariot. As a chariot has no will of its own, but accedes to the will of its driver, the Patriarchs' intellectual and emotional energy were so devoted to God that the Sages called them "the Divine chariot." This metaphor conveys the idea that even their bodies were holy and detached from mundane matters, enabling them to serve as pure vehicles for the Divine Will.

**More to Explore**

Torah Ohr, Vaera, p. 55; Likkutei Sichot, vol. 3 p. 856; ibid. vol. 10, p. 89; ibid. vol. 20, p. 408; ibid. vol. 25, p. 206; Torat Menachem, vol. 4, pp. 2116 and 2484; ibid. vol. 9, p. 160; ibid. vol. 43, p. 27; ibid. 5745, vol. 1, p. 253; Sichot Kodesh, Vayeshev 5715, chap. 7; ibid. Vayechi 5730, chap. 1; ibid. Vaera 5732, chap. 1; ibid. Bo 5737, chap. 2.

### Bottom Line

Just as a child inherits his or her parents' qualities, so too, every Jew has inherited a great treasure of noble qualities and capabilities from our Patriarchs. The purpose of this treasure is to enable us to succeed in our service of God.

### Ponder/Action

▸ Our Sages taught that the world stands on three pillars: the study of Torah, the . of God, and deeds of kindness. Abraham reflects deeds of kindness. Issac reflects the service of God, and Jacob reflects the study of Torah. We inherited from them all three qualities and they are within our reach to utilize and strengthen every day.

# מתן תורה

# The Giving of the Torah

The Torah was given to the Jewish people on Mount Sinai on the sixth of *Sivan* of the year 2448 from creation (1313 BCE). During this moment of unprecedented Godly revelation, the Jewish nation became a kingdom of priests and a holy nation. They accepted the responsibility to uphold and live by the Torah's laws, and they modified their lifestyles accordingly. According to the Midrash, every Jewish soul that ever has or will exist witnessed the Giving of the Torah and committed to following its commandments.

The account of the giving of the Torah and its acceptance by the entire Jewish people was recounted not just by a single group of people, but by the millions of Jewish people who experienced it firsthand. People of varying mentalities, intellect, backgrounds, and interests would charge their children to follow the same path, and, in turn, their offspring would pass it on to the next generation—and often under extremely trying circumstances—until our present times.

Indeed, throughout history, Jews have always known that the Torah with all its laws, as we know and practice them, was given by God at Mount Sinai, and today, we follow the same tradition based upon this uninterrupted chain of active and involved Jews. (This is fundamentally different from any other faith, for they are based on the claims of a single or small group of individuals, scenarios with potential for human error and other motives.)

The Torah states that, at the Giving of the Torah, the whole of Mount Sinai was covered with smoke because God had descended upon it. Chassidut explains that *"oshon,"* the Hebrew word for smoke, is also an acronym for the words *olam*, *shana*, *nefesh* (place, time, and person) to convey that the Torah affected all three dimensions of creation.

Further, "Mount" signifies a significant height, yet Sinai is among the lowest mountains. This teaches us that in matters of Torah and mitzvot, we need to stand tall with the strength and self-assurance symbolized by a mountain, while in relating to others, conducting ourselves in a modest and humble manner. Also, the word "Sinai" means "spite." With the Giving of the Torah, the Jewish people attained the ability and energy needed to spite, i.e., contravene or disregard, the evil inclination.

### Bottom Line

At the giving of the Torah the Jewish nation accepted the responsibility to uphold and live by the Torah's laws and modified their lifestyles accordingly. The Torah and all its laws as we know and practice them today are exactly the same as those given by God at *Har Sinai* (Mount Sinai).

### Ponder/Action

- The blessing "Blessed are You, Lord, Who gives the Torah" teaches that just as God gives us the Torah every day (the word used in the blessing is in the present tense) so, too, we accept it daily. Additionally, when fulfilling a mitzvah, we should do it with the utmost confidence. After all, we are emissaries of the Almighty!

### More to Explore

Torah, Shemot 19:18; Ohr HaTorah, Yisro, p. 816; Biurim L'Pirkei Avot, p. 12; Likkutei Sichot, vol. 22, p. 159; Torat Menachem, vol. 25, p. 309; "The Letter and the Spirit," vol. 1, p. 53;

# ארץ ישראל
# The Land of Israel

The cradle of the Jewish people and home to the holiest place on earth is *Eretz Yisrael*, the Land of Israel, given by the Almighty to the Jewish nation as a perpetual inheritance. From the first verse of the Torah, Rabbi Shlomo Yitzchaki (1040–1105), known as Rashi, the foremost commentator on the Torah, quotes the sage Rabbi Yitzchok, who asks, "Why does the Torah, a book of law, begin with creation instead of commandments?" So that if the nations of the nations of the world should ever say to the Jewish people, "You are thieves, for you conquered by force the lands of the seven nations [of Canaan]," they may reply, "The earth belongs to the Holy One, blessed be He; He created it and gave it to whomever He deemed was fit. According to His wish He gave it to them, and according to His wish He took it from them and gave it to us." Indeed, the land, the borders of which are defined in the Torah, belongs to every single Jew.

Kabbalah explains that the Land of Israel receives its vitality from a higher spiritual source than all other lands, and thus at its core is holier and more spiritually potent. Further, the seven nations that inhabited the land before it became the Land of Israel mirror the seven archetypal attributes of the human experience (see *"Sefirat HaOmer,"* p. 163). In this sense, our Patriarchs not only refined their own traits, but elevated those of the secular lands, by infusing them with great sanctity. Chassidut teaches that the words *"Eretz Yisrael"* also have a figurative meaning. The word *"Eretz"* has the root letters of the Hebrew word *ratzon*, which means "will" or "desire." The word *"Yisrael"* can also be read as an acronym for the Hebrew statement, "There are 600,000 letters in the Torah." Taken together, *Eretz Yisrael* embodies the will and desire of the Jewish people to fulfill the commandments of the Torah, continuing our forefathers' work of refining the world and revealing its latent Godliness.

The Rebbe encouraged us to have faith in God's constant protection of the Land of Israel, quoting the Torah, "The land that God's eyes are constantly upon it, from the beginning of the year until the end." He assured that it is the safest place on earth, and emphasized that through steadfast adherence to Torah principles, it can achieve lasting peace. The Rebbe also encouraged us to bolster the security of Israel through renewed commitment to mitzvot that elicit God's blessings, such as Torah study, prayer, charity, and acts of kindness, *tefillin*, *mezuzah*, and acquiring a letter in a Torah that is being written, thereby uniting with other Jewish people and hastening the final redemption.

**More to Explore**

Torah, Bereishit 15:18; ibid. Devorim 11:12; Rashi, Bereishit 1:1; Likutei Torah, Maasai, p.89b; Shuchan Aruch, chap. 329; Likkutei Sichot, vol. 18, p.404 (see footnote); Torat Menachem vol. 19, p. 294; Sichot Kodesh, Vayelech 5738, p. 21.

**Bottom Line**

Israel is the holiest—and safest place—on earth, where, as the Torah tells us, *"God's eyes are constantly upon it, from the beginning of the year until the end."*

**Ponder/Action**

▸ Until the final redemption and the complete ingathering of exiles occur, one can create *"Eretz Yisrael"* in their personal environment by connecting with God through learning His Torah and observing its mitzvot.

**Bottom Line**

The Holy Temples continue to live within the hearts of every Jew. Just as the spiritual holiness never departed from them, so too each Jew remains Godly at his core and is always able to spread spiritual light into the world regardless of his present spiritual state.

**Ponder/Action**

▸ None of us is ever too forgone to tap his or her Jewish soul and spread Godly light in the world, beginning with studying the Torah and fulfilling its mitzvot.

# בית המקדש

# The Holy Temple

The Holy Temple, known as the *Beit Hamikdash*, stood atop Mount Moriah, also known as Mount Zion, adjacent to the eastern part of the Old City of Jerusalem. It was built by King Solomon, beginning in the year 832 BCE, and its construction took seven years, utilizing the work of tens of thousands of people. The first Temple stood for 410 years until it was destroyed by the Babylonian king, Nebuchadnezzar. Seventy years later, the Jews began building the Second Temple, which stood for 420 years until it was razed by the Romans in 70 CE. Embodying the very purpose of creation and archetypes of the "dwelling for God in the physical world," both Temples drew the Divine presence into our midst. At the Temples, the Jewish people would pray, bring daily offerings, and gather during the three major festivals to "see and to be seen" by God.

It is written in the Torah, "They shall make Me a sanctuary and I shall dwell within them." Chassidut explains that "within them" means "within every Jewish person," for every Jew's essence is fit to be a sanctuary for His dwelling.

The *Midrash* explains that the Godly emanations penetrated the stones of the Holy Temple, the latter referring to the inanimate world. Therefore, even during times of exile and desolation, they remain sacred and holy. Chassidut extends this idea to the "personal sanctuary" within every Jew— the Divine core of the Jewish soul. The light that permeates and elevates our physical nature always remains.

This idea is supported by the verse in Song of Songs *(Shir Hashirim)*: "I am asleep, yet my heart is awake." The *Midrash Rabba* comments, "I am asleep for mitzvot, but my heart is awake for acts of kindness; I am asleep for charities, but my heart is awake to perform them." Any spiritual "dormancy" experienced during our lifetime affects only the "stones and walls." However, the core of every Jew remains forever intact and holy, ready to serve through the study of Torah and observance of its mitzvot.

The presence of the Holy Temples is sorely missed and their absence deeply mourned. Our prayers are replete with yearning for their rebuilding. Our consolation is the knowledge that very soon, we will merit to see the Third Temple, an edifice which will last for all eternity (see *"Moshiach,"* p. 39).

**More to Explore**

Talmud, Yoma 21a; Pirkei Avot, chap. 5, par. 5; Rambam, Hilchot Beit HaBechira; Midrash, Sh'mot Rabba, chap. 2; Shir Hashirim, chap. 5, par. 2; Torah Ohr, Vayigash, p. 86; Introduction to Imrei Binah; Sefer Hamaamorim, 5680, p. 184; ibid. 5716, Mizmor L'Dovid; Likkutei Sichot, vol. 4, p. 1346 and footnotes; ibid. vol. 3, pp. 906-908; ibid. vol. 17, p. 91; ibid. vol. 18, p. 414 and footnotes; ibid. vol. 20, p. 94; ibid. vol. 21, p. 261; ibid. vol. 24, p. 84; Sichot Kodesh, Noso 5736, chap. 3; Torat Menachem, vol. 24, p. 94; ibid. vol. 57, p. 265.

# כהן לוי וישראל

# *Kohen, Levi, Yisrael*

The Talmud titles the Jewish people a "three-fold nation" comprised of the *Kohen* (Priest), *Levi* (Levite), and *Yisrael* (Israelite). In the times of the Holy Temple, each group had its own function. From a mystical perspective, these three groups reflect the *sefirot* (spiritual "vessels" which reflect divinity) found in the higher worlds. Kohanim represent the *sefira* of *chesed*, "giving." Leviim symbolize the *sefira* of *Gevura*, which express "judgment" or "severity." *Yisraelim* represent the middle attribute of *tiferet* or *rachamin*, "beauty" and "mercy."

The cosmic alignment of the three *sefirot* is reflected by their roles in the Holy Temple. The *Kohanim* conducted the services and presented the sacrifices, bringing supernal Godly revelations into the world. The *Leviim* had several roles in the Holy Temple, including guarding its premises and singing Psalms during services. The *Yisraelim* provided material support for their brethren in Holy Temple.

Chassidut teaches that the levels of *Kohen*, *Levi*, and *Yisrael* exist spiritually in every Jewish person's soul. The three groups reflect, in turn, thought, speech, and deed. The *Kohanim* had to have proper intentions—in other words, thoughts—for their sacrifices to be accepted Above. The *Leviim* sang, a form of speech. The *Yisraelim* performed actions, i.e., deeds, by supplying sacrificial animals and contributing money to maintain the Holy Temple.

As Jews practicing our faith, we perform these three functions every day. First, we recite the morning prayers, which include descriptions of the service of the *Kohen* in the Holy Temple, drawing blessings down into the world as the *Kohanim* did. Then, just as the *Leviim* sang in the Holy Temple, we elevate our prayers by fulfilling this mitzvah with joy. Lastly, throughout the day, even while pursuing a livelihood, we further fulfill mitzvot by raising our actions to the spiritual plane. From a different perspective, *Kohen*, *Levi*, and *Yisrael* correspond to the three modes of service represented by Torah, mitzvot, and self-sacrifice.

Today, *Kohanim* have the privilege of being called up first to say the blessing over the Torah, recite the priestly blessing for the congregation (the *Leviim* wash their hands). They also play a critical role in the ceremony of *Pidyon Haben* (Redemption of the Firstborn (see *"Pidyon Haben,"* p. 97).

**More to Explore**

Talmud, Shabbat, p. 88a; Likkutei Sichot, vol. 18 p. 193; ibid. vol. 19 p. 319; Torat Menachem, 5749, vol. 2 p. 317; ibid. 5750, vol. 3 p. 211; Sichot Kodesh, Yud Shevat 5731, chap. 3; ibid. Bamidbar 5734 chap. 6; ibid. Bamidbar 5739, chap. 51; ibid. Shlach 5740, chap. 55.

**Bottom Line**

All of us have within our soul the modes of *Kohen*, *Levi* and *Yisrael*. They are reflected in the daily service of the Almighty through one's thought speech and deed.

**Ponder/Action**

▸ The service that took place in the Holy Temple can be fulfilled in a spiritual state on a daily basis through the study of Torah, prayer, and the performance of mitzvot.

## Bottom Line

Offerings and sacrifices helped elevate the material and draw down blessings upon the community. On a practical level, it refers to refining our character traits and using them in positive ways.

## Ponder/Action

▸ Although the Holy Temple doesn't stand physically, we can bring a spiritual offering every day through prayer, as well as by expressing vigor and zest in studying Torah and fulfilling its mitzvot, thereby strengthening our connection with the Almighty.

# קרבנות
# Sacrifices

The act of presenting a sacrifice to God as a means of strengthening the relationship between man and his Creator dates back to the earliest times of man. In Jewish tradition, sacrifices were brought either to thank God for His blessings, or to petition God for forgiveness of a misdeed.

An offering, *korban* in Hebrew, literally means "coming closer," to draw us near to the Almighty. This is true for all sacrifices, whether they be brought by an individual, community, or as part of the Temple services as ordained by the Almighty. The effect of offerings was two-fold: turning the individual towards God, and eliciting God's blessings toward the people. From a mystical perspective, when spiritual deficiency comes about due to lack of fulfillment of Torah and its commandments, spiritual energy from a higher level must be drawn down to repair the deficit. When a sacrifice consisted of offerings from the four domains of the world—from the inanimate, plant, animal, and heartfelt human meditations—a new revelation came from above to repair the insufficiency in each affected domain.

The section of the Torah relating to sacrificial offerings starts out, "A man who offers of you an offering to God." It seems the logical order of the words should be, "A man of you who offers." The Alter Rebbe, however, translates the verse this way: "A man who offers," i.e., for a man to become closer to God, "of you must be the offering," meaning he must bring the offering of himself. This means that man must sacrifice his own "animal," referring to the desire for transgression emanating from his animal soul. Further, the offering service often entailed sprinkling or placing some of the animal's blood and fat on the Altar. "Blood" symbolizes the vigor and zest that exist in a person's soul and body. Likewise, "fat" accumulates, symbolizing excessive indulgence in physical pleasures. Offering both represents redirecting our vigor and zest to sacred matters, and taking pleasure in serving God through His mitzvot.

Although we may sometimes feel distant from God due to certain actions or inactions on our part, the Torah assures us that nearness to God is "of you"—it lies within each of us. No limitations or obstacles can prevent a Jew from spiritually elevating himself and attaining closeness with God. Moreover, our Sages taught that God does not confront us with unattainable demands, and, therefore, it is within every person's reach to mend his or her ways and restore spiritual equilibrium in all areas of our life.

**More to Explore**

Ramban, Vayikra 1:9; Tanya, chap. 34; Likkutei Torah, Shlach pp. 42a-b and d; Sefer HaMaamorim, 5653, pp. 184-7; Likkutei Sichot, vol. 3 p. 948; ibid. vol. 16 p. 19; ibid. vol. 17, p. 12; ibid. vol. 22 p. 17; Sichot Kodesh, Bamidbar 5733, chap. 1; ibid. Tzav 5736, chap. 1; Hayom Yom, 12 Adar II.

# גלות

# Exile

The concept of exile (in Hebrew, *galut*) is—sadly—a familiar concept for the Jewish people. The concept of exile began with Adam, after he ate from the Tree of Knowledge and was banished from the Garden of Eden (in Hebrew, *Gan Eden*). Our Patriarchs, Abraham, Isaac, and Jacob also experienced times of wandering and exile. All told, following the root of all exiles which began in Egypt (1523 BCE–1313 BCE), the Jewish nation has endured four major exiles: Babylon (423 BCE–372 BCE), Persia/Media (372 BCE–348 BCE), Greece (371 BCE–140 BCE), and Rome (69 CE–present). Even though exile affects us both spiritually and physically, it is a temporary state, no matter how long-lasting.

As we are taught, everything in this world has a spiritual root. The Midrash states that before the world was created, a spiritual world called *Olam HaTohu* ("World of Chaos") existed. When this world shattered, "sparks" of spirituality "fell" into this physical world and landed in regions where the Jewish nation were destined to be exiled. In a way, therefore, God too "experiences" our exile and shares our suffering. When the Jews were driven from their home, their spiritual task was to elevate these sacred sparks, and every soul has a unique mission in this regard. This mission is accomplished by learning Torah and particularly by fulfilling mitzvot. In this way, our exile is an opportunity to bring redemption not only to ourselves but to those entrapped sparks of Godliness.

In the prayer service on Jewish holidays we recite, "Because of our sins we were exiled from our land." A question arises: punishment for a sin is legitimate, but why exile? The explanation is that the Jews were liberated from Egypt on one condition—that they serve the Almighty by fulfilling His commandments. If this were neglected, the reason to leave Egypt would disappear. The end result is that instead of "leaving Egypt," those not fulfilling God's commandments bring exile upon themselves and the rest of the Jewish people. Since the spiritual Land of Israel cannot tolerate the ignoble "Egyptian" morals and values, the outcome is, unfortunately, being exiled from our land.

In Hebrew, our homeland is called "*Eretz Yisrael.*" *Eretz* also means "will" or "desire." A lack in carrying out the Almighty's will results in being driven away from *Eretz Yisrael.* We are promised, however, that our exile will eventually end. Indeed, we pray every day that God hasten the final redemption through the Messiah (see "*Moshiach,*" p. 39), ushering in the ingathering of exiles and the restoration of the Temple services.

**More to Explore**

Talmud, Brachot, 3a; Sefer Hamaamorim, 5670, p. 213; ibid. 5735, Ach Bgorol; Likkutei Sichot, vol. 3, p. 824 and on; Torat Menachem, vol. 4, p. 136; ibid. vol. 33, p. 349; ibid. vol. 56, 332; ibid. 5742, vol. 3, p. 1382; Sichot Kodesh, 15 Shevat 5739, chap. 39; ibid. Metzoro 5741, chap. 53.

**Bottom Line**

The long exile is painful spiritually as it is physically. The spiritual task is to elevate the exiled "sparks" of Godliness by learning Torah and fulfilling its mitzvot.

**Ponder/Action**

▸ Our Sages compare the exile to a father hiding from his child. The father waits for his child to seek and find him. As long as the child looks for his father, there is a ray of hope that he will be found. So, too, we need to seek and find our Father by learning Torah and fulfilling its mitzvot.

**Bottom Line**

Jews are spread out by Divine providence, each in a specific place, in order to improve something specific in his or her area of influence.

**Ponder/Action**

▸ All Jews are united from the perspective of their soul. When one Jew unites with another, this helps all Jews in their spiritual work. It also removes the physical distance between Jews and serves to hasten the Redemption.

# תפוצות

# Dispersion

The Talmud tells us that the Almighty acted charitably toward the Jewish people by scattering them among the nations of the world. Although the dispersion of our people may seem more a curse than a blessing, a more positive outcome might be that, by being spread out in this manner, the Jewish people can never be easily destroyed.

Another Talmudic verse states that Jews were exiled among the nations so that converts would join. The fact is, however, not very many people have converted to Judaism over the years, so how can the Talmud's statement help us understand, much less justify, such a long history of Jewish dispersion? The explanation given in Chassidut is that the word "converts" also refers to Godly sparks throughout the world that need to be collected and refined. The Jewish nation accomplishes this by learning Torah and fulfilling its mitzvot; we become "partners" with the Almighty in perfecting creation.

Dispersion can also be viewed positively if we think of every Jewish person, though a unique individual, as sharing something in common that joins each of us into a single collective entity, similar to the way various limbs and organs make up one body. Despite external differences that appear to exist between one Jew and another, the Torah binds them with an unbreakable unity that has nourished and sustained our nation. Therefore, when Jews in one community or country are unable to fulfill Torah and its commandments for some reason, Jews in other locales do so and support their brethren, eliciting blessings upon the entire Jewish nation.

Further, we are taught that man's steps are set by God, meaning that we are placed where we are by Divine providence because our particular soul must purify and improve something specific in that particular place. For centuries—ever since the world's creation—that which needs purification or improvement in our circle of influence awaits each of us to accomplish this. The soul also waits from the time it comes into being to fulfill its unique task.

We can counteract physical dispersion with continued love, concern, and support for our fellow Jews wherever they may be. Although separated by continents and vast oceans, we know that at our core we are all one, united through God and His Torah.

**More to Explore**

Talmud, Pesachim 87b; Torat Chaim, Chaye Sarah, p. 121c; Sefer HaMaamorim, 5689, p. 127; ibid. 5729 Omar Reb Osiya; Likkutei Sichot, vol. 3, p. 825; Torat Menachem, vol. 33, p. 249; ibid. vol. 49, p. 217; ibid. 5742, vol. 4, pp. 2037-2039; ibid. 5751 vol. 3, p. 151; Sichot Kodesh, Metzora 5741, chap. 53; Hayom Yom, 3 Elul.

# משיח

# Moshiach

The redemption of the Jewish nation from exile (in Hebrew, *galut*) will be marked by the arrival of the Messiah *("Moshiach")*. He will herald the actualization of the reason our world was created, wherein Godliness will be perceived by all, when an era of global peace and prosperity will begin, and the righteous resurrected.

The Hebrew word "*Moshiach*" means "anointed." Since creation, a Jewish person in each generation could potentially be the *Moshiach*. According to tradition, he will be a human being born of Jewish parents from the tribe of Judah, descended from King David and his son, King Solomon. He will rebuild the Holy Temple in Jerusalem and gather the Jewish people from all corners of the earth to the Land of Israel *(Eretz Yisrael)*.

Belief in the coming of the *Moshiach* is a longstanding and integral part of Judaism. The Torah, especially the prophetic texts, is replete with references to the Messianic redemption. Jewish liturgy is also filled with prayers for the Redemption and coming of the *Moshiach*.

Our Sages throughout history have discussed the topic of *Moshiach*, including the great Maimonides, who wrote about this at length in his book of Jewish law, "*Mishneh Torah*". He codified the belief in *Moshiach* and the ultimate resurrection of the dead as essential principles of Jewish faith, going so far as to state that one who does not believe in these denies not only the prophets, but also the entire Torah.

Chassidut teaches that the Hebrew word *gola* (exile) and *geula* (redemption) are opposite concepts, even though in Hebrew both words are spelled with most of the same letters. The difference is that the word "*gola*" does not have the Hebrew letter *alef*. The *alef* symbolizes the Master of the world, the Almighty. The purpose of creation will be achieved by "inserting" the *alef* into *gola*, thereby turning it into the *geula*, the revelation of the Godliness inherent in the world.

The Rebbe has regularly called for awareness of *Moshiach's* imminent arrival, encouraging the study of the laws of *geula* and *Moshiach*, and fervent prayer for its actualization in our times. As he stated, we stand at the threshold of redemption, and one more good deed may be all that is needed to usher in the final *geula*.

### More to Explore

Rambam, Mishneh Torah, Hilchot Melachim, chap. 11-12; Tanya, chap. 37; Likkutei Torah, Tzav, p. 34; Sefer HaMaamorim, 5699, p. 207 and on; Torat Menachem, vol. 33, p. 349; ibid. 5746, vol. 3, p. 145.

### Bottom Line

The Jewish Messiah will be a human being who has free will. Through his leadership, the world will come to recognize that God is the Creator and sole Ruler of all.

### Ponder/Action

- Every person has the ability to hasten *Moshiach's* arrival and the ultimate Redemption. It depends on everyone's personal spiritual commitment and contribution in terms of fulfilling Torah and mitzvot, and performing acts of goodness and kindness.

# *Torah & Mitzvot*

## Bottom Line

Torah is considered nourishment for the soul, while mitzvot are considered its garments. Whenever and wherever we learn Torah properly, we bond with the Almighty.

## Ponder/Action

▸ Prior to studying Torah we should think about the greatness of God and how God's infinite light rests upon those who study His Torah. This reflection inspires a sense of awe and fear, as well as gratitude for the opportunity to connect to God.

# התורה

# The Torah

The Torah, which in Hebrew means "instruction" or "guide," is composed of two parts: the written law (in Hebrew, *Torah SheB'chtav*) and the oral law (*Torah SheBaal Peh*). The written law contains the Five Books of Moses, the Prophets, and the Writings. Along with the written law, Moses was given the oral law which explains and clarifies the written law.

The Torah reveals the will and wisdom of God. It is the channel through which Godliness is connected to the world, both uniting God's infinite light with creation and giving creation the means to connect and unite with God. Before the giving of the Torah, the coarseness of the physical body concealed the essence of the soul. With the giving of the Torah, however, the barriers between the higher and lower spheres were penetrated, enabling mankind to break free from their physical limitations and connect with the Infinite. In this context, the Torah has two facets, *nigleh* (the "revealed" part of Torah), which is "limited" to words and ideas; and *nistar* (the "concealed" part of Torah), which reflects a higher level of reality.

The Talmud states that when Moses ascended Mount Sinai to receive the Torah, he was challenged by the angels: "Why should the Torah be given to human beings?" Moses replied to the Almighty, "What is written in the Torah that You are giving me?—'I am the Lord your God, who brought you out of the Land of Egypt.'" Moses then turned to the angels and said, "Did you go down to Egypt? Were you enslaved to Pharaoh? Why then should the Torah be yours?" Moses gave another example, "In the Torah it is written 'You shall have no other gods.' Do you dwell among people who engage in idol worship?" He continued in this fashion, asking more questions to prove his point—the Torah belongs with us on earth and not in the heavens.

According to our Sages, God placed the Jewish soul in a human form to refine and elevate both the body and the physical world around it. The body, however, is driven by an animal soul with its own agenda of satisfying its desires for food, clothing, money, power, and so on. Following the path of Torah strengthens the Godly soul while weakening the animal soul. Over time, the animal soul learns to appreciate Godliness and willingly serves the ends of Godly soul. In all areas of living, it is through Torah that we connect ourselves and our surroundings to God.

**More to Explore**

Tanya, chap. 4, 5 and 23; Torah Ohr, Bachodesh Hashlishi (Parshas Yisro); Sefer HaMaamorim, 5672 and 5696, Rosh Hashana; ibid. 5739, Vayomar Lo Yehonoson.

# התורה שבעל פה

# The Oral Torah

The "oral law" (in Hebrew, *Torah SheBaal Peh*) is the part of the Torah not written in the "written law" (*Torah SheB'chtav*). The oral law elaborates upon, explains, and clarifies the many details of the commandments only briefly mentioned in the written law. These teachings were verbally transmitted from father to son and from teacher to student, so that any ambiguities could be immediately elucidated. This method of transmission endured for over a thousand years after the Giving of the Torah.

Around 130 years after the destruction of the Second Holy Temple, the great sage Judah the Prince (*Yehuda HaNasi*), fearing that the oral law would be forgotten, gathered the scholars of his generation and compiled the Mishnah ("teachings"). This monumental compendium contained a condensed collection of all the oral teachings passed down to date. Divided into six sections called *sedarim* (orders), they covered the gamut of human life and interaction. The first section dealt with agricultural laws and the laws of blessings and prayers. The second discussed the laws of the Shabbat and the holidays. The third was about marriage and divorce. The fourth dealt with civil and criminal law, as well as ethics. The fifth covered laws about the sacrifices, the Holy Temple, and the laws of kosher. The sixth section discussed the laws of ritual purity.

Over the next three centuries, the divinely inspired discussions of the Sages who learned, expounded, and elucidated the Mishnah were recorded in the thousands of pages of the Talmud, resulting in an authoritative recording of the oral tradition which became binding on all Jews to this day.

A symbiotic relationship exists between the fixed words of God in the written Torah and the profuse elaborations and interpretations by the Sages as recorded in the oral law (i.e., Mishnah, Talmud, including later authoritative *halachic* writings and responsa). The written law nourishes the faith of the soul from on high, while the oral law is the physical manifestation of the Supreme Will, for the elders of the Jewish nation were granted the ability to reveal, understand, and explain His Wisdom and Will, reflecting how mankind "partners" with God in completing and perfecting Creation.

**Bottom Line**

The Oral Torah (i.e., the Mishnah, Talmud, etc.) elaborates, explains, and clarifies the many details of the commandments that are only briefly mentioned in the Torah. They are all divinely inspired and binding on all Jews.

**Ponder/Action**

- Learning Torah nourishes the soul and enlightens the world around us.

**More to Explore**

Torah, Shmos 34:27 (incl. Rashi); Tehillim, 119:126; Talmud, Temura 14b; ibid. Chaggiga 9b; ibid. Eiruvin 13b; ibid. Menochot 29b (incl. Maharsha); Hilchos Talmud Torah of the Alter Rebbe, chapt. 2:13 and 1:4; Tanya, Iggeres Hakodesh, chapt. 1 and 29; Torat Shmuel 5627, Vayedaber Elokim; Likutei Sichos, vol. 36, p.43; Torat Menachem vol. 14, p. 83; Sichos Kodesh, Noso 5736, no. 1; ibid. 19th of Kislev 5733, sicha 8; Hayom Yom, 6th Shvat.

# מצוות

# Mitzvot

In the Torah, the Almighty charged the Jewish people to obey and fulfill 613 mitzvot. These are comprised of 248 positive commandments ("do's") and 365 negative commandments ("do not's"). Our Sages teach that these numbers mirror the 248 organs and 365 vessels of the human body. Since the mitzvot of the Torah relate to material matters, they serve as an intermediary between the infinite revelation of God and the more limited nature of the body and soul. The Torah is considered the soul's nourishment and mitzvot its garments. In fulfilling the positive commandments, we bring about a state in which God "embraces" us, and honoring the directives of the negative commandments helps us purify and sanctify ourselves. Also, the fulfillment of mitzvot creates a powerful spiritual energy for overcoming the darkness and tribulations of exile.

Generally, before fulfilling certain mitzvot we make a blessing that typically involves the phrase, "Blessed are You, Lord our God, King of the universe, Who has sanctified us with His commandments and commanded us concerning…[the mitzvah is named]." The words "Who has sanctified us," (in Hebrew, *kidshanu*) is related to the Hebrew word *kiddushin*, meaning "Who has betrothed us." Betrothal leads to a perfect bond. Also, the root word *kadosh* means "holy." A biblically permitted marriage between two people is a sanctified union. Moreover, God has chosen us as His "partner" and "betrothed us" with His Torah. Our relationship with Him is as sacred as that of a marriage, and is actualized, nurtured, and fulfilled through the observance of the mitzvot of the Torah.

God is concerned with our wellbeing and has given us these commandments in order for us to build a relationship with Him. Just as in a marriage relationship, each partner has a responsibility to the other. As Jews, our responsibility in the sacred relationship between us and the Almighty is to observe the mitzvot of the Torah. God's role consists of His promise to sanctify and protect the Jewish people.

The word "mitzvah" is also related to the Hebrew word *tzavta*, meaning "joining" or "attachment." Every time we perform a mitzvah, we become attached to the essence of God. Thus our Sages taught that "the reward of a mitzvah is the mitzvah," expressing that our ability as mortal and finite creatures to cling to the infinite God, Who Himself ordained the mitzvah, is the ultimate reward.

**More to Explore**

Tanya, chap. 4, 46, and 52; Tanya, Iggeret Hakodesh, chap. 29; Likkutei Torah, Matot, p. 85a; Sefer Hamaamorim, 5680, p. 157; Sefer HaMaamorim, 5652, Vayechi; ibid. 5732 and 5733, Bsho'oh Shehikdimu; ibid. 5746, Yehi Hashem; Likkutei Sichot, vol. 4 p. 1026 and on; Hayom Yom, 8 Cheshvan.

### Bottom Line

Mitzvot have multiple positive effects on a person. They connect us with the Almighty, refine and shield us in this world, and prepare spiritual garments for the soul in the world to come.

According to our Sages, God "desired" to have a dwelling place in the lower realms. Every mitzvah helps to perfect the world, eventually enabling it to serve as a "home" for the revealed Essence of God.

From the soul's perspective, the world can be compared to a "fair" or "marketplace." Only during its lifetime on Earth, (i.e., "at the fair,") can the soul simultaneously elevate the physical and earn spiritual rewards.

### Ponder/Action

▸ A mitzvah is a direct connection with the Almighty. The bond can be accomplished only while the soul is enclosed in a physical body.

# מנהגי ישראל

# Jewish Customs

*Minhagim*, or customs, are religious observances that were adopted by various, and sometimes all Jewish communities over time. The Torah's mitzvot possess a defined structure and framework, including time, location, and other practical details. *Minhagim* express our desire to enhance our connection with God, above and beyond that accomplished through fulfilling mitzvot.

The concept of *minhagim* goes all the way back to the era of King Solomon (circa 829 BCE). Some customs simply reflected local traditions and over time faded into history. Others were adopted by the entire Jewish nation, or large sections thereof, and were eventually set in the *Shulchan Aruch* (Code of the Jewish Law).

Chassidut provides an insight into the concept of a *minhag*: In the Torah, there are 248 positive mitzvot ("do's") and 365 negative mitzvot ("do not's"). Each mitzvah is a "channel" for expressing our relationship with the Almighty (see previous page). When the Jewish people were exiled to different parts of the world and underwent challenges and tribulations, the Sages of the time felt a need to further strengthen the nations' connection with God. Therefore, they established certain *minhagim* based strictly on Torah principles to reinforce the people's spiritual bond with Him. These *minhagim* served to fortify the observance of Torah and the fulfillment of mitzvot. Once adapted and established as law by the Sages, a *minhag* is considered as sacred as a commandment of the Torah.

During the last years of the Rebbe Rayatz's life he revealed and taught many *minhagim*, including those that, up until then, he practiced inconspicuously. Chassidim would thirstily adopt and put these *minhagim* into practice, and teach them to others as well. Regarding the teaching of these *minhagim* to everyone and not just Chassidim, the Rebbe Rayatz once stated that just as the teachings of Chassidut are relevant to every Jewish person, as the Alter Rebbe declared, so are the *minhagim* and ways of Chassidut.

Should one claim that certain Chassidic *minhagim* are too lofty relative to his or her current spiritual level, the Rebbe quoted a letter of the Rebbe Rashab, where he wrote that one should remember that all things happen by Divine providence, thus the fact that one reads about or encounters a certain Chassidic practice indicates it has some personal relevance to his or her life.

### Bottom Line

Jewish customs enhances the fulfillment of Torah and mitzvot and bolsters our connection to God. When we perform a Jewish custom, an exceptional Godly illumination is revealed. Chassidic customs are relevant to all Jewish people.

### Ponder/Action

- Children should be taught to have affection and respect for Jewish customs, so that this attitude becomes ingrained. They should feel how each custom serves as a spiritual illumination and gives deeper meaning to fulfilling Torah and mitzvot.

**More to Explore**

Talmud, Menochot, p. 20; ibid. Menochot, p. 20; Rama on Choshen Mishpat, chap. 46:4; Shulchan Aruch, chap. 232, para. 19; Tanya, pt. 3, chap. 6; Likkutei Torah, Matot, p. 85a, ibid. Sukkot, p. 80c; Likkutei Sichot, vol. 1, p. 245 and 523; ibid. vol. 22, p. 57; ibid. vol. 26, p. 216; Torat Menachem vol. 10, p. 196; Sefer HaMaftechos L'Sichot Kodesh, p. 605; Hayom Yom, 22 Tammuz; Hiskashrus (weekly), no. 880, p. 8.

# בחירה חפשית

# Free Choice

As partners with God in creating a world that reflects the Almighty's infinite goodness and perfection, mankind is held responsible for its actions and is ultimately required to account for them before the Creator. The ability for mankind to consciously choose their own thoughts and actions is, indeed, one of the most precious gifts granted by God. In fact, this characteristic distinguishes humans from all other creatures.

The dynamic function of free choice can, of course, be harnessed for the good and productive, or the converse, affecting the physical world on a personal and communal level. In bestowing free choice, God, in effect, "cedes" to mankind control over matters of small and great consequence, while assisting and supporting those who desire to improve the world and to transcend natural and selfish inclinations.

It is only by distinguishing between two options that we can intelligently choose between them. Thus God, in His ultimate kindness, gave the Torah to humanity so that the essential nature of right and wrong, good and evil, would allow for true freedom of choice.

Maimonides writes that freedom of choice is a core principle of the Torah, upon which the whole doctrine of reward and punishment rests (see *"Rewards & Punishment"* on the following page). He further explained that even though man's deeds are ultimately in God's hands, God does not compel our actions, regardless of His omniscience in world matters.

The Alter Rebbe assures that practicing freedom of choice in our thought, speech, and deed in accordance with the Torah's precepts is within the reach of every single Jew. He stated that every person can turn away from evil and do good by evoking the soul's innate desire to unite with God through its "three garments" of thought, speech, and deed. In other words, choosing good over bad, right over wrong, creation over destruction, is a natural state for the Jew, and one to be nurtured and inspired.

At the same time, to ensure that our actions are meaningful and not merely mechanical functions based on a binary system of cause-and-effect, God keeps the paths of our lives a mystery, leaving the choice for us to make.

**Bottom Line**

Free choice is a gift from God. Therefore, we should always make wise choices, especially in matters of serving God.

**Ponder/Action**

▸ Our soul naturally desires to unite with God through its three garments of thought, speech, and deed (action). Thus we are all given the potential to choose what is positive and thereby draw down an abundance of blessings, both physically and spiritually.

**More to Explore**

Rambam, Mishneh Torah, Laws of Repentance, ch. 5; Tanya, chap. 14; Shaar Habchira, by Rebbe DovBer of Lubavitch, chap. 13; Sefer HaMaamorim, Zeh Hayom 5744; Torat Menachem vol. 27, p. 27; Hitvaaduyot, 5744, vol. 1, p. 501; ibid. vol. 3, pp. 1701-6; ibid. 5745, vol. 1, p. 256.

# שכר ועונש

# Reward & Punishment

The path of Torah and mitzvot lead to material blessings in this world, so we may fulfill our religious obligations without worry and disturbance. Following a person's passing, the soul ascends on high to paradise (in Hebrew, *Gan Eden*), to reap the benefit of what has been spiritually achieved during its lifetime. A culminating reward awaits the arrival of the World to Come (in Hebrew, *Olam Habah*), which is the time of *Moshiach* (the Messiah), when all Jews will receive the ultimate reward for fulfilling Torah and mitzvot (see *"Moshiach,"* p. 39).

Chassidut explains that there are multiple levels of paradise, which the mystics discuss more generally in terms of an upper and lower paradise. The lower level is in the spiritual world of *yetzira*, where emotions dominate; thus, we are rewarded there for serving God with the feelings of the heart. The higher level exists in the spiritual world of *briah*, known as the Intellectual World. There, we are rewarded for serving the Almighty with emotion resulting from intellectual meditation.

During an ideal lifetime, the soul performs the tasks assigned to it by Divine providence, learning Torah, fulfilling mitzvot, and performing acts of goodness and kindness. In so doing, it forges links to the higher worlds and build new, deeper connections to God. As the Alter Rebbe taught, the reward for a mitzvah is the mitzvah itself, because it promotes a closer relationship with God, even while we are still here on earth.

Regarding punishment, the Torah teaches that when one neglects or transgresses its commandments, God forbid, a punishment ensues for the sake of awakening the person to repent and reconnect with God. The Alter Rebbe explained that the precepts of the Torah are, after all, about developing honorable character traits. In a sense, therefore, even punishments can be understood as acts of kindness.

Regarding the state of the soul after a person's passing, if it departs the body in a spiritually intact state, requiring no cleansing in purgatory (in Hebrew, *Gehinom*) of spiritual blemishes caused by careless observance of the Torah or transgressions thereof, it is elevated directly to paradise, where it is fittingly rewarded.

### Bottom Line

The path of Torah and mitzvot lead to blessings in this world, and following a person's passing, reward on high for the soul. Punishment for transgressions are intended to awake us to repent and correct our ways, and reconnect with God.

### Ponder/Action

- The ultimate revelation of the spiritual energies revealed through our observance of Torah and the performance of its mitzvot will take place in the time of Redemption with *Moshiach* (the Messiah).

**More to Explore**

Tanya chap. 48, p. 134; ibid. Iggeret Hakodesh, chap. 17 and 29; Likkutei Torah, Nitzavim, p. 48a; Torah Ohr, p. 49a; Sefer HaLikutim of the Tzemach Tzedek, Os Gimel, p. 238; Sefer Pirush Hamilos, p. 106c; Sefer Shaarei Teshuvah, Shaar Habchira, p. 17d; Derech Mitzvosecha, Tzizit, p. 28 and on; Sefer HaMaamorim, 5733, Kol Yisrael; ibid. 5746, Lehovin Inyan T'chiat Hameitim; Likkutei Sichot, vol. 17, pp. 87, 387 and 404; ibid. vol. 19, pp. 7 and 204; Torat Menachem, 5746, vol. 3, p. 172; ibid. Simchat Torah 5737, chap. 1; ibid. 5742, vol. 1, p. 123; Sichot Kodesh, Miketz 5734, chap. 2; ibid. Bechukosai 5741, chap. 5; Hayom Yom, 23 Elul; ibid. 25 Iyar.

# תשובה

# *Repentance*

In general, there are four parts to repentance (in Hebrew, *teshuvah*): awareness of the lapse, acknowledgment of same; sincere regret and resolution to not repeat the transgression. The Torah views repentance as a return to our source—to one's very essence. Proper repentance not only restores the compromised spirit to its pristine state, but also elevates every aspect related to the transgression as a result. This stronger and more principled spiritual expression is manifest in the person involved, and in the world at large.

Repentance also encompasses both intermittent moments of regret and subsequent desire to return to spiritual righteousness, in addition to day-to-day efforts at spiritual growth. Chassidut explains that a comparison can be made to the founding of a wellspring, which requires effort to excavate it; however, once the surface layers are breached, the living waters gush forth. Metaphorically, every Jew is deeply connected to the Almighty's "wellspring of living waters," the Torah and mitzvot. Often, some work to "dig through" outer layers of resistance is all that is required to reap the reward of the heavenly wellspring that supports the individual in his spiritual service.

The Mishnah states, "Repent one day before your death," meaning that repentance is the completion of our service of God. And because we don't know when our time on earth will end, we should examine our deeds and repent daily, pursuant to the Talmud, "All of one's days should be spent in repentance." If so advised by the Mishnah, however, we might question why we need to repent additionally today when we already repented yesterday? The Sages provide further explanation by distinguishing between a "lower repentance" and a "higher repentance." The lower repentance characterizes the person who has newly become aware of his spiritual decline and distance from God, and who desires to return to a holy state. Chassidut compares this person to someone struggling in deep water, when his survival is at stake and he will do whatever it takes to avoid drowning. At the higher level of repentance we choose to enhance our connection with God by constantly striving to be ever closer.

Moreover, a person exists within a limited framework in this physical world, yet God is infinite. Thus, even if we have attained the highest spiritual levels, when compared to God's infinity, there is always room to reach higher and draw even closer to Him.

### Bottom Line

A sincere thought of repentance can raise a person to the level of a *tzaddik* (righteous person). This is because true repentance reaches beyond all limitations, including time; thus, it can be done "in one instant."

### Ponder/Action

▸ While the concept of "Repent one day before your death" can motivate one to repent, it is preferable to repent out of love for God and with a desire for joy.

### More to Explore

Talmud, 153a; Pirkei Avot, 2:10; Tanya, Iggeret HaTeshuva, chap. 4; Derech Mitzvosecha, p. 78; Sefer HaMaamorim, 5708, p. 83; Torat Menachem, vol. 24, p. 30; ibid. vol. 29, p. 65; Sichot Kodesh, Haazinu 5733, chap. 1; ibid. Haazinu 5735, chap. 2; ibid. Balak 5741 chap. 17; ibid. Simchat Torah 5736, chap. 1, end; ibid. 5742, p. 48; Igrot of the Rebbe, 25 Elul, 5731.

# תפילה

# Prayer

Prayer is a positive commandment in the Torah. We are told to pray to God for our needs in order to establish firmly that God takes notice of our ways, that He can make them successful if we serve Him, or the opposite, God forbid, if we disobey Him, and that success and failure are not the result of chance or accident. The Hebrew word *tefillah* is generally translated as "prayer," but this is not its only translation. The word *"tefillah"* comes from the verb *pallel*, which means "to judge." The reflexive verb, *le-hitpallel*, meaning "to pray," also means "to judge oneself." Thus, prayer is also a time of self-judgment and self-evaluation, during which we ask for God's forgiveness and resolve to better ourselves.

On a higher level, prayer becomes *avodah*, or "service" meant to purify our nature. The plain Hebrew meaning of *avodah* is "work." Think of working with a raw material to transform and refine it into a finished product. In so doing, we remove its impurities and roughness. Similarly, every Jew is endowed with wonderful treasures of character that can be worked to the fore. This refinement is achieved through prayer.

The highest level of prayer is reached when we are so inspired as to want nothing but the feeling of attachment with God. On this level, *tefillah* is related to the verb *tofel*, which is used in Mishnahic Hebrew and means "to attach," "to join," or "bind together." The connotation here is that the soul and God are as two parts of one whole that, through prayer, unite again.

During prayer, our Divine soul speaks to God, and even the animal soul is filled with holiness. We realize that we stand before the Almighty and the whole material world, with all its pains and pleasures, seems to melt away. We become aware of things that really matter and are truly important; even as we pray for life, health and sustenance, we think of these things in their deeper sense: a life that is worthy to be called "living"; health that is not only physical, but above all spiritual; and for sustenance, the things that truly sustain us in this world and in the world to come—Torah and mitzvot. Knowing that God is ultimately good and that nothing is impossible for Him, we can go about life with a deep sense of confidence and security. Even during times of distress we need not despair, knowing that, in some way best known to God, whatever happens is for our own good, and that during any and all, we can reach God through the gift of prayer.

**More to Explore**

Likkutei Torah, Lo Hibit (Balak); Maamorim Kuntreisim of Rabbi DovBer of Lubavitch, p. 579; Derech Mitzvosecha, Shoresh Mitzvahs Hatfila; Sefer HaMaamorim, 5708, p. 94; ibid. 5712, Ani L'dodi; ibid. 5712, Bosi Legani; see also "My Prayer," by Nissan Mindel (Kehot Publication Society).

**Bottom Line**

We pray to God for our needs to affirm within our hearts that God takes notice of our ways and can affect our life. Prayer is a time of self-judgment and self-evaluation, during which we ask for God's forgiveness and resolve to better ourselves.

**Ponder/Action**

- Through prayer, we attach ourselves to God "spirit to spirit," and unify our soul with Him.

**Bottom Line**

The shul and study hall are sacred areas. In effect, they represent God's house and mini-sanctuary.

**Ponder/Action**

▸ Our Sages state that when gathering for prayer, the person who arrives first receives a reward equal to the collective reward of all the congregants that follow.

# בית הכנסת

# The Synagogue

A *beit hakneset* or *shul* (synagogue) and a *beit hamidrash* (study hall), are sacred places that play a vital role in the Jewish community. They reflect the Holy Temple that stood in the holy city of Jerusalem, and are often referred to in Jewish writings as a "miniature" Holy Temple. These edifices are revered and are to be treated with utmost respect.

The creation of houses of worship and study wherever the Jewish people have found themselves, has added a communal element to the obligation for every Jew to pray and to learn Torah. In addition, they serve as a vital locus for Jewish communal life.

Inside the synagogue there is a holy ark (in Hebrew, *Aron Kodesh*) at the front wall, in which the Torah scrolls are kept. In most synagogues, the ark is set on the Eastern wall, so that one's prayers are directed toward Jerusalem. Also inside the synagogue is the reading table *(Bimah)*, upon which the Torah is read, and the prayer stand *(Amud)*, where the prayer leader stands to conduct the services. A shul also requires a *halachically* (i.e., Jewish law) acceptable tall divider (in Hebrew, *mechitza*) separating men and women so that each one can pray focused solely on God.

Just as only the finest materials were used in the building of the Holy Temple, shuls and study halls should be planned and constructed to be as esthetically pleasing as possible. Ideally, they should be open 24-hours a day to be available as a positive spiritual environment for prayer and study.

During prayer in shul, we stand as if before the Master of the World, focusing on the thought, "Know for Whom you are standing." Nothing else exists! Following prayer, it is best to study some Torah in order to linger in a spiritual atmosphere. After this process, we become fortified and ready to step "outside" into the mundane world. Chassidut adds that the world outside is, specifically, where the spiritual strength gained during prayer and learning can be harnessed for the performance of mitzvot and to positively influence others in the service of God.

Bringing children to shul enables us to be positive role models of proper decorum and the practice of meaningful prayer.

**More to Explore**

Talmud, Brochot, 5b; ibid. Moed Katan, end; Sichot Kodesh, 20 Menachem Av, 5718, chap. 1; ibid. Bamidbar 5736, chap. 5; ibid. 29 Elul, 5736, chap. 2; ibid. 11 Nissan, 5738, chs. 39 and 47; ibid. 20 Menachem Av 5739, chap. 66; Torat Menachem, vol. 26, p. 123; ibid. vol. 32, p. 281; ibid. vol. 47, 62; ibid. 5742, vol. 4, p. 1980; ibid. 5749, vol. 1, p. 39; ibid. vol. 2, pp. 67 and 102; ibid. 5751, vol. 1, p. 120.

# תפילין

# Tefillin

The mitzvah of *tefillin* (phylacteries) was among the first commandments given to the Jewish nation while they were still in Egypt, just prior to the Exodus. The Hebrew word *"tefillin"* is related to the word *"tefillah,"* which means "prayer." Both words share the root *tofel*, which means "to attach," "to join," or "bind together." Prayer and *tefillin* signify our connection and commitment to God.

*Tefillin* are donned by Jewish men from the age of thirteen before the morning prayers, and promote a state of awareness and humility before the Almighty. Wearing *tefillin* demonstrates acceptance of the "Yoke of Heaven" and the release of our mind and heart to the Will of God. These ideas are represented by the fact that we put *tefillin* on the arm, facing the heart—seat of our emotions, and on the head—seat of our intellect. In committing our emotions, deeds, and intellect to the Almighty, we elevate our entire being.

Kosher *tefillin* are made by a God-fearing scribe, and have been checked by a reliable scribe at intervals and found to be in order. Wearing kosher *tefillin*, we are taught, elicits deep intellectual capabilities from Higher spheres and also enhances the wearer's mental capacity during Torah study.

The *tefillin* are comprised of two specially constructed leather boxes containing scrolls inside of them. The *shel yad* (literally interpreted, "of the arm") is bound to the arm and hand with the attached leather strap, and the *shel rosh* (literally interpreted, "of the head") is put on the head, secured by its attached leather straps. The head *tefillin* consists of four compartments, each containing a tiny scroll of parchment with a specific section of Torah written on it in a special Hebrew script. In the hand *tefillin*, four sections are written on one long parchment scroll that is carefully rolled up.

In response to letters from people requesting advice for health, family, or business issues, the Rebbe often advised them to have their *tefillin* checked to ensure that they are still kosher and to repair or buy new kosher ones when necessary. All *Tefillin* should be checked by a qualified scribe at least twice every seven years, to make sure that the boxes and parchments within, as well as the straps, are still kosher.

**More to Explore**

Talmud, Brochot 6a; Zohar, part 2, p. 283a; Shulchan Aruch Harav, chap. 25, par. 11; Likkutei Sichot, vol. 9, p. 11 and 55; ibid. vol. 14, p. 152; Torat Menachem, vol. 8, p. 208; ibid. vol. 24, p. 290; ibid. vol. 49, p. 429; ibid. vol. 55, p. 200; ibid. vol. 57, p. 165; ibid. 5742, vol. 2, p. 823; Sichot Kodesh, Yud Shevat 5735, chap. 5; ibid. Purim 5731, chap. 2; ibid. Purim, 5735, chap. 5; ibid. Rosh Chodesh Iyar 5735, chap. 3; ibid. 16th Tammuz, 5735, chap. 3; ibid. Bamidbar 5732, chap. 6; ibid. ibid. Voeschanan 5734, chap. 2; ibid. R'eh 5734, chap. 3; Hamelech Bemisibo, vol. 1, p. 252.

**Bottom Line**

While he is wearing *Tefillin*, a man should have the intention of subjugating and "attaching" his mind and heart to the Almighty and to His will.

**Ponder/Action**

▸ *Tefillin* is one of the first commandments that connected us to God as Jews, and it enables men to express their deep connection to the Almighty on a daily basis.

## Bottom Line

The mitzvah of honoring parents applies to when they are living as well as after they have passed away. Those who honor and revere their parents merit long life. The Sages equate honoring parents with honoring the Almighty.

## Ponder/Action

▶ By honoring parents, we merit to receive honor from our own children.

# כיבוד הורים

# Honoring Parents

When God gave the Ten Commandments to the Jewish nation, half of the commandments addressed matters between man and God, and the other half addressed matters between man and man. The Fifth Commandment, honoring our parents, appropriately bridges the God/man and man/man commandments because, as our Sages taught, there are three partners in the creation of every child—the father, mother, and God, who bestows life and blessings. Therefore, respecting our parents expresses respect for God as well.

Honoring parents leads us to recognize God's tremendous kindness and goodness in granting us our bodies with its incredibly complex systems, as well as a soul capable of understanding and intuition. Honoring our parents also generates unique blessings, including the Biblical promise from God that, "Your days will be lengthened on the land that God, your God, is giving you."

The mitzvah of honoring parents makes sense once it was given. In fact, we are taught that when the nations of the world heard of this commandment, they gained additional respect for all the other commandments. Our parents not only bring us into the world, but they invest their time, money, and energy into raising us. This mitzvah is thus also a reminder to recognize and show gratitude for what others have done for us.

The Code of Jewish Law (*Shulchan Aruch*) states that this mitzvah demands both awe and honor. What defines awe? Examples include not sitting in our parents' usual seat, not contradicting their words, and not calling them by their name. What constitutes honor? This would be demonstrated by such acts as rising in their presence, and cheerfully providing all their needs, including food and drink, sufficient clothing, and transportation to places they need to go. The Talmud recognizes that this mitzvah can be difficult to follow at times, yet we are amply rewarded for our efforts.

The *Zohar* (foundational work of Kabbalah) adds that after the passing of our parents, we are obligated to respect them even more, since in the spiritual realm there are no limits to how high we can help elevate their soul through doing good deeds in their memory.

### More to Explore

Torah, Shemot 20:12; Talmud, Kiddushin, p. 30b-31a; Jerusalem Talmud, Peah 1:1; Zohar, vol. 2, end of Parshas Bchukotai; Sefer Hachinuch, Mitzvah no. 33; Shulchan Aruch, Yoreh Deah, 240:1-14; Torat Menachem, 5747, vol. 1, p. 334; ibid. 5751, vol. 1, p. 198 and 291; Sichot Kodesh, B'chukosai 5733, chap. 5; ibid. 11 Nissan 5738, chap. 5; ibid. Vayikra 5740, chap. 8; ibid. Shavuot 5734, chap. 5; ibid. Eikev 5740, chap. 58; ibid. 20 Menachem Av 5735, chap. 5; ibid. Behar-Bechukosai 5737, chap. 22; Igrot Kodesh of the Rebbe Rayatz, vol. 1, p. 203.

# צדקה

# *Tzedakah*

Throughout the entirety of the Jerusalem Talmud, charity (in Hebrew, *tzedakah*) is called simply "The Commandment," as this was the idiomatic expression commonly used to refer to it. The reason it was distinguished so singularly is that the mitzvah of *tzedakah* is the root of all mitzvot in the Torah. According to our Sages, it even surpasses them, since no other mitzvah elevates the entire soul in the way *tzedakah* does. All other mitzvot elevate aspects of the person's body, such as the use of hands for action such as donning *tefillin*, or holding an *etrog*. However, when we give *tzedakah*, we give from the proceeds of our toil in which all the faculties of our soul are invested.

The Hebrew word *tzedakah* actually means "justice" and "righteousness," suggesting that it is more of an obligation than a discretionary action. Indeed, our Sages point out that on a meaningful level, everything we own is entrusted to us by God to be put to use for our own needs and then, serving as His agent, to share the remainder with those in need. Providing food, clothing, physical help, a listening ear, good advice, and even a kind disposition, are all valid forms of *tzedakah*.

The Alter Rebbe explained that the amount of *tzedakah* given is often constrained by an individual's natural inclinations. However, he says, diligent spiritual self-refinement enables a person to "leap above and beyond" his character and give generously and happily. Furthermore, when it comes to *tzedakah*, frequency trumps quantity. Meaning, it is better to give less but often, than to give a large sum all at once, for this refines the giver to a greater degree and brings greater benefit to the world.

The Rebbe taught that although one should give *tzedakah* when asked, there are auspicious times for doing so, such as prior to morning and afternoon prayers, before Shabbat and holiday candle-lighting, and prior to performing other mitzvot.

To express the enormity of the reward for giving *tzedakah*, the Rebbe often quoted the verse of God's promise to the Prophet Malachi: "Bring the whole of the tithes into the treasury so that there may be nourishment in My House, and test Me now therewith, says the Lord of Hosts, if I will not open for you the windows of Heaven and pour down for you blessing until there be no room to suffice for it."

### Bottom Line

The Hebrew word *tzedakah* means "justice" and "righteousness," suggesting that it is more of an obligation than a discretionary action. In giving *tzedakah*, one is promised abundant blessings from God.

### Ponder/Action

▸ Our Sages taught that every mitzvah God commands us to do, He performs as well. His way of giving *tzedakah* is by caring for our material needs. However, the ultimate expression of Divine *tzedakah* will be when He takes us out of exile through the coming of *Moshiach (the Messiah)*.

**More to Explore**

Torah, Devorim 15:7-8 and 11; Malachi 3:10; Pirkei Avot 3:15; Midrash Tanchuma, chap. 15; Rambam, Hilchos Matnos Aniyim 7:2; ibid. chapt. 10:1; Tanya, chap. 37, p. 96; ibid. Iggeret Hakodesh, chap. 4 and 21; Likkutei Sichot, vol. 2, p. 410; ibid. vol. 24, p. 298 (footnote 74); Sichot Kodesh, Noach 5741, chap. 52; Sefer HaMinhagim (Chabad), pp. 7-8 (and footnotes); Igrot Kodesh of the Rebbe, 12th of Sivan 5717; Hayom Yom, 6 Tammuz; Hiskashrut (weekly) vol. 880, p. 10.

# אהבת ישראל

# *Love of a Fellow Jew*

Our Sages taught that when there is unity among the Jewish people, the Divine presence rests among them. When there is division, God forbid, it departs, because in its perfection, it cannot rest in a fragmented space. It is thus well understood why love of a fellow Jew (in Hebrew, *Ahavat Yisrael*) is a cardinal principal in Judaism, and why it is constantly accentuated and discussed in Chassidut. The *Zohar* (foundational work of Kabbalah) teaches that God, Torah, and the Jewish people are "one." It follows that love for God, for Torah, and for a fellow Jew are all interrelated. For this reason, our feelings and actions towards a fellow Jew is an excellent barometer for our feelings toward and love of God. One who loves the Father, surely loves His children.

Self-love is innate and comes naturally to most people. Love and concern for others, however, is a learned skill. How can we love a fellow Jew whom we don't even know, or one who doesn't look or act like us? The answer, according to Chassidut, is clear: at its most core level, love for a fellow Jew is an embedded characteristic of our soul. The Jewish soul is connected to all others through their common root in Godliness. As explained by Tzemach Tzedek, all Jewish souls are rooted in an aspect of the original man, Adam's soul. With the same source, all Jewish souls are inherently interconnected.

One of the teachings of the Baal Shem Tov was that a soul may descend to this world and live for a lifetime ("for seventy, eighty years"), just to do a material favor for another Jew. If this is true for a material favor, think how much greater is the mitzvah of helping a fellow Jew in the spiritual realm, for example, by imparting knowledge and spiritual support. Even better, we need not wait to become a scholar to teach or guide others. If we know the first Hebrew letter *"Alef,"* we can already teach that to others. If we know more, we relate more—each sharing according to their present knowledge and abilities.

In the physical realm, love of a fellow Jew is actualized by speaking positively about other Jews, focusing more on similarities than on differences, doing favors for one another, looking for opportunities to support needy Jews and Jewish institutions, inviting fellow Jews to share in religious experiences, such as Shabbat or Jewish holiday meals and events, etc. All such acts draw blessings from God into the world.

**More to Explore**

Torah, Vayikra 19:18; Derech Mitzvosecha, p. 56; Sefer HaSichot 5701, p. 144; Igrot Kodesh of the Rebbe, vol. 4, p. 29; Hayom Yom, 15 Kislev; ibid. 5 Iyar; ibid. 18 Menachem Av.

**Bottom Line**

The Jewish nation is considered a single body. When one Jew loves another, it reflects their deep, soul-level connection, and in turn, the health of the Jewish nation. Acting on love for a fellow Jew brings blessings from the Almighty.

**Ponder/Action**

▸ It is written, "Love your God." It is also written, "Love your fellow Jew." The Almighty says, "I will put aside the love you should have for Me, as long as love is shown to a fellow Jew."

# אומות העולם

# The Nations of the World

The Torah records that at the time of the building of the Tower of Babel, God separated mankind into 70 nations, with 70 languages, and scattered them upon the face of the earth. The purpose of the nations was to refine and civilize the world through adherence to the Seven Noachide Laws of universal morality. The renowned Biblical commentator Rashi notes that unlike the generation of The Great Flood (2,105 BCE), which had to be completely destroyed because of endemic thievery and strife, the descendants of Noah who built the Tower of Babel, behaved with love and friendship among themselves, and so instead of being annihilated, they were divided and dispersed around the world. According to the Midrash, from this we learn that discord is hateful and peace is great. It also implies a vital truth—that at a root level, all of mankind possess the ability to deal kindly and live peacefully with one another.

When Moses addressed the Jewish nation on the last day of his earthly life, he did so in a form of a 70-line ethical oration which is recorded in the Torah portion of *Haazinu*. Among the exhortative verses, Moses referred to the above-mentioned separation of nations and, according to Rashi, intimated that the Almighty did so in correspondence with the [future] number of the children of Israel who would go down to Egypt. Rashi explains that God let Noach's descendants remain, for the sake of the children of Israel who were destined to descend from them (i.e., from Noach's son, *Shem*), and ultimately, for the 70 souls of the children of Israel who would go down to Egypt and initiate the events that brought us the Torah.

The Midrash relates that, in the Heavenly spheres, each of the 70 Nations (i.e., major countries) of the world are under the dominion of one of 70 Angels who dwell near the Heavenly Throne. These Angels serve as representatives of their respective countries, and the needs of each country are channeled through them. When a Jewish person performs a mitzvah, we are taught, he elevates the Godly "spark" in the country where he dwells, drawing down blessings upon all its citizens.

In the times of the Holy Temple, during the holiday of *Sukkot* (Tabernacles), 70 offerings were brought for the merit of the nations of the world. The Midrash relates that if these nations only knew how beneficial the services of the Holy Temple were for them, they would surround it to protect it.

**More to Explore**

Torah, Bereishit, 11:1-9; Haazinu 32:8-10 (with Rashi); Midrash, Bereishit Rabbah, 38:6; Bamdibar Rabbah, 1:3; Midrash, Shir Hashirim Rabbah, chap. 4; Talmud, Sukkah 55b; Ramban, Bamidbar 11:16; Torat Shmuel 5628, p.158; Torat Sholom, p. 205; Likkutei Sichot, vol. 7, p.219; Sichot Kodesh, 19 Kislev, 5735, sicha 8.

### Bottom Line

The mission of the nations of the world is to refine and civilize the world, through adherence to the Seven Noachide Laws of universal morality. Furthermore, at a root level, mankind possesses the ability to deal kindly and live peacefully with one another.

### Ponder/Action

▸ Ponder how our actions can go beyond affecting only us and our corner of the world, but can also have a positive ripple-effect throughout the world.

Bottom Line

It is the Jews' duty to see to it that all people lead righteous and decent lives in compliance with the Noachide laws of universal morality.

Ponder/Action

▸ Even a single positive action can have far-reaching consequences, producing ever-widening ripples until their cumulative effect ushers in the ultimate Redemption.

# מצוות בני נח

# The Noachide Laws

The world, Judaism teaches, was not created to be in chaos, but to be inhabited and settled. When there are no absolute criteria by which man lives and when morals and ethics are based solely on man's ever-shifting understanding which can be influenced by motives inconsistent with reason and justice, then a chaotic world results. To avoid this outcome, G-d has given clear and absolute guidance on how the world can be made decent, productive, settled, and enduring.

The Noachide laws of universal morality which consist of six prohibitions—against murder, robbery, idolatry, adultery, blasphemy, and cruelty to animals—as well as one positive command—to establish a judicial system, were given to the nations of the world as a Divine code of conduct. These laws are general statements, the ramifications and extensions of which encompass countless details. It is through observance of the Noachide laws that the world becomes a decent, productive place, and a fitting receptacle for the Divine. Ultimately, observance of these laws will culminate in the Messianic epoch, when as the prophet Zephaniah proclaims, "All will invoke the Lord by name and serve Him with one accord."

When gentiles live in consonance with these laws, not just because human logic compels them to do so, but because they are God's commands, we can be assured that the whims of society will never be allowed to distort the Divine criteria of conduct.

The Rebbe emphasized that we, as Jews, have a crucial role to play in the world's knowledge of and adherence to the Noachide laws. He explained that, as is taught in Kabbalah and Chassidut, our mission and purpose is to make the world a fitting "dwelling place" for God. An integral part of accomplishing this is to see to it that all people, and not just Jews, acknowledge the Almighty as the Creator and Ruler of the world. In light of this responsibility, we cannot remain indifferent to the conduct of the world and must see to it that the world's nations lead a righteous and decent life in congruence with the Noachide laws.

Furthermore, a world where individuals live by no law other than that dictated by mankind will inevitably affect the Jewish people negatively. It is therefore to our benefit to promote and teach the Noachide laws. True, the task may seem immense, even impossible, given that Jews are a minuscule minority among the nations of the world, but with determined effort, the Rebbe assured, progress can be made.

**More to Explore**

Zephaniah 3:9; Rambam, Mishne Torah, Hilchot Malochim, chap. 8, par. 10-11; Likkutei Sichot, vol. 15, p. 150; 18 p. 168; 26 p. 132; Torat Menachem, 5742, vol. 1, p. 225; ibid. vol. 4, p. 2048; ibid. 5744, vol. 4, p. 2167; ibid. 5745, vol. 4, p. 2466; 5746, vol. 2, p. 44, and vol. 4, p. 252.

# גירות

# Conversion

In general, the Torah discourages gentiles from converting to Judaism. Specifically, prospective converts are told about all the negative experiences that the Jewish nation has endured throughout history, as well as the awesome yoke of responsibility of adhering the 613 commandments of the Torah. Further, considering their previous background and lifestyle, converts need to be extra careful so as to avoid falling back into old habits.

Potential converts are also advised that they may experience emotional pain as a result of leaving the ways of their family of origin, as well as from being unable to maintain the same level of relationship as they had before, including possible conflict with some relatives. (Despite this potential complication, the Rebbe always encouraged converts to maintain proper respect for their non-Jewish parents.)

If a gentile still desires to convert, qualified Orthodox rabbis teach him or her all necessary Jewish laws and commandments, in preparation for the conversion itself. This is necessary because that person becomes obligated to follow the commandments immediately upon conversion.

Required elements of a kosher conversion include intense study of Jewish tenets and faith; laws of proper daily Jewish living; receiving a proper *brit* (circumcision) for males; and immersion in a kosher *mikvah* (ritual pool). A conversion is valid only when it is done strictly according to Jewish law ("*halacha*") as codified in the Code of Jewish Law (*Shulchan Aruch*), and the entire process is overseen, and the ceremony conducted by, a qualified Orthodox *Beit Din* (Jewish court).

A convert who has converted in accordance with *Halacha* is considered a child of God. The Torah specifies thirty-six warnings and identifies three prohibitions against offending a convert. We are also taught that since gentiles are not obligated to convert, the spiritual reward for doing so on one's own volition is exceedingly great.

Interestingly, when the Talmud discusses those who convert to Judaism, it uses the phrase, "a convert who converted." Shouldn't it be "a non-Jew who converted"? This hints, our Sages teach, that their drive to convert stems from a Jewish spark already within their soul.

**More to Explore**

Likkutei Sichot, vol. 18, p. 130; Torat Menachem, vol. 30, p. 215; ibid. vol. 60, p. 461; Sichot Kodesh, 11 Nissan 5734, chap. 5; ibid. Tovo 5734, chap. 4; ibid. 12 Tammuz, 5734, chap. 17; ibid. Beshalach 5739, chap. 49; ibid. Shlach 5740, chap. 3, at end.

**Bottom Line**

In general, the Torah discourages gentiles from converting to Judaism. If a gentile still desires to convert, qualified Orthodox rabbis teach him or her all necessary Jewish laws and commandments. A conversion is valid only when it is done strictly according to the Code of Jewish Law, and the entire process is overseen, and the ceremony conducted by, a qualified Orthodox *Beit Din* (Jewish court).

**Ponder/Action**

▸ On a personal level, conversion is constantly taking place. When we perform a mitzvah involving a physical object, we are raising that object's condition to one of sanctity. The spark within the object may have been waiting for its redemption from the beginning of time.

SECTION FOUR

# *Torah Study*

## Bottom Line

A house full of sacred Jewish books has a big impact on the home and its inhabitants, both spiritually and physically.

## Ponder/Action

▸ Keeping sacred Jewish books in the house brings blessing and light into the home. Make it a habit to purchase and study Jewish books.

# ספרי קודש
# *Sacred Books*

There's a discussion in the Midrash whether a home full of *seforim* (sacred Jewish books) needs a *mezuzah*, which implies that Jewish books possess a unique quality distinct from all other kinds of books. In the same vein, The Rebbe urged all Jews, regardless of their current level of observance, to buy *seforim* and conspicuously display them throughout their homes, conveying that sacred Jewish books, along with the ideas they represent, are of utmost importance to them. The presence of sacred Jewish books also encourages family and guests to take a book or two off the shelf and study them, an act which will imbue their thoughts, speech, and actions with an added level of holiness.

Although one might argue that a wall full of Torah books in our home contains more than could be learned in a lifetime, the sanctity in the holy books themselves creates an environment reflective of their holiness. Their presence also protects the house and its residents, drawing forth the spiritual merits found among its pages.

From a Chassidic perspective, a house full of seforim has an additional meaning: the Hebrew word *seforim* has the same root as the word *sefirot* (spiritual "vessels" that reflect divinity), signifying that a home with sacred Jewish books transmits a high level of sublime Divinity.

There are several essential *seforim* that serve as the foundation of any home collection. These include a *Siddur* (Jewish prayer book), *Chumash* (the five books of the Torah), *Tehillim* (the Book of Psalms), *Mishnahyot* (authoritative collection of the oral tradition given to Moses on Mount Sinai) or Talmud (rabbinic analyses of the Mishnahic texts ), *Kitzur Shulchan Aruch* (abbreviated Code of Jewish Law), and a *Tanya* (the foundational work of Chabad Chassidic philosophy). Also, the Rebbe encouraged children to have at least a *Chumash, Tehillim, Tanya,* and charity box in their own room.

The Rebbe further advocated having at least one charity box in each Jewish home or office. Aside from being an ideal destination for spare change and for additional coins before Shabbat and Jewish holidays, having a charity box, the Rebbe said, elevates the entire space it occupies from being simply a home or office to being a center of kindness and compassion. The Rebbe also suggested affixing the charity box to a wall as a permanent fixture, expressing a permanent commitment to generosity and love.

**More to Explore**

Midrash, Korach; Likkutei Sichot, vol. 13, p. 213 and 275; Sichot Kodesh, Vayeshev, 5734, chap. 5; ibid. 15 Sivan, 5734, chap. 3; ibid. Shlach, 5734, chap. 1; ibid. Balak, 5734, chap. 4; ibid. 20 Menachem Av, 5734, chap. 2; ibid. Bereishit, 5735, chap. 7; ibid. 16 Tammuz, 5735, chap. 3; ibid. Matot-Massai, 5736, chap. 6; ibid. Devorim, 5736, chap. 4; ibid. 29 Elul, 5736, chap. 2; Hayom Yom, 17 Cheshvan.

# רוח הקודש
# Spiritual Intuition

Spiritual intuition, in Hebrew, *ruach hakodesh*, refers to Divine inspiration and insight that is granted to certain individuals. For example, according to the Talmud, Moses delivered Deuteronomy *(Chumash Devorim)* to the Israelites with spiritual intuition. In a similar vein, all the elaborations and commentaries on Torah that were revealed to the Rabbinic Sages as recorded in the Mishnah and Talmud (the *Tana'im* and *Amora'im*) are words of the Almighty. Also thus inspired are the words of all Torah-true scholars, who are referred to as the "Moses" of their generation.

Obtaining Divine inspiration requires extraordinary devotion to the Torah and self-refinement. It is told that Rashi, the foremost commentator on the Torah and Talmud, spent 613 days in fasting and prayer in preparation for writing his commentaries. Our tradition relates that his words were written with pure spiritual intuition. Although a sage may not be consciously aware of his receiving Divine inspiration, it will be reflected in the precision and meticulousness of his commentaries, wherein not so much as even one letter is superfluous or out of place.

According to Chassidut, the various rulings issued by the Mishnaic and Talmudic Sages were based upon their vision of Jewish laws existing in the higher spiritual worlds. Yet, since each sage envisioned them in accordance through the lens of their own particular soul, there is potential for controversy among the rulings.

Rabbi Yosef Karo, author of the original Code of Jewish Law (*Shulchan Aruch*) states that the spirit of the Almighty is embedded within its language, and the work reflects God's desire. We are also taught that the AriZal (Rabbi Isaac Luria), author of the *Zohar* (foundational work of Kabbalah), was endowed with Divine inspiration by virtue of the great joy with which he fulfilled mitzvot.

On some level, all Jews are blessed with spiritual intuition. It is said in the name of the Baal Shem Tov that the references our Sages make to a Heavenly voice that issues forth from Mount Sinai every day, calling for our repentance, is actually heard by all Jews with their "spiritual" ear. It is this Divine echo from Sinai that empowers us to hear the inner voice of reason and goodness and to desire repentance.

### More to Explore

Talmud, Megilah, p. 31b, incl. Tosfot; Biurei HaZohar, Vayishlach, p. 20b; Tanya, introduction; Torah Ohr, Toldot p. 20b; Tzemach Tzedek Responsa, Yoreh Deah. no. 176. pt. 3, chap. 1; ibid. Orach Chaim, no. 115, chap. 1; Likkutei Sichot, vol. 4, pp. 1087-1088; ibid. vol. 5 p. 341; ibid. vol. 7, p. 170; ibid. vol. 19, p. 9; vol. 23, p. 40, footnotes 27-28 and 78; Torat Menachem, 5745, vol. 3, p. 1503; ibid. 5749, vol. 2, p. 118, footnote 67; Hayom Yom, 6 Shevat. Sichot Kodesh, Haazinu 5731, chap. 5; ibid. 11 Nissan, 5733, chap. 6; ibid. Teruma, 5740, chap. 40; ibid. Metzora 5733, chap. 4; ibid. Acharei, 5733, chap. 4.

### Bottom Line

Spiritual intuition is given from Above to certain righteous individuals. Although a sage may not be consciously aware of his receiving Divine inspiration, it will be reflected in the precision and meticulousness of his commentaries, wherein not so much as even one letter is superfluous or out of place.

### Ponder/Action

▸ The words of the Torah, Mishnah, Talmud, Kaballah, *Shulchan Aruch* (Code of Jewish Law), and all authentic rabbinic commentaries were written under Divine inspiration.

### Bottom Line

Kabbalah relates to the most elevated levels of Torah understanding. When studying Chabad Chassidut, the student acquires knowledge from all levels of Torah, as is obligatory for all Jews.

### Ponder/Action

▸ When we learn Torah, and the study is informed by the teachings of Chassidut, we receive the essentials of Kabbalah and can connect with the most exalted concepts in Torah, drawing down Godliness from the highest spiritual realms.

# קבלה

# Kabbalah

The Hebrew word "*Kabbalah*" means "that which has been received." In general, it refers to the body of knowledge passed down from the time of the revelation at Mount Sinai and even earlier, conveying the most elevated understanding of the Torah and the spiritual nature of God's presence and interaction with the world.

There are various schools of thought in Kabbalah, primarily represented by the AriZal and the Ramak (Rabbi Moshe Cordovero). Chabad Chassidut aligns more with the Kabbalah of the AriZal, as elucidated by his student Rabbi Chaim Vital in his works, *Etz Chaim* and *Pri Etz Chaim*. Even though during most of Jewish history, learning Kabbalah was restricted to those over forty years of age and in possession of a firm foundation in all other areas of Torah, the AriZal taught that in our times, it is a mitzvah to spread the teachings of Kabbalah.

In general, there are four levels of Torah study: *Pshat*—the simple, textual understanding, *Remez*—its allegorical meaning, *Drush*—its metaphorical meaning, and *Sod*—its secret or esoteric meaning; i.e., Kabbalah. The first letters of the four words spell the Hebrew word *Pardes*, which means "Garden," as in the "Garden of Torah." Essentially, the Torah was given from on High in a multifaceted, summarized form. Through the levels above, however, complete comprehension by mankind is possible.

A fifth level, Chassidut, primarily Chabad Chassidut with its systematic and exegetical teachings, contains the essence of all four levels of *Pardes*, providing an energizing and intellectual context for both scholar and layman. Thus, when a person studies Chassidut, he is acquiring knowledge from all levels of Torah, as is obligatory for all Jews.

Several specific Kabbalah works considered to be authentic are *Shmona Sh'orim*, *Sefer Hagilgulim*, and those from *Mahari Tzemach*. Today, there are a number of individuals and organizations who teach Kabbalah. One must choose a mentor wisely, because Kabbalah goes hand-in-hand with *mesorah* (tradition; the "Oral Torah"), and both must be central to the daily life and conduct of the person teaching it. Also, Kabbalah cannot be grasped in a fragmented manner, for it is incumbent on us to study all areas of Torah.

### More to Explore

Tanya, Iggeret Hakodesh, chap. 26; Hilchot Talmud Torah of the Alter Rebbe, Ch. 1:4; Sefer HaMaamorim, 5718, Tzion; Likkutei Sichot, vol. 26 p. 35; Torat Menachem, vol. 21, p. 235; ibid. 5742, vol. 1, p. 357; ibid. vol. 4, p. 2061; ibid. 5744, vol. 3, p. 1753; Sichot Kodesh, Tetzave 5732, chap. 6; ibid. 19 Kislev 5733, chap. 4; ibid. Vayeshev 5735, chap. 2; ibid. Tetzave 5739, chap. 34; ibid. 2 Cheshvan 5740, chap. 2; ibid. Chukas 5740, chap. 5; ibid. Matot 5741, chap. 20; Hamelech Bemisibo, vol. 1, p. 238; Kfar Chabad (weekly), no. 827, p. 38.

# קבלה מעשית
# *Practical* Kabbalah

The concept of "Practical Kabbalah" refers to the use of incantations of specific Divine names, amulets, and deep-level guided meditations for the purpose of changing natural states or events, e.g. inducing "paranormal" activities, in addition to influencing the configuration of Divine energies and thus affecting reality. These powerful abilities were to be solely employed by extremely holy Jewish Sages, and only for the benefit of mankind. Comprehensive knowledge of the proper application of many of the preternatural activities found in the writings of Kabbalah, such as palm reading, stargazing, and the like, has been lost over history.

In more recent times (i.e., the past 400–500 years), the loss of knowledge of the original practices has led the AriZal, along with many other many Kabbalists, to shun the use of Practical Kabbalah, due to the general lack of ritual purity and dangers of misapplication. Even though the Rebbes of Chabad were familiar with aspects of Practical Kabbalah, they did not draw attention to this field in their actions or writings.

Recently there has been a proliferation of Kabbalistic knowledge peddlers, who prey on the uninformed public by offering to teach the "Traditions of Kabbalah" or "Practical Kabbalah" in a few lessons, or over a few days, for a fee—or sometimes even for "free" albeit with mandatory purchase of their high-priced books, DVD's, etc. Be aware that in an area so deeply involving a person's soul, plenty of caution should be taken regarding what is being proffered, and by whom. Clearly, a true understanding of authentic Kabbalah cannot be made based on books and theory alone, let alone in lessons from individuals with little or no genuine knowledge.

To ensure that professed teachers of Kabbalah are not superficial at best, or deceitful at worst, you should ascertain whether they lead their personal lives in accordance with the precepts of the Written and Oral Torah as codified in the Mishnah, Talmud, and the Code of Jewish Law (*Shulchan Aruch*), and that they do so in such a way as to demonstrate that the principles are an integral part of their life. The seeker should also evaluate his or her motivations for studying Kabbalah. Many newcomers don't realize that for the Jew, reaching true spiritual heights comes from living Jewishly in accordance with all aspects of Torah in a practical, day-to-day manner. Embellishing one's faith with intriguing rituals and adornments is but secondary to a true Torah-filled life.

**More to Explore**

Zohar, part 3, p. 43b; ibid. part 2, p. 76a; Igrot Kodesh of the Rebbe, vol. 9, p. 32; ibid. vol. 15, p. 64; Kfar Chabad (weekly), no. 1097, p. 20.

**Bottom Line**

Practical Kabbalah relates to changing natural states or events by using incantations of specific Divine names, amulets, and deep-level, guided meditation. The genuine knowledge regarding this field has been lost over history. Be cautious where and from whom any aspect of Kabbalah is studied.

**Ponder/Action**

▸ Refrain from visiting purveyors of "paranormal" offerings, and instead study Chassidut which delivers the heart of the Torah in a proper, wholesome, and genuine manner, thereby meaningfully invoking all of God's blessings that one may need.

## Bottom Line

The Mishnah (written record of the oral tradition) and Gemara (rabbinic analyses of the Mishnahic texts) constitute the Talmud. The Babylonian Talmud demands exertion for the student to reach the highest levels of scholarship. The Jerusalem Talmud provides clarity without confusion.

## Ponder/Action

▸ Learning the Babylonian Talmud affords a person the unique opportunity to uncover and reflect Godly light into the world.

# התלמוד

# *The* Talmud

The Mishnah (literally interpreted, "review") records the oral tradition given to Moses on Mount Sinai. It was compiled by Judah the Prince *(Yehuda HaNasi)* around the year 200 CE. The Gemara (literally interpreted, "conclusion") consists of rabbinic analyses of the Mishnahic texts and was written over the next three centuries (200 – 500 CE). Together, the Mishnah and Gemara constitute the Talmud (literally interpreted, "Instruction"). The Talmud Yerushalmi ("Jerusalem Talmud") was compiled by Rabbi Yochanan and reflects the understanding of the Sages in the Land of Israel. Regarding this edition of the Talmud, we are taught that the holiness of the land contributed to a clarity in learning. Therefore, questions are asked and answered in a relatively direct manner. The Talmud Bavli ("Babylonian Talmud") was compiled by the Sages Rav Ashi and Ravina and reflects the learning of the Jewish academies in Sura and Pumpedita, in Babylon. Here, every subject is marked by differences of opinion, requiring clarification. At times, the discussion extends over many pages, often with various digressions.

From a Chassidic perspective, illumination and revelation can occur from "below to Above," and its converse, from "Above to below." From "below to Above" refers to the Godliness that is concealed within the words of the Torah, and revealed by individuals who put significant effort and time into learning and understanding Torah, at times even completely changing their approach. The other means of illumination, from "Above to below," refers to Godliness in a revealed state, wherein the student simply receives spiritual light. The Talmud Bavli forces students to address obscurity and confusion to achieve clarity. Students must immerse themselves in the experience and use various techniques to acquire a deeper understanding of the text and the various positions of the rabbis. On the other hand, the easily comprehensible question-and-answer format of the Talmud Yerushalmi symbolizes light given from Above. The learning experience is not as intense, nor does it require as much effort on the part of students.

When there is a dispute between the Talmud Bavli and Talmud Yerushalmi, the Talmud Bavli is given precedence because it addresses the topic with all its details, therefore, it yields Jewish law (the *"Halacha"*). However, we are taught that in the upcoming Redemption, our study will follow the approach of Talmud Yerushalmi—i.e., light that comes directly from Above.

**More to Explore**

Tanya, p. 316; Sefer Hamaamorim, 5708, p. 121; Likkutei Sichot, vol. 4, p. 1337; ibid. vol. 24, p. 168; ibid. vol. 34, p. 30; Torat Menachem, vol. 9, p. 146; ibid. vol. 10, p. 274; ibid. vol. 11, p. 89; ibid. vol. 14, p. 150; ibid. vol. 46, p. 59; ibid. vol. 50, p. 170.

# ראשונים ואחרונים

# *Rishonim & Acharonim*

The Torah Sages who explained the Torah and codified Jewish law are called the *Rishonim* and *Acharonim*. The *Rishonim* ("early scholars"; literally interpreted, "first ones") lived between the 11th and 15th centuries, a span of nearly 500 years, and provided much-needed commentary on the Talmud and many other areas of the Torah during turbulent times for the Jewish people. The staggering scholarly output of the hundreds of brilliant *Rishonim* produced vast authoritative commentaries on the Torah, Talmud, *Halacha* (Jewish law), and philosophy, providing the basis for much of our current liturgy. Notable among the *Rishonim* are Rabbi Yitzchok Alfasi (the *Rif*), Rabbi Oshri (the *Rosh*), and Rabbeinu Nissim (the *Ran*).

All of current Torah scholarship is based on the work of the *Rishonim*. Being so close to the original source, both historically and spiritually, their writings are held as indisputable. It is unthinkable for a later student or scholar to say, "The *Rishon* was wrong," God forbid, or "He made a mistake." Instead, the student labors to reveal the intent of the *Rishon*. The Era of the *Acharonim* (literally interpreted, "later ones"; also known as *poskim* or "adjudicators of *Halacha*"), began in 1563 CE with the publication of the Code of Jewish Law (*Shulchan Aruch*) by Rabbi Yosef Karo. This era includes all Torah true scholars to the present day and in the future.

The *Rishonim* and *Acharonim* differ in their style and use of language. *Rishonim* typically wrote in a short, direct manner. The *Acharonim* provided their analyses in a much more extensive style. Tradition emphasizes that both *Rishonim* and *Acharonim* authored their works with Divine inspiration, imbuing the texts with holiness and spiritual import.

The *Halachic* rulings of the *Acharonim* are understood as the "final word," yet throughout the generations there has often appeared exceptionally erudite Torah giants, whose *Halachic* analyses and decisions are further accepted across all Torah circles. Two such semi-recent scholars are Rabbi Sholomo Ganzfried (1804–1886), author of the *"Kitzur Shulchan Aruch"* (Abbreviated Code of Jewish Law), and Rabbi Moshe Feinstein (1895–1996). Some communities continue to follow the rulings of the same *Acharonim* to which their parents or grandparents had access in their town of origin. In all cases, rulings of an authentic *Acharon* are considered part of Torah.

### Bottom Line

*Rishonim* and *Acharonim* guide our understanding of the Talmud and many other areas of Torah.

### Ponder/Action

▸ Unlike in previous times, today we have the benefit of a plethora of published books enabling us to study the *Rishonim* and *Acharonim* together on one page. We are thus able to learn more comprehensively by following the development of a theme from beginning to end.

**More to Explore**

Torat Menachem, vol. 4, p. 281; ibid. vol. 25, p. 144; ibid. vol. 48, p. 213; ibid. 5742, vol. 4; ibid. 5743, vol. 1, pp. 293 and 388; Sichot Kodesh, Purim 5724, chap. 8; ibid. Purim 5733, chap. 7; ibid. 11 Nissan 5733, chap. 6; ibid. Tetzave 5739, chap. 34; Igrot Kodesh of the Rebbe, vol. 20, p. 338.

## Bottom Line

By studying the Talmud, a person becomes acquainted with the methodology and logic underlying *Halacha* (Jewish law). Clear understanding of these foundational concepts of *Halacha* adds deeper meaning and joy to our performance of mitzvot.

## Ponder/Action

▸ Familiarize yourself with the approaches taught by Chassidut to facilitate your learning of *Nigleh* (i.e., Mishnah, Talmud, and *Halacha*).

# לימוד התלמוד

# *The Study of* Talmud

Jews throughout the ages have always studied Torah, which includes the study of the Mishnah, Talmud, and all related commentaries. The Torah itself instructs the Jewish people to dive fully into its depths in order to learn how to properly lead life as a Jew. By studying the Torah, with all its branches, we not only fulfill the mitzvah to study Torah, but also becomes acquainted with the methodology and logic underlying Jewish law (in Hebrew, *Halacha).* Our learning allows us to infuse our performance of mitzvot with profound meaning and joy. Just as importantly, the study of the Talmud, including its discussions, homilies, and moral lessons, draws God's wisdom into our minds, elevating and purifying us and our surroundings. By immersing ourselves in understanding Torah, we, in fact, unite our thoughts with God's "thoughts," connecting our deepest self with Him.

We find in the Torah the words *"zot hatorah adam,"* which can be understood to mean, "This is the Torah of man." Our Sages explain this expression to mean that, just as man has a body and soul, so too does the Torah. Its "body" is the *niglah* (literally interpreted, "the revealed") part of Torah, and its "soul" is *pnimiut hatorah* (literally interpreted, "the inner [mystical] part"). Just as man's body and his soul are connected at the core, the two aspects of Torah are inseparably bound to one another.

*Niglah* relates to the physical world, characterized by the dualities of permitted and forbidden, positive and negative, pure and impure, and which ultimately addresses man's role in perfecting his surroundings. *Pnimiut hatorah* consists of Kabbalah and Chassidut, which introduce a spiritual reality above and beyond the physical world. On this level, there is no evil or arrogance; physical creations are used toward spiritual purposes and are elevated by their supportive role in the performance of mitzvot.

Also, just as the soul energizes the body, the study of *pnimiut hatorah* enhances the study of *nigleh*, enabling its spiritual enlightenment to be internalized, thereby transforming physical existence. Finally, learning *pnimiut hatorah* evokes awe and love for God, which serves to fortify successful study of all other areas of Torah.

**More to Explore**

Talmud, Nedarim 81a; Zohar, Bhaaloscho 152a; Torah Ohr, Mishpatim, pp. 154-156; Preface to Shulchan Aruch Harav; Bach on Shulchan Aruch Orach Chaim, chap. 47; Kuntres Etz Hachaim, chap. 3-4 and 28 (English); Likkutei Sichot, vol. 10, p. 252; ibid. vol. 14 p. 321, 405; ibid. vol. 19, p. 41; ibid. vol. 20, p. 468; ibid. vol. 21, p. 279; ibid. vol. 28, p. 58; Torat Menachem, vol. 2, p. 116; ibid. vol. 4, pp. 186 and 241; ibid. vol. 7, p.44-48; ibid. vol. 8, p. 156. Sichot Kodesh 5749, vol. 2, p. 116; ibid. 5750, vol. 2, p. 263; ibid. 5752, vol. 1, p. 437; see also, "On the Essence of Chassidus," by the Rebbe.

# לימוד יומי של חת"ת

# The Daily Study of Chitat

In addition to an individual's regular Torah studies, the Rebbe Rayatz instituted a daily regimen of Torah learning fit for all Jews to follow. The study schedule, which repeats annually, incorporates portions of the *Chumash* (the five books of the Torah), *Tehillim* (the Book of Psalms), and *Tanya* (The foundational work of Chabad Chassidic philosophy). The first letters of these three titles form the Hebrew acronym *Chitat*. For Chumash, one of the seven sections of the weekly Torah portion is studied each day of the week, along with Rashi's commentary. For *Tehillim,* several psalms are recited each day in accord with the traditional monthly division of chapters, culminating in completion of the entire *Tehillim* in one month. For *Tanya,* a daily portion is studied following the order established by the Rebbe Rayatz. Today, there are books and easy-to-read weekly pamphlets that contain everything needed for each day's study and thus make it easier for all to participate in the global study of *Chitat*.

The value of learning *Chitat*, compared to other daily Torah study programs, lies in the fact that its contents encompass a broad range of Torah fields. "*Chumash*" is the "revealed" part of Torah; *Tehillim* relates to both Torah and prayer; and "*Tanya*" relates to the mystical, "concealed" aspects of Torah. Therefore, several major areas of Torah learning are enveloped through study of the daily *Chitat*.

The Rebbe also pointed out that *Chumash, Tehillim,* and *Tanya* reflect the three great Jewish leaders who are connected to the festival of *Shavuot*, the holiday commemorating the Giving of the Torah: *Chumash* relates to Moses; *Tehillim* relates to King David, who passed away on Shavuot; and *Tanya,* which is based upon and explains the teachings of the Baal Shem Tov, who also passed away on Shavuot. Thus, the Rebbe pointed out that in studying *Chitat*, one connects to the holy essence of these three great Jewish leaders, drawing forth abundant blessings for the student and all Jewish people. *Chitat* study also follows and encompasses familiar and sensible time cycles, with each portion (in Hebrew, *Parsha)* of *Chumash* being divided weekly, *Tehillim* monthly, and *Tanya* yearly.

Regarding daily study of the weekly Torah portion, the Alter Rebbe once said to his disciples, "One must live with the times." He clarified this by explaining that each day, we should "live with," i.e., viscerally experience, the messages from the Torah portion connected to that date as a means of elevating our day-to-day life.

**More to Explore**

Torat Menachem, 5744, vol. 4, p. 2194; ibid. 5745, vol. 4, p. 2193; Sichot Kodesh, Bereishit (2), 5724, chap. 45; ibid. Acharon Shel Pesach, 5726, chap. 14; ibid. Bereishit (2) 5728, chap. 16; ibid. 10 Shevat 5729, chap. 8; ibid. Simchat Torah 5740, chap. 37; ibid. Bereishit (2) 5741, chap. 44; Hayom Yom, 2 Cheshvan.

**Bottom Line**

The daily *Chitat* studies (*Chumash*, *Tehillim*, and *Tanya*) mirror various aspects of Torah and serve as channels for blessings we can receive in a "daily dose" of spiritual energy. Furthermore, *Chitat* studies unite Jewish people worldwide.

**Ponder/Action**

▸ Copies of the *Chumash*, *Tehillim*, and *Tanya* are available in many languages. Classes covering the daily *Chitat* readings are also available, either locally or online. Now is a good time to begin!

## Bottom Line

Studying the Rambam every day is unique in that it unites Jews through learning something that encompasses the whole Torah. Learning Rambam enables Jews to become familiar with the Written and Oral Torah, and gives us the knowledge needed to perform mitzvot properly.

## Ponder/Action

▸ Copies of the *"Mishneh Torah"* and *"Sefer Hamitzvot"* are available in many languages. Classes covering the daily Rambam are also available, either locally or online. Each year, a calendar is published that contains the learning schedule, making it easy to start at any time.

# לימוד יומי של הרמב"ם

# The Daily Study of Rambam

In the early 1980's, the Rebbe called for an addition to be made to the daily Torah study schedule of every Jewish man, woman, and child. He suggested that everyone study of a portion of *"Mishneh Torah,"* a compendium of Jewish law authored by Maimonides (*Rambam*). This work gathers and presents the entire *Torah Shebal Peh* (the "Oral Law'), i.e., all of Jewish law, in a clear, concise way that enables the average Jewish person to fulfill the mitzvah of learning and understanding "the entire Torah."

The Rebbe suggested that the *"Mishneh Torah"* be studied straight through, from beginning to end, according to an organized, three-track schedule. For those capable, this equates to learning three chapters per day, thereby completing the entire work in just under a year. For those who cannot commit to studying three chapters per day, one chapter per day can be studies to finish the entire work in approximately three years. For those unable to commit to either of the above schedules, the Rebbe suggested study of the Rambam's *"Sefer Hamitzvot"* (the "Book of Commandments"), which briefly, but comprehensively, enumerates all of the Torah's commandments. This track can be completed in just under one year.

The Rebbe related what our Sages taught, that when a Jew studies Torah, he and what he learns are united in a supernal union like no other. Thus, when a number of Jews study the same Torah topic, all of them collectively become part of this unique union. And just as Torah is eternal, the bond forged among those studying it together also endures eternally.

Besides serving as a way to unite all of Jewry, learning the Rambam daily enables everyone to fulfill the mitzvah of studying Torah on several levels. First, it provides study that leads to deed, relating to the fact that the *"Mishneh Torah"* contains laws that every person needs to know in order to observe the mitzvot properly. This study also allows familiarity with both the "Written Torah" and the "Oral Torah," for the work touches upon all of *Talmud Bavli* and *Yerushalmi*, *Mechilta*, *Sifra*, *Sifri*, *Tosafot*, and *Midrashim*. It also familiarizes us with the laws that will apply in the era of *Moshiach*. The *"Mishneh Torah"* is unique in this regard as it covers these comprehensively. And finally, this cycle of study helps engrave the words of Torah in a person's memory. The Rebbe taught that the ongoing study of the Rambam's *"Mishneh Torah"* will help usher in the final redemption through *Moshiach*.

**More to Explore**

Likkutei Sichot, vol. 27, pp. 230-233; ibid. vol 32, pp. 257 and 271; ibid. vol. 36, pp. 22-24; Sichot Kodesh, Acharon Shel Pesach 5744; ibid. 12 Sivan, 5744; ibid. 12 Tammuz, 5744; ibid Pinchas 5744; ibid. 15 Menachem Av 5744; ibid. 14 Kislev, 5745; ibid. Shavuot 5745.

# Chabad Chassidut

## Bottom Line

Chassidut is a unique, Divine knowledge that shows man how small he is and yet how great he can become. It guides each Jew in enhancing his life, his family, and the world around him by serving God with deep understanding and joy.

## Ponder/Action

▸ One should study Chassidut every day. This will enhance and uplift the person in all areas.

# חסידות

# Chassidut

The Chassidic movement was founded in the early 18th century by Rabbi Yisrael Baal Shem Tov, whose contribution infused life into a fading Jewish communal spirit. Reeling from devastating pogroms that had rained death and destruction on thousands of European Jewish communities, myriad Jewish families had been left broken and destitute, compelled to set aside their Torah study and education of their children to seek basic physical sustenance. The inevitable result was a generation of largely ignorant, yet pious and devoted Jews.

The lack of extensive Jewish knowledge among those adversely affected led, sadly, to their being scorned and neglected by the few wealthy, learned elite. This disparity eventually turned into a widespread rift between learned and unlearned Jews, to the point where in many towns, the two groups even prayed in separate synagogues.

Amid this troubling backdrop, the Baal Shem Tov rose and transformed the crumbling Jewish landscape, introducing fresh ideas rooted in passionate love for the simple and scholarly alike. He traveled from village to village, talking about the eternal unity of God, Torah, and the Jewish people, as well as about finding Godliness in all aspects of people's existence, rather than just at set times as during daily prayer, on Sabbath and Jewish holidays. Every Jew, he emphasized, is vital to the whole of Jewish people, no matter their present state of religious knowledge or observance. He expounded on God's infinite love and care for every individual Jew and the immense value of a simple Jew's heartfelt spiritual service. He further espoused the power of individual Divine providence, explaining that all events that occur in a person's life—both large and small—are orchestrated by God with utmost kindness and benevolence.

The Baal Shem Tov's life-affirming, Torah-based revelations lifted thousands from deep despair and provided them hope and courage to serve the Almighty with renewed joy and fervor. As a result, Jewish pride, knowledge, and observance underwent a powerful resurgence. Developed further by his successors, Chassidut came to be more than a mere classic philosophy, but an entire way of life that offered spiritually insightful guidance into every facet of our daily affairs. Jews from all walks of life were stimulated and inspired to serve God with eager devotion, even during times of great difficulty.

In the context of other prominent schools of Jewish thought, such as *Mussar* (ethics; or discipline), which advocates nullification of the material by emphasizing the repulsive and abhorrent nature of all that is bodily and physical, and *Chakira* (Jewish philosophical doctrine), which stresses the superiority of the spiritual dimension of character traits and intellectuality, thus encouraging avoidance of immersion in worldly activities, Chassidut focuses on the predominance of form over matter, soul over body. Chassidut has been compared to oil, characterized by two extremes: it rises above other liquids, yet when it comes in contact with something it penetrates and permeates it entirely. So too, while Chassidut deals in very lofty spiritual matters—a Godly philosophy of the highest caliber—it engages the physical world in an elevated and Torah-appropriate way. Refining one's character, redirecting the energy of the evil inclination toward sacred and spiritual matters, serving God with love and joy, and demonstrating emotional involvement through prayer, are all at the core of Chassidic teachings.

Depriving the body its basic needs as a spiritual approach is not the correct path to serving the Almighty. To the contrary, the body's total and active participation in Torah and mitzvot will be singularly rewarded, as a person then becomes a whole or complete sanctuary for the Almighty, in fulfillment of the verse, "Make me a sanctuary and I will dwell amongst them," with "amongst them" referring to every individual Jew.

Indeed, the Alter Rebbe once commented on the verse in Ethics of Our Fathers, "Know what is above you," which is an exhortation to awareness of God, denoting that everything "above" in the spiritual hemispheres of Divine emanation derives "from you" in an individual's personal service. Chassidut places the person as the central figure in the Creation, showing how each Jew has a unique impact on the physical, as well as spiritual worlds. It focuses on the distinctive quality of material things once they are elevated and also the singular significance of "form," when matter and form are so thoroughly fused that the end of one is indiscernible from the beginning of the other. Other central aspects of Chassidut include the understanding of every Torah law on its spiritual plane, i.e., its root and source, as explained according to Chassidut principles as well as translating the core of every practice through *avoda* (lit. work; the service of God) to improve our daily conduct and spiritual service.

Studying Chabad Chassidut inspires contemplation on the inner meaning and personal and global effects of Torah and mitzvot. It also provides insight and reflection on the higher spiritual worlds, enriching our intellect and emotions, leading to a refinement of our thoughts, speech and deeds. Its study instills a uniquely uplifting and spiritually productive worldview, leading to and nourishing a fervent love and awe for the Almighty, which are the two basic elements required in His service.

As the Baal Shem Tov wrote in a letter to his brother-in-law in the year 5507 (1747), he ascended to the chamber of *Moshiach* and asked him, "Master, when will you come?" *Moshiach* replied, "When your wellsprings will spread to the outside." Today, the teachings of Chabad Chassidut have indeed permeated Jewish communities across the globe, illuminating for millions the importance of Torah study and inspired daily practice of the Jewish faith.

**More to Explore**

Pirkei Avot, 2:1; Sefer HaMaamorim, 5663, p. 142; Likkutei Sichot, vol. 2, p. 463 and p. 472 and on; ibid. vol. 5 p. 280; ibid. vol. 26, p. 173 footnote 45; Sichot Kodesh, 19 Kislev 5731, chap. 8; 3rd of Slichos 5735, chap. 6; Igrot Kodesh of the Rebbe, vol. 14 p. 288; Hayom Yom, 7 Kislev; ibid. 13 Iyar; "On the Essence of Chassidus"; "Philosophy of Chabad," vol. 2.

# חסידות חב"ד

# Chabad Chassidut

The founder of the Chassidic movement, Rabbi Yisrael Baal Shem Tov, had many illustrious students, among them the greatest minds and spirits of the time. His primary disciple, the Maggid of Mezritch (literally interpreted, "preacher"; religious leader in the town of Mezritch, in Eastern Europe), succeeded him and further developed the teachings of Chassidut into a comprehensive system. Under his leadership, Chassidism laid deep and widespread roots. Following the Maggid's passing, many of his students returned to their respective communities and continued to spread Chassidut teachings. Each student focused on a particular aspect of serving God, such as warmth in prayer, humility, asceticism, and so on, leading to development of the various branches of the Chassidic movement.

The Alter Rebbe, founder of Chabad Chassidut, was the youngest disciple of the Maggid of Mezritch. He was a master of the revealed and mystical facets of the Torah, and over the years integrated his intellectual rigor with the mystical tradition taught by the Maggid. Fusing these concepts with the teachings of the AriZal, he gave birth to Chabad Chassidut, one of the strongest and most dynamic branches of the Chassidic movement.

"Chabad" is an acronym for three Hebrew words: *Chochma* (wisdom), *bina* (understanding), and *daat* (knowledge). In the Alter Rebbe's view, the intellect is necessary to drive and direct our service of God. The Alter Rebbe applied this unique approach to his role as Rebbe.

In general, Chassidim relied on their Rebbes to "carry" them on their shoulders, or in other words, to be responsible for understanding deep Godly concepts and practice lofty spiritual meditations on their behalf. The Alter Rebbe, however, insisted that every individual can and should exert himself personally in these matters.

As an analogy, there is a Jewish law that when immersing oneself in a *mikvah* (ritual pool), the person must be totally covered in order to attain a state of purity. If a single hair remains outside the water, it will disqualify the immersion. Chabad Chassidut takes the same approach to serving the Almighty. When fulfilling a mitzvah solely with *koach hamaaseh* (literally interpreted, "deed"; action) and emotion, sometimes the intellect remains "outside." Although Chassidut greatly extols the value of mitzvot done with simplicity and pure faith, applying our full wisdom, understanding, knowledge and emotion ensures its complete perfection, which additionally aids us in overcoming any challenges in our service of God.

### Bottom Line

The Alter Rebbe developed Chabad Chassidut as an all-inclusive "general" course of Divine service, incorporating the essential principles from all streams of authentic Jewish thought. When a person studies Chabad Chassidut, his mind is filled with a deep understanding of Godly concepts, thus connecting him to holiness and practical character refinement.

### Ponder/Action

- Chabad philosophy stresses full involvement of the mind, heart, and limbs in service of the Almighty, thus enabling a person to become a complete channel through which Godliness is drawn into the world.
- There are hundreds of books and classes, in many languages, both printed and online, that can help one study and absorb the teachings of Chabad Chassidut.

The Alter Rebbe taught that it is not enough for recent generations to merely "Know the God of your father and serve Him with a whole heart." Each Jew needs to study Torah and fulfill mitzvot employing his or her intellectual abilities. Substantiating this principle is the fact that even in oppressive countries where Jews have faced fierce opposition to their study of Torah and practice of mitzvot, those who persisted in learning and following Chabad Chassidut mostly overcame their difficulties with their religious commitment intact.

Chabad Chassidut is described as "the light and life of our soul." When a person fulfills a mitzvah or learns with enthusiasm and joy, the amount of his or her service will inevitably grow. From a psychological standpoint, the more a person derives positive feelings from fulfilling mitzvot, the less interest he or she is likely to have in negativity. Studying Chabad Chassidut also serves as a preparation for the time when, as the prophet Habakkuk prophesied, "The knowledge of God will overflow like water covers the seas," when all the Jewish people will have a comprehensive understanding of Godliness. And in the words of the prophet Jeremiah, "They will all know Me."

During his leadership, the Alter Rebbe wrote a foundational text of Chabad philosophy called the *Tanya*, which derived its title from the first word of the first chapter. Based on the teachings of the AriZal, the Baal Shem Tov, and the Maggid of Mezritch, the *Tanya* was written to provide Jewish religious guidance to those who needed guidance in their religious beliefs. It essentially addresses the forces of good and evil in human nature and the world, with the objective of offering guidance toward the highest good. The Alter Rebbe worked on the *Tanya* for twenty years, punctilious to the point that every word and letter was fraught with meaning and intent.

The *Tanya* was written in such a way that it would satisfy the analytical and searching mind, as well as provide meaning for the less scholarly. Its comprehensive nature led it to be regarded as the "written Torah" of Chabad, and accounts for the widespread recognition it has commanded in Jewish communities to the present day.

In addition to the *Tanya*, the Alter Rebbe and his successors, the subsequent Rebbes of Chabad, left staggeringly voluminous written teachings on both Chassidic thought and Jewish law. Tens of thousands of essays, profound discourses, letters of guidance, and published talks provide effectively limitless study material to inform, inspire and perfect their service of God.

Because each individual soul is challenged to identify its own unique path of Torah and prayer, the Rebbes taught that Chabad Chassidut was developed as an all-inclusive, "general" course of Divine service, incorporating the essential principles from all streams of authentic Jewish thought. Thus, Chabad Chassidut represents a genuine pathway for all Jews toward the highest good and greatest service of the Almighty.

**More to Explore**

Prophets, Yishayahu, 11:9; ibid. Yirmiyahu 31:33; ibid. Habakkuk, 2:14; Likkutei Sichot, vol. 4, pp. 1148-1149; ibid. vol. 2, pp. 474-475 and 500; ibid. vol. 20, p. 171; Torat Menachem, vol. 11, p. 153; ibid. 5750, vol. p. 163; Sichot Kodesh, 19 Kislev 5739, chap. 15; ibid. Miketz 5741, chap. 54; see also "On the Essence of the Chassidus," by the Lubavitcher Rebbe.

## Bottom Line

The word "Rebbe" is an acronym for *Rosh B'nei Yisrael*, meaning "head" or leader of the Jewish people. A Rebbe illuminates the path by which each Jew can utilize his or her individual strengths and capabilities to connect with God.

## Ponder/Action

▸ Connecting to the Rebbe—by learning his teachings and following his directives—joins an individual to the powerful flow of spiritual energy that circulates throughout the entire body of the Jewish people.

# תפקידו של רבי

# *The Role of a* Rebbe

The Hebrew word Rebbe means "my master" or "my teacher." Chassidut teaches that a Rebbe has a *neshama klolit* (a "general" soul), i.e., a soul that encompasses all the souls of the generation. In this context, the word "Rebbe" is an acronym for the Hebrew words *Rosh B'nei Yisrael*, meaning "head," or leader of the Jewish people.

Moses was the first Rebbe, serving as intermediary between God and the Jewish people even to the point of self-sacrifice. In general, an intermediary may be a gatekeeper before the master, or a facilitator connecting a person directly with the master. A Rebbe is defined by the latter, illuminating the path by which each Jew can utilize his or her individual strengths and capabilities to connect with God.

There's another meaning to the title of Rebbe: a teacher who not only invigorates the mind and heart, but who can guide us in finding our true essence and thus igniting within us a passion to serve the Almighty. In this context, a Rebbe is also a servant of his people.

In addition to serving as a "soul-specialist" and providing people with a blessing or advice to enhance their spiritual and physical lives, a Rebbe also functions as an advocate for the Jewish people before Heaven. On a global level, the Rebbe uses his spiritual intuition to sense areas needing spiritual strengthening, as well as issues needing attention for protection of the world as a whole and the Jewish people in particular.

The Rebbe's deep connection to the souls of his generation has been compared to a power station that serves a metropolis. Every lamp, whether a streetlight or night light, needs to be connected to the generator and receive the right amount of electrical current. Supply too much voltage and the device will blow; supply too little and it won't illuminate. Similarly, the Rebbe intuitively knows what each individual needs so that the light of their Jewish soul might shine as brightly as possible.

Connecting to the Rebbe—by learning his teachings and following his directives—joins an individual to the powerful flow of spiritual energy which circulates throughout the entire body of the Jewish people.

**More to Explore**

Tanya, chap. 2; Torat Menachem, vol. 2, p. 32; Sichot Kodesh, Yitro 5733, Sicha 3; see responsa Minchas Elazar, Orech Chaim, chap. 68.

# תפקידו של חסיד

# The Role of a Chassid

The term *"Chassid"* is ancient, and was applied by the Sages to the very first man, Adam. In its purest meaning, the word *"Chassid"* describes a person who has attained perfection or excellence in the areas of intellect and emotional disposition. The term is also used in reference to followers of the Baal Shem Tov and his disciples. In the introduction to *Tikunei Zohar*, a foundational work of Kabbalah, its author Rabbi Shimon Bar Yochai writes, "Who is a Chassid? One who conducts himself with benevolence (from the Hebrew word *Chessed* which means "kindness") towards his Creator." A Chassid goes beyond the letter of the law to unite the Holy One and His Divine presence with those who dwell in this world. Going beyond the quenching of his own spiritual thirst, a Chassid also seeks to elevate others around him.

The Alter Rebbe defined a Chassid as a person who forgoes his personal interest, and even his personal safety at times, to do a material and spiritual favor for another. The Rebbe Rashab further described the Chassid as a lamplighter, drawing a spiritual analogy between the Jewish soul and a candle. Even though the soul lives to illuminate its environment, sometimes its flame needs rekindling. A Chassid seeks out and ignites those lamps. In Chabad thought, a Chassid shows great diligence in *kabbalat ol malchut shomayim*—that is, in accepting the yoke of the Kingship of Heaven. He truthfully recognizes his essential character traits, his standing in knowledge and study of Torah, and his level of observing mitzvot. He knows what he lacks and takes pains to fill that void, constantly striving to refine himself and raise his level of observance to the highest standard possible. In this context, the Rebbe once wrote, "To one who improves in a given area today over the day before, it gives me great joy to call him my Chassid."

When one encounters a Jew who follows the Code of Jewish Law (*Shulchan Aruch*), faithfully observes Shabbat, fulfills mitzvot *b'hidur* (in the most beautiful manner), (if male) dons *Rashi* and *Rabbeinu Tam Tefillin* for morning services, is particular in fulfilling the commandment of *Tzitzit,* and wears an untrimmed beard, (for both male and female) attentively observes *Tzniut* (laws of modesty), *Taharat Hamishpacha* (laws of family purity), and provides a robust *Chinuch* (Jewish education) for their children, as well as caring for and helping others with their physical and spiritual needs, and follows the Rebbe's directives, it can be assumed this person is a Chassid.

### Bottom Line

A Chassid is a Jew who studies Chassidut and follows its teachings. In so doing, the individual opens himself to deeper insights in Torah, enhances his fulfillment of its commandments, and develops a more meaningful and complete relationship with the Almighty.

### Ponder/Action

▸ A Chassid does not postpone a good thing until tomorrow. Furthermore, a Chassid works to infuse his life with joy and a positive attitude.

**More to Explore**

Talmud, Eiruvin p. 18b; Niddah p. 17a; Tikunei Zohar, Introduction, p. 1b, Sefer HaMaamorim, 5726, Podo B'sholom; Torat Menachem, vol. 7, p. 114; ibid. vol. 29, p. 270; ibid. vol. 32, pp. 120 and 144; ibid. vol. 52, p. 65; Sichot Kodesh, 29 Elul 5736, chap. 5; ibid. 24 Tevet 5741, chap. 45; Hayom Yom, 14 Kislev; ibid. 21 Adar I; ibid. 15 Iyar; Kfar Chabad (weekly), no 1300, p. 40; see also "On the Essence of the Chassidus," by the Lubavitcher Rebbe.

## Bottom Line

Each soul has been entrusted with a mission from God: the privilege and responsibility to enhance and elevate itself and its surroundings.

## Ponder/Action

▸ The soul, being a part of God, shares all His attributes—it is Infinite, All-Powerful, Holy, and Enduring, to name a few. The body, by comparison, is comprised of physical matter. It is temporary, and therefore here today but rapidly disintegrates as soon as the soul leaves. Thus, it is easy to understand the Torah's call for us to be concerned with the soul over the body. The soul endures, while the body returns to dust.

# תכלית הנשמה

# The Soul's Purpose

A soul descends from the Heavenly spheres into a physical body for the purpose of spiritually elevating itself and the world around it, through the study of Torah and the fulfillment of its mitzvot. While on its earthly mission, the soul radiates the light of God through its bodily "lamp." The Alter Rebbe explains in his foundational Chassidic work, the *Tanya*, that every Jewish soul is composed of two parts: a *nefesh habehamit* (an "animating soul"), which animates and enlivens the body and is the store of all its desires, including negative character traits such as anger, apathy, and arrogance; and the *nefesh elokit* (literally interpreted, "Godly soul"), described as an "actual part of God." This second part of the soul exists solely to enable the body to transcend its animal nature. It creates within the body a yearning to escape the limits of physical existence and to connect with the Eternal, ultimately revealing the innate Godliness and goodness of the material world.

Before its descent into this world, the Godly soul is given an oath that she will remain righteous, and is then fortified and armed with enough spiritual energy to transform the animal soul and its portion in the physical world. During a person's lifetime, the two souls compete vigorously for control of his or her attention. It is up to the individual to harness the immense spiritual stores latent within every Jewish person, to surmount the pull of the animal soul and heed the call of the Godly soul.

King Solomon offered a hint of how this can be accomplished, saying, "The world was placed in their hearts." Chassidut explains this to mean that just as the physical world is comprised of different domains, i.e., inanimate objects, plants, animals, and man, these categories are similarly found within man himself. Thus, there may be times in life when our thoughts, speech, or actions are likened to one or more of the above domains. For example, during certain periods of time, we might feel apathetic in our service of God—as though stuck in a numb, cold stasis not unlike the state of an inanimate stone. Other times, we might become overly focused on satiating physical appetites, reminiscent of animal behavior, and so on.

By working on refining our internal "domains" from within, through being aware of any undesirable tendencies and diligently working to rise above them, we allow the light of our soul to shine through and illuminate ourselves and our world with profound holiness. Herein the soul accomplishes its sacred purpose.

### More to Explore

Ecclesiastes 3:11; Rambam, Mishneh Torah, Hilchos Teshuvah, chap. 3, par. 4; Tanya, chap. 36-37; Likkutei Sichot, vol. 6 p. 113; vol. 9 pp. 411 and 425; Torat Menachem, vol. 57, p. 241; Sichot Kodesh, 5752, vol. 1 p. 342; Hayom Yom, 18 Elul; ibid. 14 Cheshvan.

# תכליתו של היהודי

# The Purpose of the Jew

The basic function of a Jew is to be a catalyst for positive change in the world. Each person has a unique mission in the Divine plan, which remains unaffected by the dross of the physical universe. Using an analogy from the field of chemistry, small quantities of reactants can propel a large reaction, yet the catalyst remains unchanged and capable of generating future reactions. Through the lens of Kabbalah and Chassidut, the purpose of the Jew is to create a *dirah betachtonim*, an abode for Godliness within the material dimension of this world, and to elevate and connect it to the Almighty, thereby revealing its Godly essence. This is primarily achieved by aligning oneself with the Will of the Creator through study of Torah and performance of its mitzvot with joyful love and intent.

In Hebrew, man is called *"adam,"* which is related to the Hebrew phrase, *"Adameh l'Elyon"* (literally interpreted, "an emulation of Above"). Although created from the lowliest of materials, *adama* (literally interpreted, "earth" or "dust"), man has the potential to reflect the "Supernal Man," God, and rise to great spiritual heights. Being a composite of two extremes, material body and spiritual soul, mankind has the ability to elevate the lowest forms to the highest levels. Thus, even under the most trying circumstances a Jew need not despair, for his soul is infinite and exceptionally powerful, especially when in alignment with God's will.

According to the Midrash, in the first conscious moments of the first man, Adam, he gathered all the creatures in the Garden of Eden and proclaimed, "Let us bow in awe and thanksgiving before our Creator," in a demonstration of his nullification before the Almighty. Similarly, we are all charged with recognizing God and "bowing in awe," i.e., bending our will to His service. Maimonides teaches that every man should view his merits as equally balanced—half good and half evil. Likewise, he should see the entire world's merits as half good and half evil, so that a single virtuous deed on his part may tip the scales for himself and the entire world to the side of good.

Indeed, our Sages taught that each person is providently born at a specific time in history and placed in a specific geographic location, so that this corner of the world can be refined in a way only that individual can accomplish. Therefore, we should never underestimate our ability to have lasting influence on ourselves and on our surroundings.

### Bottom Line

The purpose of the Jew is to create an abode for Godliness within the material dimension of this world and to elevate and connect it to the Almighty, thereby revealing its Godly essence. This is achieved by aligning ourselves with the Will of the Creator through study of Torah and performance of its mitzvot with joyful love and intent.

### Ponder/Action

- As a reflection of Supernal Man, you can elevate the lowest levels to the highest and most sublime levels of holiness by living your life in accordance with God's Will.

**More to Explore**

Torat Menachem, vol. 24, p. 324; ibid. vol. 25, p. 209; ibid. vol. 28, p. 22; Sichot Kodesh, 12 Tammuz 5733; ibid. Yud shvat 5743; ibid. 11 Nissan 5742; ibid. Nitzavim 5745; ibid. Chaye Sarah 5749; Hayom Yom, 18 Elul; ibid. 14 Cheshvan.

Bottom Line

When Jewish people involve themselves deeply in the service of God, their acts bring great pleasure to Him, and contribute to vanquishing the darkness of evil in the world.

Ponder/Action

▸ Ponder areas in your life in which you can make improvements to raise your level of service of God. Do this, and do it with joy.

# עבודת השם

# Serving the Almighty

The Jewish nation serves God as servants to a king, adhering to His guidance to make manifest His objectives. *Avodat hashem*, which in Hebrew means "Serving God," refers to leading our life in accordance with the Will of God. This is achieved by refining our character to be sensitive to the Divine, studying the Torah, and performing mitzvot with joyful love and intent. In devoting ourselves to *avodat hashem*, we bring unique pleasure to the Almighty, stimulating elevation in the upper spiritual worlds, thereby positively affecting the physical world as well.

As discussed earlier (see *"Prayer,"* p. 49), the plain Hebrew meaning of *avodah* is "work." Think of working with a raw material to refine it into a finished product, in the course of which we remove its impurities and smooth its roughness. Similarly, every Jew is endowed with wonderful treasures of character that may require effort to reveal and fortify. The "work" herein involves honest self-reflection, thoughtful prayer, learning Torah, performing mitzvot, and encouraging others to do the same. Chassidut teaches that the Almighty especially cherishes those who undertake the effort of personal *avoda*, and through doing so transform their inner darkness into light. Uncultivated human potential thus becomes a vehicle for the spiritual. This level of dedication to spiritual enhancement not only elevates the person and his immediate surroundings, but contributes greatly to vanquishing the darkness of evil on a global level.

In Chassidic thought, an essential factor in serving God is joy (see *"Serving God With Joy,"* p. 87). The Alter Rebbe writes that it is impossible to surmount our animalistic nature sluggishly and passively. Success in this regard requires enthusiasm and excitement born of joy, and a heart unblocked by worry or sadness. As we are taught by the Sages, joy pushes past all barriers and limitations.

Yet, how do we attain this type of joy? We can connect with it by considering the great privilege we have been given in serving the King of kings. Think about the awesome kindness of the Creator demonstrated every day in our lives and in the world and events around us. Ponder the amazing fact that although we are small, insignificant beings in comparison to His infinite greatness, we are able to bring delight to the Greatest of all great, of whom it is written in the Book of Psalms, "There is no delving into His greatness."

**More to Explore**

Tehillim, 145:3; Tanya, chap. 26; ibid. chap. 41; Derech Mitzvosecha, p. 9; Sefer HaMaamorim, 5657, p. 223; ibid. 5712, Lo Tehya Mshakelo; Torat Menachem, Nitzavim 5716, chap. 13; vol. 6, p. 144; ibid. vol. 8, pp. 135-137; Sichot Kodesh, Mishpatim 5736, chap. 2; Hayom Yom, 8 Cheshvan; ibid. 8 Kislev.

# שעבוד החומר

# *Harnessing the Physical*

The universe was created *yeish m'ayin* (literally interpreted, "something from nothing"). In essence, God transformed the spiritual into something material. The work of the Jewish people in the ongoing perfection of Creation is to transform the physical into an instrument for the spiritual. This process affects not only the individual himself, but his family, his community, and in fact, the entire planet. In the view of Chassidut, transformation does not imply we must pulverize mountains and shatter boulders, turning the world upside down—rather, the work of harnessing the physical for the spiritual is satisfied in the simple, consistent efforts of day-to-day life, performed with true *kavana* (intent).

This idea is based on the teachings of the Baal Shem Tov, who emphasized the importance of embracing and working with physical matter in this world, elevating whatever is permissible and capable of being elevated according to the Torah, versus denouncing materialism and advocating a life of abstinence and religious isolation.

In this context, the Rebbe expounded on the verses of our Sages: "In all your ways, you shall know him," and "All your deeds should be for the sake of heaven." He explained the view of the Code of Jewish Law (*Shulchan Aruch*) that "your ways" and "your deeds" do not only refer to mitzvot, or even to Jewish customs, but to the multitude of mundane facets comprising a physical life—how we live and act every day. Indeed, every part of the Jew's existence needs to be permeated with the mission of serving God.

Reciting a blessing over kosher food with concentration and intent; praying as it should be done, with a prepared heart and awareness of before Whom you stand; studying a passage in the *Chumash* (the five books of the Torah) with recognition that it is the word of God; reciting verses of *Tehillim* (the Book of Psalms); demonstrating kindness by lovingly befriending another—are all valid examples of harnessing the physical toward a spiritual purpose, and is within the reach of every Jew to accomplish.

Studying Chassidut nourishes this spiritual awareness and devotion, leaving the individual secure in the knowledge that God will enable him or her to overcome any and all obstacles and limitations.

**Bottom Line**

With the creation of the world, God transformed the spiritual into something material. The work of the Jewish people is to transform the physical into an instrument for the spiritual, and this ability is within the reach of every Jew to do so.

**Ponder/Action**

▸ As we transform the material into the spiritual, we transform ourselves along the way.

**More to Explore**

Mishlei 3:6; Avot, 2:12; Tanya, Iggeret Hakodesh, no. 20; Likkutei Sichot, vol. 17 p. 48; Sichot Kodesh, Tzav 5724, chap. 19; ibid. Bereishit (2) 5727, chap. 20; ibid. 10 Shevat, 5742; Hayom Yom, 7 Kislev; ibid. 27 Tevet; ibid. 28 Shevat; ibid. 29 Adar II; ibid. 5th Iyar.

**Bottom Line**

The soul and the body need to work in harmony in the service of God. One should not shun the other.

**Ponder/Action**

▸ Ponder ways to elevate the mundane aspects of life, e.g. setting time aside at work to learn Torah, infusing Torah values into day-to-day decisions, and seeking ways to inspire others to do the same.

# שילוב הצורה והחומר

# Integrating Form & Material

The Rebbe once related that there are some people who go to work carrying two briefcases: one for sacred books and the other for their business materials. The Rebbe used this analogy to underline the erroneous notion that life and its material trappings are somehow disparate and incongruent with Torah. The truth, the Rebbe continued, is that all of the physical world is a vessel and instrument through which the greatness of the Almighty is revealed and expressed.

The Almighty created the soul (i.e., "form") and the body (i.e., "material") for the singular purpose of revealing the light of His holiness in this world. This spiritual revelation emerges from the unique quality of the material when it is purified, and of "form" when so integrated with the material that the end of one and beginning of the other is undetectable. Achievement of this end requires the soul and the body to work together in true harmony toward spiritual integration. This idea is further substantiated in the verses of our Sages: "In all your ways, you shall know him," and "All your deeds should be for the sake of heaven"—all of our actions, including material concerns, should be aligned for the sake of heaven, and that by leading life in this manner, we are in the perpetual service of God. The concept of spiritual integration of form and matter was further illuminated by the Baal Shem Tov, who expounded on the deeper meaning of a seemingly unrelated verse from the Torah. In a section discussing various civil laws, the Torah states, "When you see the donkey of your enemy collapsing under its load and are inclined to turn away from helping him, you shall surely help along with him."

As explained by the Baal Shem Tov: "When you see the donkey—" meaning, when you examine your materiality; "—of your enemy," denoting the materialistic body which opposes and even loathes the Divine soul, with its longing for Godliness and the spiritual; "—collapsing under its load," referring to the yoke of Torah and mitzvot put into place by God to refine and elevate the person and the world; "—and are inclined to turn away from helping him," or wish to shun the material/physical, refuse to provide the body assistance in fulfilling its mission and, in so doing, break the body; it is not in this approach that the light of Torah resides. Rather, the Baal Shem Tov clarifies, "You shall surely help along with him," which directs us to nourish the body, inspire it, refine it, and elevate it, so that body and soul complement, fulfill, and aid each other in the all-encompassing service of God.

**More to Explore**

Torah, Shmos, 23:5; Prophets, Mishlei 3:6; Pirkei Avot 2:12; Shulchan Aruch, Orech Chaim, chap. 231; Sefer HaMaamorim, 5657, p. 45 and on; Likkutei Sichot, vol. 3, p. 907; Torat Menachem, 5744, vol. 1, p. 136; ibid. 5748, vol. 2, p. 478; Hayom Yom, 27 Elul; ibid. 22 Cheshvan; ibid. 7 Kislev; ibid. 27 Tevet; ibid. 28 Shevat; ibid. 29 Adar II; Kfar Chabad (weekly), issue 1096, suppl. Alei Osor, p. 51.

# אין עוד מלבדו

# *There is None Beside Him*

The premise of *Ain Od Milvaado*—that nothing exists beside the Almighty—is a core belief of Chassidic thought. Everything created contains a Godly "spark" that constantly sustains it, in the absence of which all would return to nothingness. According to the Midrash, the "word" referred to in the Psalm, "Forever, O Lord, Your word stands firm in the Heavens," refers to the *Asara Maamarot*, the ten declarations used by God in bringing about creation, i.e., "Let there be light," "Let the earth sprout vegetation," etc. Chassidut explains that these commands were not one-time utterances, but instead remain "suspended," actively sustaining creation. If their perpetual utterance were to stop, even for an instant, the world would revert to nothingness. Thus, since God is the One infusing the ongoing life-force of the world, all of creation is totally nullified and subservient (in Hebrew, *batul*) before Him; ergo there is nothing beside Him.

Yet, in order for the world to have a physical existence and for mankind to sense a level of independence, God filters and conceals His emanation through various spiritual constrictions (in Hebrew, *tzimtzumim*), thereby enabling sustainable life. Otherwise, the world would be consumed in the overpowering Godly revelation just as a ray of light is totally nullified within a greater light. These *tzimtzumim* enable mankind to regard itself as independent beings that exist within the dimensions of time and space, much like a well-defined ray of light shines on Earth because it seems to exist "far away" from the sun.

Nevertheless, although God transcends space and time, He is also present within space and time—that is, He remains united with the spiritual constrictions through which space and time come into existence.

When a person obtains a comprehension that there is nothing beside the Almighty, that God does everything for our ultimate good, and that nothing can occur that is not God's will, he is able to lead his life without fear or excessive anxiety, and to enthusiastically fulfill God's commandments from the depth of his being. This is why Chassidim would often exclaim, *"ain od milvaado,"* even in song, when faced with difficulties, to remind themselves of the transitory nature of all-that-is-physical, lift their spirits, and alleviate their material anxieties.

**Bottom Line**

The entire creation exists and is constantly sustained by the word of the Almighty.

**Ponder/Action**

▸ When a person obtains a comprehension that there is nothing beside the Almighty, he fulfills God's commandments enthusiastically from the depth of his being.

**More to Explore**

Bereishit, 1:1; Keter Shem Tov, Hosafot, 395; Tanya, Part 2, chap. 7; ibid. Part 4, Igeret 11; Sefer HaMaamorim, 5629, Mi Komocho; ibid. 5657, p. 45; ibid. 5734 B'Chol Dor; Torat Menachem, 5742, vol. 4 p. 1792; ibid. 5749, vol. 1, p. 237.

## Bottom Line

We exist within the intimate purview of the Almighty at all times, and He constantly sustains our existence.

## Ponder/Action

▸ Judaism doesn't believe in coincidences. Reflect upon the moments in your life where you knew the Hand of God was guiding you or events, bringing opportunity or solutions to your doorstep. Notice the moments like this are yet to come.

# השגחה פרטית

# Divine Providence

Belief in individual Divine providence (in Hebrew, *hashgacha pratit*) is central to Judaism. From classic Jewish texts we find two general approaches to understanding this idea. One posits that the Almighty, being infinite and thus "above" creation, runs the world from afar, so to speak, and any measure of His focus and personal providence is matched only to the level of an individual's Divine service. Thus, a holy tzaddik, by virtue of his intense devotion and spiritual service, draws the Almighty's providence into every detail of his life; whereas the fate of the less spiritually refined is relegated to that of "subordinates," reliant on the natural order of cause and effect.

A second approach, and the one taught by Chabad Chassidut based on the teaching of the Baal Shem Tov, and on the plain meaning of scriptural, Talmudic, and Midrashic texts, puts forward that He Who is Infinite in the most absolute sense must be capable of transcending all bounds, including those of transcendence itself. Even though logically, God as Creator is above and beyond all that He has created, He is nevertheless neither apart nor removed from the world. To place limitation on His providential abilities is to deny His very omniscience. God is intimately and directly involved with all the happenings in the world, down to the minutest details, and each entity and event is shepherded to its ultimate purpose by His wisdom and desire. As King David wrote in Psalms, "He covers the heavens with clouds, prepares rain for the earth, causes the mountains to sprout grass. He provides the animal its food, to the fledgling ravens that for which they cry."

Chassidut enriches our understanding of these Divine patterns of causation and destiny. The Baal Shem Tov taught that even the movement of a single leaf in the wind is a part of the Divine plan. Indeed, Divine providence directs not only every particular occurrence affecting mankind, but also those affecting inanimate matter, plants, and animals. Thus, the Almighty's direct providence is the very life-energy maintaining the existence of all created entities.

The knowledge that God is right there and intimately involved in whatever we may be going through brings tremendous comfort. Furthermore, as God is the ultimate source of good, we can rest assured that everything that comes to us from Him is for our ultimate good. This awareness confers deep inner peace, enthusiasm, and great joy to us in our service of the Almighty.

**More to Explore**

Tehillim 147:7–9; Tanya, Part 4, Igeret 11; Sefer HaMaamorim, 5690, Yehi; ibid. 5694, HaTei Eloka; ibid. 5696, Al Kein Yomru; ibid. 5717, Mayim Rabim; Likkutei Sichot, vol. 8, p. 277; Likkutei Dibburim, 19 Kislev, 5694 (sec. 3-4); Igrot Kodesh of the Rebbe Rayatz, vol. 9, p. 272. vol. 7, p. 21; Hayom Yom 28 Cheshvan; ibid. 29 Sivan.

# פנימיות

# *Inward Simplicity*

In Chassidic thought, there are two types of individuals: "*pnimi*" and "*chitzon.*" Loosely translated, these Hebrew terms mean, respectively, "inward-focused" and "superficial." The *pnimi* goes about life with great clarity, knowing the difference between what is important and what is not, and the value of the journey versus the destination. He is consistent and genuine to the core: he pours his entire self into the moment, focuses on the essence of things, and fulfills his spiritual service with inner conviction and commitment. For example, when performing a mitzvah or learning Torah, he does so without pomposity but with earnestness and humility. Enveloping himself completely in the effort, it is as though nothing else in the world exists at the time. He knows that mastery over time comes from minding the present; each minute must be a fully utilized unit of time. Patience and a non-conflicted mind are basic to being a *pnimi.*

By contrast, the *chitzon* is more concerned with meeting minimum requirements and gauging his efforts according to others who may be watching. He is internally inconsistent and lacks depth of feeling. He is mainly focused with externalities, missing the wisdom and conviction that result from being deeply connected to what one is doing.

In Chabad thought, Divine service through the path of the *pnimi* is essential. Chassidim tirelessly strive to be a *pnimi*, seeking to root out any semblance of *chitzon* in their personality. In our times, with so many worldly distractions competing for attention, it may seem harder than ever to be a true *pnimi.*

Chabad Chassidut teaches, however, that we should not despair. It is only when we are totally wrapped up in ourselves that we cannot see beyond our ego. Once surrendered to a higher objective, such as our service of God, we free ourselves to reach outside our self-centeredness, to give and serve genuinely. Living and serving on the level of a *pnimi* can be attained by each and every Jew through regular study of Chassidut (*Pnimiyut HaTorah*) with sincerity and understanding, praying with deep concentration, and interacting with the world in a humble and sincere manner. These actions infuse all of a person's faculties—thought, speech, and deed—with Godliness, which refines their character and sets him on the path of the *pnimi.*

**More to Explore**

Torat Sholom, p. 39; Sefer HaSichot, 5688-5691, p. 175; ibid. 5700, p. 113; Torat Menachem, vol. 52, p. 368; ibid. 5751 4, p. 56; Sichot Kodesh, Bereishit 5733, chap. 1 ibid. Bamidbar 5734, ch.2 (end); ibid. 7 Adar 5736, chap. 1; ibid. Lag B'omer 5738, chap. 17; ibid. Maasai 5741 chap. 27; ibid. 3 Sivan, 5748; see also "The Mystical Dimension," vol. 3, by Jacob Emanuel Schochet.

**Bottom Line**

Divine service through the path of the *pnimi* (inwardly focused; sincere) is essential. Chassidim tirelessly strive to be a *pnimi*, seeking to root out any semblance of being a *chitzon* (superficial; pompous).

**Ponder/Action**

▸ Be genuine and present in all spiritual and physical interactions, redirecting self-serving motives to an attitude of humility in the service of a higher Godly cause.

## Bottom Line

Honest self-examination of character, addressing deficiencies with joy instead of sadness and shame, liberates us to serve God properly.

## Ponder/Action

▸ When involved in studying Torah or in a mitzvah project, a person should act with boldness and enthusiasm. On the other hand, when dealing with other people, our conduct must be infused with humility.

# מודעות עצמית

# Self-Awareness

The Talmud instructs every person to say, "For my sake the world was created," meaning that all of creation exists to enable him to perfect himself and his world through the path of Torah. At the same time, our Sages taught that one should be like our Patriarch Abraham, who proclaimed, "I am but dust and ashes." How do we reconcile these two seemingly contradictory statements? According to Chassidut, both ideas are true. Serving God demands that each person be genuinely aware of his own character, which involves honest recognition of deficiencies, yet at the same time conscious awareness of his or her immeasurable significance, including reasonable estimation of one's good qualities.

While self evaluation is important, Chassidut cautions that we should not be excessively self-critical as this will impede our serving God with joy and a contented heart. In this regard, there are designated times on the Jewish calendar for evaluating personal deficiencies, such as during the recitation of the bedtime *Shema*, on fast days such as Yom Kippur, and during unexplained moments of spiritual revival when feeling a sudden spiritual tug or awakening. During all other times, Chassidut teaches, we must be dedicated to serving God with joy.

Although every individual's unique personal strengths and weaknesses serve as valuable guideposts to his or her unique mission in this world, a person is cautioned not to brood over personal deficiencies excessively. Sadness over a character deficiency often instills an impenetrable stone-like dullness of heart which prevents the deficiency from being corrected. Instead, enlisting the power of the Almighty enables us to obtain the enthusiasm, warmth, and fullness of authentic joy, empowering an individual to move past personal limitations. Conversely, a person should not suppress recognition of his good qualities out of fear of falling into excessive pride. Rather, true humility brings understanding that one's special qualities are a gift from God, meant to be utilized in His service.

Reb Zusha of Anipoli, a disciple of the Maggid of Mezritch, once told his students: "When I come to Heaven and they ask me, 'Why weren't you like Abraham our forefather?' I will answer, 'Because I wasn't Abraham.' If they inquire, 'Why didn't you match the greatness of Moses?' I can answer that I wasn't Moses. However, if they ask me why I wasn't the way Zusha needed to be…to that I have no answer." In a world where we can be anything, Judaism implores us to be our best selves.

### More to Explore

Talmud, Sanhedrin 37a (bottom); Tanya, Introduction, chap. 1 and chap. 26; Likkutei Sichot, vol. 17, p. 4 and 8; Sichot Kodesh, Shlach 5736, chap. 1; ibid. 20 Menachem Av 5737, chap. 60; Hitvaaduyot, 5742, vol. 3, p. 1521; ibid. 5752, vol. 1, p. 241. Igrot Kodesh of the Rebbe Rayatz, vol. 4, p. 468; Hayom Yom, 26 Cheshvan; ibid. 17 Iyar.

# תיקון המדות

# Character Refinement

The refinement and enhancement of our character (in Hebrew, *tikkun hamiddot*) is a central theme of Torah and at the root of its mitzvot. According to Kabbalah, and as further explained in Chassidut, the noble work of self-improvement is one of the primary Divine purposes of creation and the reason for the soul's descent into this world. While traits such as modesty, compassion, and benevolence, along with arrogance, anger, laziness, and depression, are present to some degree within every person, it is our duty to address and either correct or sublimate them.

Our Sages taught that, on a higher level, each individual's basic character traits derive from the *sefirot* (spiritual "vessels" which reflect Divinity). Namely, these consist of *Chessed* (kindness), *Gevurah* (strength or judgment), *Tiferet* (mercy or harmony), *Netzach* (victory), *Hod* (glory), *Yesod* (foundation) and *Malchut* (kingship). Each can be positive when moderated and appropriately expressed, but negative if taken to extremes. The seven *sefirot*, we are taught, reflect the "Seven Nations" that were conquered when the Jewish people entered the Land of Israel. In the same way, the seven *middot* of a person's soul are to be "conquered" and cultivated. Developing our positive traits and transforming the negative are an integral part of Chassidic teaching.

This process is compared to that of nurturing a tree. Initially, when a tree is young and flexible, it is propped up to help it weather tempestuous winds and storms. Similarly, while an individual's character traits are still "young" and immature, they require nurturing, guidance, and direction. As the person grows into an adult, his character traits must continue to evolve and mature along with him. Deep roots can be moral supports anchored and developed by training the mind from a young age to control the heart so that our intellect and behavior are not influenced or driven by our base instincts.

The study of Torah and performance of its mitzvot, along with the regular study of Chassidut, nurtures our ability to direct their instinctual drives with intellect and reason. Our Sages affirm that each individual refinement, each correction of thought, speech, or deed—even in a seemingly "small" matter, or however slowly or irregularly—contributes powerfully to the overall spiritual refinement of the world and greatly enhances the beautiful color of the cosmic orchard.

**Bottom Line**

Refining character traits is a vital process in the service of God.

**Ponder/Action**

▸ For the "mind to rule the heart," we must monitor our character traits to make sure they are appropriate at all times.

**More to Explore**

Tanya, p. 96; Maamorei Admur HoEmtzo'i, Devorim, vol. 1, pp. 8 and on; Kuntres HaTefilla, chap. 15; Likkutei Dibburim, vol. 1, pp. 56a-b; Sefer HaMaamorim, 5716, Podo Bsholom; Likkutei Sichot, vol. 4, p. 1116; Torat Menachem, vol. 38, p. 54; ibid. vol. 39, p. 300; Sichot Kodesh, Bamidbar 5734, Sicha 6; Igrot Kodesh of the Rebbe Rayatz, vol. 3, pp. 458 and on; Hayom Yom, 26 Cheshvan.

**Bottom Line**

The mind can govern the heart, allowing each individual mastery over his or her temporal desires and thoughts. Filling our mind with Torah ideas and words, spending time in thoughtful prayer, and seizing opportunities to demonstrate goodness, help develop and nurture the human capability to direct instinctual urges arising from core needs.

**Ponder/Action**

▸ Thoughts, speech, and deed are considered garments of the soul. Just as a person switches from one garment to another, so may a person ultimately manage his thoughts, speech, and deeds.

# מוח שליט על הלב

# Mind Over Emotions

In the *Tanya*, the foundational text of Chabad philosophy, the Alter Rebbe writes that the mind is capable of governing the heart (in Hebrew, *mo-ach shalit al ha-lev*), giving each individual mastery over his temporal desires and thoughts. This self-control extends to peripheral body parts such as the mouth, involved with speech and eating, and other organs used for all other forms of action. Though the mind—by nature cool and detached—and the heart, which is fiery and passionate, seem so contrary to each other that no interrelation could be possible, this is not so. In fact, they work in tandem, both driving human development. A person's general volitions stem from his intellectual faculties which contain the power to restrain and direct the heart's urgings. Hence, through our self-awareness we can limit inadvertent indulgence in an inappropriate thought, word, or action, and rouse the soul's infinite power to help choose right over wrong, good over evil, and the holy over the profane.

The capacity to marshal intellect to moderate and control emotion-based responses is the hallmark of mankind's superiority over animals. Members of the animal kingdom, for the most part, respond instinctively and immediately to stimuli that signal the opportunity to gratify a basic biological need. For example, when hungry, an animal searches for the quickest route to food. The reverse can be expected of humankind, whose mind has the capability to direct actions related to basic needs and instincts. Conscientiousness, moderation, and self-control are all vital in leading a physically passionate and deeply meaningful spiritual life.

In no way does this signify that we must revile or shun the materiality of the world. Rather, each and every bit of life can and must be channeled along a path guided by the Torah. Ultimately, explains Chassidut, this is what it means to serve God in "totality," as the Torah implores the Jewish people to love God "with all your heart, and with all your soul..."

The human ability to harness the intellect to elevate and transform instinctual urges stems from every person's pure and infinite Godly soul. It is true that filtering and wrestling with the incessant demands of the flesh, based in the animal soul, takes more than a little training and practice. However, Chassidut assures that every person has the potential to attain this level of control. Filling our mind with Torah ideas and words, spending time in thoughtful prayer, and seizing opportunities to demonstrate goodness, are examples of ways to develop and nurture this special capacity.

**More to Explore**

Torah, Devorim 5:5; Tanya chap. 12, 17, and 30; Sefer HaMaamorim, 5660, p. 9; ibid. 5716, L'fichoch; "The Philosophy of Chabad," vol. 2.

# עבודת ה' בשמחה

# Serving God with Joy

Joy is a state of happiness accompanied by feelings of great delight. A person experiencing joy (in Hebrew, *simcha*) is uplifted beyond his usual emotional condition and able to surmount all types of barriers and personal limitations. For this reason, the Baal Shem Tov placed great emphasis on the mitzvah of serving the Almighty with joy and gladness of heart.

Chassidut teaches that joy is generated by deep awareness that all of mortal existence is nothing more than a revelation of God's essence, lovingly surrounding and enveloping us. Also, joy comes from realizing that we, finite creations, have been given an incredible opportunity to connect with the infinite and unknowable Creator through learning Torah and observing its mitzvot. Further, we rejoice knowing that our spiritual efforts and positive deeds give God great pleasure, generating blessings for ourselves and our entire household, including the main reward to be revealed with the ultimate redemption (see "*Moshiach*," p. 39).

As finite creations, we may find ourselves at times approaching Torah and mitzvot dryly and fulfilling religious obligations by rote, with no particular elation or consciousness of a spiritual experience. We do so because we don't readily perceive the infinite flow of spiritual revelation generated by our deeds. The Maggid of Mezritch illuminated this idea by expounding on the inner meaning of a verse from Ethics of Our Fathers (*Pirkei Avot*), "Know what is above from you: a seeing eye, a listening ear, and all your deeds being inscribed in a book." The Maggid explained the inner-meaning of this verse as follows: "Know what is above you," denoting everything "above" in the spiritual hemispheres of Divine emanation, derives "from you," in an individual's personal service. Each of us has the potential to influence the most elevated spiritual realms through our service of the Almighty. Indeed, every expression of our being, whether in thought, word, or action, has a spiritual effect which can change the world.

It follows that when a person is joyous, he not only uplifts people nearby, but also generates joy in the spiritual realm as well. This joy can reverberate in the heavens and effect radical changes—eliciting blessings which might not have occurred in the absence of such joy and delight.

### Bottom Line

Torah and mitzvot need to be fulfilled with joy, in which state a person is uplifted beyond his usual emotional condition and able to surmount all types of barriers and personal limitations. This joy is generated through contemplation that our deeds count, and that as finite creations, we are given the incredible opportunity to connect with the infinite and unknowable Creator through learning Torah and observing its mitzvot.

### Ponder/Action

- Aside from being a healthy way to traverse through life, joy and positivity have a tremendous impact on both our immediate environment and the entire world.

### More to Explore

Torah, Bereishit 1:31; Avot, 2:1; Zohar, chap. 2, p. 184b. Maamorei Admur Hazoken, 5568, vol. 1, p. 122; Sefer HaMaamorim, 5657, p. 221; ibid. 5689, pp. 92-93; Likkutei Sichot, vol. 14, p. 403; Torat Menachem, vol. 2, pp. 242-243; ibid. vol. 9, pp. 158 and 186; ibid. vol. 15, p. 203; ibid. 19 Tishrei 5741; ibid. Lech Lcho 5741, chap. 83; ibid. 5748, vol. 4, p. 268; ibid. 5745, vol. 1 p. 369; Hayom Yom 13 Iyar; Igrot Kodesh of the Rebbe, vol. 11, p. 70; Hiskashrus (weekly), no. 502, pp. 8 and 10; "The Chassidic Approach to Joy (Sichos in English)."

**Bottom Line**

Every Jew, without exception, is like a land in which the Almighty finds endless treasures. Therefore, we should regard every Jew as such, treating all with kindness and respect.

**Ponder/Action**

▸ When meeting a fellow Jew who is different from you, do not forsake or ignore him, for by engaging or teaching him, he may also reveal a treasure within you that you didn't know existed.

# כל נפש יהודי חשובה

# Every Jew Matters

Every single Jew counts, the fact of which was evidenced at the Giving of the Torah. If even one Jew had been absent at Mount Sinai, the Torah would not have been given, God forbid. The Tzemach Tzedek related, in the name of the Baal Shem Tov, an interpretation of the verse in Prophets, "For you (the Jewish people) shall be a land of desire." He explained that just as the greatest scientists will never discover the limits of the enormous natural resources that the Almighty placed into the world, neither can anyone fully grasp the incredible innate treasures that lie within every Jewish person. The Baal Shem Tov wanted to help every Jew fully realize their innate gifts, likened to the yield of the Almighty's "Land of Desire."

Therefore, when encountering a Jewish person who is deficient in knowledge or observance of Torah and its mitzvot, for whatever the reason, remember the treasure buried within them: their Godly soul and potential to rise fully to the service of God. Though at present that person may be "slumbering," a Jewish heart is always open to inspiration that will rouse it from the indifference induced by its environment and natural inclinations.

The fact that at the Giving of Torah, the Almighty Himself descended to all of creation—not just to the scholars—imparts an important lesson about all Jews' vital obligation to treat each other with respect, affection and responsibility. No one should ever think that it is beneath his spiritual stature to engage with a seemingly errant or unlettered Jew. In action, this means going outside our comfort zones and "spiritual boundaries" to relate to every Jew, introducing them to Torah and mitzvot with sensitivity and kindness.

This idea is further bolstered by the Chassidic explanation of the laws of *Tzara'at*, a spiritual type of leprosy. The laws reveal the Torah's concern that we preserve even vessels of little value. Extrapolating from this, Chassidut teaches that we must show all the more compassion, love, and attention to a Jewish person who is unaware of his or her Judaism. Though externally, he or she may appear to be of lesser "value" to the Jewish people, within them lies tremendous power and potential.

Furthermore, Chassidut espouses that when meeting a fellow Jew who seems different from you, do not disdain or ignore him, for by pleasantly engaging or teaching him, he may also reveal a treasure within yourself that you never knew existed.

**More to Explore**

Prophets, Malachi 3:12; Sichot Kodesh, Purim 5732, chap. 2; ibid. Mishpatim 5732, chap. 2; ibid. Beshalach 5733, chap. 1-end; ibid. 20th Menachem Av 5736, chap. 5; ibid. Shemot 5733, chap. 3; ibid. Shemini 5738, chap. 23; Hayom Yom, 17 Iyar.

# היהודי הפשוט

# The Simple Jew

In Torah thought, the Jewish nation is likened to a physical body, with the levels within the stratum of Jewish people corresponding to the body's various limbs and organs. In the past, several major schools of Jewish thought extended this idea to mean that the simple Jew (in Hebrew, *ish poshut,* or *am haaretz*) reflected "lowly" parts of the body, such as the feet. It is the feet which are most involved with action, as opposed to the higher faculties of intellect or emotion, signified by such parts as the head or heart. In this context, these schools of thought purported that the "head" and the "heart" correspond to Jews who are devoted to Torah study and to deep prayer, and as such, are of foremost value to the function and survival of the entire Jewish people. Over time, however, this concept became increasingly divisive, with some Jews not wanting to associate with the "lower" kinds.

Distraught over these self-made barriers, the Baal Shem Tov presented a unifying understanding of the concept. He taught that only God knows what is in another's heart, and that it is never appropriate to denigrate a fellow Jew, for one cannot truly judge the value of another Jew's spiritual service. He exemplified this by pointing out that the layman, the "simple Jew," is actually on a very high level. He further explained that Divine service driven by deep intellect and fiery emotions, while ideal and admirable, is limited by the capacity of the scholar's character and natural abilities. However, an ordinary Jew who serves God solely to fulfill the Almighty's will and desire (in Hebrew, *kabbalat ol*), and connects to the Almighty with genuine, simple faith—not based on great logic or painstakingly developed character traits—he avails himself of the pure simplicity of God's essence. This is a very high spiritual level indeed. In this light, the "feet" of the Jewish body of people are like "soldiers" who fulfill commands simply and directly. Moreover, all mitzvot are equal; it is not what one is doing, but rather for Whom one is doing it. When a scholar acquires this sort of *kabbalat ol*, he can also attain the height of the service of the simple, sincere Jew.

On a related note, we are taught that the era prior to the Redemption is called the "heels of the *Moshiach*." This hints, in light of the above, that the Redemption will be ushered in by simple folk doing what needs to be done with total commitment.

**Bottom Line**

The earnest, simple Jewish person is, in essence, on a very high spiritual level. This simplicity is independent of intellectual status or particular character traits. It emulates absolute Godliness, which is beyond any characterization.

**Ponder/Action**

▸ The "simple Jew" within everyone can be elicited by serving God with a purity and sincerity neither born of nor confined to personal considerations, but grounded in a basic desire to do God's Will.

**More to Explore**

Sefer HaMaamorim, 5636, p. 13 and footnotes; ibid. 5646-5650, p. 187; Sefer HaSichot of the Rebbe Rayatz, 5707, p. 73; Torat Menachem, vol. 12, p. 28; ibid. vol. 28, pp. 43, 60, and 131; ibid. vol. 36, p. 254; ibid. vol. 37, p. 27; ibid. 5742, vol. 3 p. 1573; ibid. 5743, vol. 1, p. 25; ibid. 5745, vol. 2, p. 799; ibid. 5742, vol. 4, pp. 2107-2113; ibid. 5745, vol. 5, p. 292; Sichot Kodesh, Vayikra 5741 chap. 36; Hayom Yom, 3 Adar II.

Bottom Line

There's no such thing as a Jew who is "far." Every Jew is near and connected, but at times their Jewish heart needs to be rekindled through performing a mitzvah. We should look for occasions to remind or teach another Jew about Torah and mitzvot.

Ponder/Action

▸ We can transform a soul by simply informing and inspiring a fellow Jew to do a mitzvah.

# קירוב
# Outreach

In most dictionaries, the word "outreach" is defined as "to reach out." In Chabad vernacular, however, it colloquially means "to reach beyond"—helping others learn Torah and perform mitzvot without any judgments. Indeed, the Rebbe did not like or use the term commonly used for Jewish outreach, *kiruv rechokim*, literally interpreted, "drawing close those who are distant," or colloquially, "outreach," which implies that some Jews are "out" or "distant." Continuing in the spirit of the Baal Shem Tov and the Chabad Rebbes that followed, the Rebbe maintained that all Jews are eternally "in" and "connected," and that no one can really judge who is close and who is far. When finding a Jew lacking in Torah knowledge or observance, it is most often due to his or her having been raised with no or little Jewish education, a circumstance beyond the person's control. Or perhaps that individual knew about various mitzvot, but was never encouraged to follow them. In all cases, the Rebbe taught that we must remember the mitzvah of loving a fellow Jew, since what is lacking in one causes a deficiency in all.

The proper approach begins with a foundation of love and respect. One person informs the other, in a peaceful and positive way, that there is a Torah and, as Jews, we are beholden to follow its commandments. The individual is also encouraged to fulfill at least one mitzvah. This single mitzvah acts as a catalyst to bring many others in its train. One should never denounce another Jew for their current spiritual standing. If a person responds that they feel no connection to Torah and mitzvot, God forbid, they are told in a supportive manner about their infinite Jewish soul which is connected to all other Jewish souls, and that even one mitzvah can awaken and restore their feeling of connection. Additionally, a mitzvah done with a leap of faith and self-sacrifice is much cherished in the Heavens above.

Indeed, if today a Jewish family finds a community where they feel welcome—or a Jewish student on a remote school campus discovers a home away from home where he or she feels loved and cared for—or a young Jewish girl in public school has knowledge of how and when to light Shabbat candles—or a lonely Jewish soldier on the battlefront and a dejected Jewish prisoner is blessed with a visitor for the holidays—or a special-needs child is included in Jewish life and regarded with respect and even awe, etc.—it is because of dedicated people who exemplify in its fullest sense the mitzvah of "Loving your fellow Jew as yourself."

More to Explore

Likkutei Sichot, vol. 13, pp. 69-70; ibid. vol. 20, p. 357; Torat Menachem, vol. 11, p. 135; ibid. 5742, vol. 4, p. 2157; Sichot Kodesh, Shavuot 5736, chap. 5; ibid. Yisro, 5737, chap. 28.

# מבצעים

# The Mitzvah Campaigns

In 1967, the Rebbe initiated the first of a ten-point mitzvah campaign, known in Chabad vernacular as "*mivtzoyim*" (literally interpreted, "campaigns"). On a very basic level, the mitzvah campaign's goal was to awaken the *pintele yid* (literally interpreted, "Jewish spark") which exists within every Jew. The Rebbe followed the precedent set by previous Jewish leaders, or "shepherds" of the Jewish nation, who would nourish individual Jews by helping them overcome spiritual and physical challenges, in addition to dealing with issues affecting the Jewish nation as a whole.

In the spring of 1967, two days before the Six-Day War broke out in Israel, the Rebbe launched "*Mivtzah Tefillin*," encouraging all Jewish men to lay *tefillin*, especially those who didn't usually observe this mitzvah, as a means of securing God's blessings for success in protecting the Land of Israel from its enemies.

In late 1973, the Rebbe advanced "*Mivtzah Torah*," urging all Jews to learn Torah every day. As part of this campaign, the Rebbe also encouraged "*Mivtzah Yavneh V'chachomeho*," encouraging communities to establish Yeshivot.

This was followed by "*Mivtzah Mezuza*," encouraging the observance of the mitzvah of affixing *mezuzot* on the doorposts of Jewish homes and offices. "*Mivtzah Tzedakah*" instructed people to place a charity box in their homes. "*Mivtzah Bayit Molei Sforim*" encouraged people to fill their homes with Jewish books to study. "*Mivtzah Neshek*" called on Jewish women and girls aged three and older to light Shabbat and Jewish holiday candles. "*Mivtzah Kashrut*" encouraged Jews to keep a kosher home. "*Mivtzah Taharat Hamishpacha*" stressed the importance of married couples observing the laws of mikvah and family purity.

In 1976, the Rebbe added "*Mivtzah Ahavat Yisrael*," to instill and bolster in all a love of every Jew. This was followed by "*Mivtzah Chinuch*," ensuring that every Jewish child had access to a Jewish education.

From its launch until today, in cities and towns across the globe, Chassidim and lay people go "on *mivtzoyim*," visiting Jews of all stripes in their shops, homes, offices, city squares, or college campuses, driving an unprecedented resurgence of Jewish awareness and observance.

**More to Explore**

Likkutei Sichot, vol. 13, pp. 214; Igrot Kodesh of the Rebbe Rayatz, vol. 4, p. 279; "The Thought for the Week," vol. 10.

**Bottom Line**

In Egypt, the Jews were advised to focus on specific commandments in order to prepare them for their exodus. So it is in our time, with the mitzvah campaigns helping prepare every Jew for the final Redemption.

**Ponder/Action**

▸ Encourage fellow Jews to participate in the mitzvah campaign.

# Section Six

## *Lifecycles*

# הריון ולידה
# Pregnancy & Birth

The birth of a child represents far more than adding a member to a family or increasing the number of Jewish people. Rather, it is the arrival of the unique Godly revelation that each soul brings into this world and the launch of its singular purpose for descending from Above. Indeed, each soul's particular spiritual expression is a gift from God to the world—a gift to be developed during the parents' lifetime and eventually perpetuated by their children, grandchildren, and all future descendants.

In Jewish thought, bringing a child into the world is the truest expression of God's blessings and one of the greatest mitzvot of all. In fact, it is the very first mitzvah written in the Torah. Our Sages point out that bearing children is the one area where man and woman are invited to partner with God in the wondrous creation of a new being. Coupled with this privilege, however, comes the responsibility to raise children in a healthy environment, one conducive to their growth and ability to thrive both spiritually and materially.

As with all other aspects of life, the processes of pregnancy, birth, and childrearing are guided by Jewish law. This begins with the Jewish approach to intimacy and marriage, and includes the customs and mitzvot observed during pregnancy and those following birth, such as a *brit milah* (religious circumcision) for boys (see following page), choosing a name (see, *"Naming a Child,"* p. 96), redemption of the firstborn son (see, *"Pidyon Haben,"* p. 97), the first haircut for boys (see, *"Upshernish,"* p. 98), and more.

The Rebbe would often remind couples that just as the healthy development of a fetus is largely dependent on the expectant mother's nutritional choices, behavior and mindset, the parents' spiritual choices during pregnancy also have profound effects on the developing life. The Rebbe thus encouraged expectant couples to increase their mitzvah observance, in particular, enhancing observance of kosher dietary laws, giving more to charity, and having an expert scribe inspect their mezuzot to ensure they are all in a kosher state.

Additionally, pregnant women should strive to maintain a spiritually wholesome environment during pregnancy, which includes appropriate musical and visual influences. Finally, it is customary to have available a copy of Psalm 121 during the birth.

**Bottom Line**

Birth heralds the beginning of a newborn's mission for which its soul has entered the body. As with all aspects of life, pregnancy, childbirth, and childrearing are guided by Jewish law. A pregnant woman should exert extra effort to maintain a spiritually healthy environment during her pregnancy.

**Ponder/Action**

▸ Your soul has been dispatched to this world to fulfill a mission assigned to it by God. Recognize its inherent power and capabilities, and use them wisely.

**More to Explore**

Talmud, Niddah 30b; Tanya, Iggeret Hakodesh, chap. 20; Torah Ohr, Vaera, p. 55a; Sefer HaMaamorim, 5657, pp. 175-177; Likkutei Sichot, vol. 24, p. 179; Torat Menachem, 5744, vol. 2, p. 961; Sichot Kodesh, Kedoshim 5736, chap. 5; ibid. Chukas 5740, chap. 49.

# ברית מילה

# Circumcision

The first commandment God gave to our Patriarch Abraham was the mitzvah of circumcision (in Hebrew, *brit milah*), an everlasting sign of the Covenant between God and the Jewish people and a tangible reminder of their innate ability to master and harness all of our physical drives for holy purposes. Bringing completion to the male body through circumcision represents the essence of the Jewish mission—to improve the physical world by imbuing our physical life with sanctity and holiness. Females are born "spiritually circumcised" — i.e., naturally bonded to their Creator, thus they do not require circumcision.

For thousands of years, Jews have circumcised their sons using the services of a trained and qualified Jewish *mohel* (ritual circumciser), even under the most trying circumstances such as during times of religious persecution. When a child is properly circumcised by a *mohel*, he enters into God's covenant with Abraham and his descendants, and is part of a chain linking him to the very beginnings of our nation.

Chassidut points out a difference between commandments performed by our Patriarchs, such as the mitzvah of *brit milah*, and the commandments fulfilled by Jews after the Giving of the Torah at Mount Sinai. Prior to Sinai, spiritual energy which radiated into the world when mitzvot were performed by our Patriarchs and the Jewish people, did not dwell in the world permanently. With the Giving of the Torah, however, the Jews received the power to draw down with each mitzvah a new spiritual energy that remains permanently in the physical world.

A *brit milah* is performed on the eighth day from birth—or as soon as possible thereafter in cases where there is illness or another significant impediment. This signifies access to a spiritual elevation that transcends time's normal framework. In the natural cycle of time, seven days make up one week; seven years make up a sabbatical cycle; seven sabbatical cycles conclude with a Jubilee. Having a *brit milah* on the eighth day evokes the Jewish people's ability to soar above nature's limitations, connecting the child directly with the infinite Almighty in an eternal covenant.

A Jewish man who has not had a proper *brit milah*, for whatever reason, should seek to have one done by a trained mohel as soon as possible, as it is vital for one's spiritual wellbeing. A knowledgeable rabbi can offer guidance in this respect.

**More to Explore**

Torah, Bereishit 17:11-12; Tehillim 119:162; Zohar, vol. 3, p. 44a; Midrash Vayikra Rabbah 27:10; Talmud, Sanhedrin 110b; Sefer Hamaamorim, 5657, p. 103; ibid. 5723, V'chol Adam, chap. 8; ibid. 5742, Vayehi Bayom HaShmini; ibid. 5743, Vayehi Bayom HaShmini; Likkutei Sichot, vol. 1, pp. 20 and on; ibid. vol. 3, pp. 757-764; ibid. vol. 10, pp. 45-47; Sichot Kodesh, Acharon Shel Pesach 5740, chap. 4.

**Bottom Line**

Circumcision connects the body of the Jew with the infinite Almighty in an eternal covenant.

**Ponder/Action**

▸ When a Jew becomes connected with the Almighty in the eternal bond of circumcision, his entire life is guided by the Almighty's blessings.

# קריאת שם לרך הנולד

# Naming a Child

A Jewish Hebrew name reflects the essence of a person's soul and channels life and vitality from Above. A baby girl is named at the first public Torah reading in the synagogue following her birth (i.e., Shabbat, Monday or Thursday, or on Jewish holidays). A boy is named at his *brit milah* (religious circumcision) ceremony. Kabbalah teaches that the name chosen by the parent is relayed by spiritual intuition *(ruach hakodesh)* and reflects the unique spiritual energy of the newborn's soul. Furthermore, just as the Hebrew name of every object is the conduit for its Divine energy, the same is true of a Hebrew name. Thus, addressing a person by that name draws spiritual energy from the soul to the physical body. This is also why when individuals are distracted or confused, calling them by name helps draw them from their reverie. Indeed, Jews throughout history have made great efforts to publicly maintain their Jewish names, because in addition to demonstrating pride in their Jewish identity and heritage, using one's Hebrew name continually summons new spiritual vitality by virtue of its soul connection.

The Rebbe writes that unless parents have a specific familial or communal custom, they should follow the ancient custom whereby they alternate choosing a name, i.e., the father chooses the name of the first child, the mother that of the second, and so on. In all cases, although one parent may prefer a particular name, both should ultimately agree on the final choice. Traditionally, names of departed relatives or holy Jewish Sages are given to perpetuate their memories and inspire the child to emulate the virtues of their namesake. Sefardic Jews also have the custom of honoring living grandparents by naming children for them. Our Sages teach that a spiritual radiance from the soul of the person after whom the child is named glows in that child's soul and inspires him or her throughout their lifetime.

When the Jewish people were exiled in Egypt in the times of Pharaoh, they remained a cohesive people and merited redemption primarily because they didn't change their Jewish names. In the same way today, proudly using your Jewish name, both privately and publicly, opens a channel for blessings to flow to the individual and contributes to the strength of the Jewish people as a whole. If a Jewish person wasn't given a Hebrew name, it is never too late to receive one. A knowledgeable rabbi can help guide you in this respect.

**Bottom Line**

A Jewish name is deeply connected to the person's soul and draws spiritual energy into the body whenever it's used. Kabbalah teaches that the name chosen for someone by his parent is relayed by spiritual intuition and reflects the unique spiritual energy of the newborn's soul.

**Ponder/Action**

- Use your Jewish name with pride. Don't have one yet? Ask a knowledgeable Rabbi to give you one.

**More to Explore**

Talmud, Yoma 4b and 83b; Tanya, Shaar Hayichud VhoEmuna, chap. 1; Sefer HaMaamorim, 5740, Zos Torat; ibid. 5741, Im B'chukotai; Likkutei Sichot, vol. 16, p. 37; vol. 17, p. 5; Torat Menachem, vol. 11, p. 70; ibid. vol. 38, p. 208; ibid. 5742, vol. 4, p. 1780; ibid. 5747, vol. 2, p. 384; Sichot Kodesh, Purim 5731, chap. 6; ibid. Motzoei B'shalach 5731, chap. 2; ibid. Emor 5740, chap. 58; ibid. Shlach 5740, chap. 40 and on; Igrot Kodesh of the Rebbe, vol. 1, p. 289; "Ziv HaShemot"; Shaarei Halachah UMinhag, vol. 3, pg. 295.

# פדיון הבן

# *Pidyon Haben*

Judaism grants a special status to firstborn male children, including certain rights related to inheritance and a religious obligation for them to fast on the eve of Passover. This assignment stems from God's sanctification of all Jewish firstborn males as a priestly class at the time they were still in bondage in Egypt.

The *pidyon haben* ("redemption of the [firstborn] son"), is performed on the 31st day from the natural birth (i.e., not caesarean) of any firstborn male child to a mother whose father, as well as father of the child, is an Israelite (i.e., Yisrael, and not a Kohen or Levite). The occasion is celebrated with a festive meal at which the child's father gives a Kohen (a priestly descendant of Aaron) five *Sela'im* (a measure totaling approximately 101 grams of pure silver), while reciting certain passages.

The primary reason for the mitzvah of *pidyon haben* is that during the last plague visited upon Egypt by God, when all Egyptian firstborn sons died, God protected and spared the firstborn Jews. Regarding this, the Torah states, "For every firstborn is Mine: On the day I struck down every firstborn in the land of Egypt, I sanctified every firstborn in Israel for Myself."

Another reason given by our Sages also harks back to Biblical times, when the brothers of Joseph—who was Rachel's firstborn son—sold him to a passing caravan of Ishmaelite merchants for twenty pieces of silver, equivalent to the five *sela'im* measurement used today. Fulfilling the mitzvah of *pidyon haben* serves as a form of atonement for the brothers' misdeed.

Practically speaking, it is not often that all *halachic* requirements requiring a *pidyon haben* are met, and therefore it is wise to consult a knowledgeable rabbi. If parents neglect to arrange a *pidyon haben* for a firstborn child who requires it, then the child must arrange one for himself upon reaching adulthood.

Chassidut explains that, on a personal level, the "first" or primary characteristic in every soul is *chochma* ("wisdom"). It represents the beginning of the inherent *sefirot* (spiritual vessels that reflect Divinity), similar to the first thought that comes to one's mind. On a practical level, the focus of *chochma* and its effects (i.e., the first thought, word, deed) should be positive and exclusively connected with God's will. Thus, our "oldest, first and foremost" will be in an elevated state of holiness.

**More to Explore**

Torah, Bereishit 37:28; ibid. Shemot 13:13–16; Talmud, Shekalim 2:3; Likkutei Torah, Bhaaloscho, p. 33a.

**Bottom Line**

Judaism grants a special status to firstborn male children; as such, the firstborn is consecrated to God and is redeemed through the *Pidyon Haben* ceremony.

**Ponder/Action**

- Consecrate each "newborn" day by starting it with thoughtful prayer and meaningful Jewish study.

# תספורת ראשונה

# *Upshernish*

It is an ancient Jewish custom to refrain from cutting a boy's hair until his third birthday. The hair-cutting ceremony is known as *upsherenish* (Yiddish for "haircut"). At that time, family and friends are honored with cutting a snip of his hair. The essence of the custom is the act of leaving certain portions of the *peyot* ("sidelocks") uncut.

From the day of his *upsherenish*, tradition dictates that the child be trained to begin wearing *tzitzit* (special four-cornered garment worn by Jewish males) and to recite the early-morning *b'rachot* (blessings), *birkat hamazon* (Grace after meals), and bedtime *shema*. Although the child may have already been trained to wear a *yarmulka* (i.e., *kippah*), and *tzitzit*, and to recite certain blessings and prayers, it is at this age that he is encouraged to gain appreciation of the meaning behind his actions and to take a more participatory role in his own religious development. Indeed, according to Chassidut, the *upsherenish* signifies the child's receiving unique spiritual revelation from a higher world. In the same vein, the first fruits of the child's education emerge.

Another insight draws on the Torah's comparison of mankind to a tree, hence we can derive a lesson from the Torah's laws relating to trees. Accordingly, in Jewish law, the fruit of a new tree may not be eaten or enjoyed for the first three years. The produce is called *orla*, meaning "closed" and "concealed." In the fourth year, the farmer jubilantly takes portions of his harvest to Jerusalem to enjoy them in an environment of holiness. Similarly, at the age of three, a child's mind begins a new stage of development during which he becomes open to learning about integrity, kindness, and Jewish values on a more mature level. Indeed, the Talmud relates that our Patriarch Abraham was three years old when he recognized his Creator, which eventually led him to become the father of the Jewish nation.

Another lesson taught from leaving the traditional *peyot* at the *upsherenish* is that, although the child is young and still has much to learn, he should never be embarrassed to act and dress as a Jew, and furthermore, he should be proud and happy of his heritage so deeply rooted in glorious history and ethical standards.

The formal education of daughters begins at age three as well, as signified by the fact that many begin to light Shabbat and Jewish holiday candles—with the help of an adult—at this age.

**Bottom Line**

A boy's hair is not cut until his third birthday, at which time he is encouraged to gain appreciation of the meaning behind his actions and to take a more participatory role in his own religious development.

**Ponder/Action**

▸ No matter our age, we are always growing and maturing, and like a tree, our branches spread and our roots deepen with each passing day and year. Actively engaging with and connecting to the Torah—the "fountain of life"—by studying it and fulfilling its mitzvot, ensures that the "shade" we provide brings comfort and lasting protection to those who count on us, and that all our "fruit" is sweet, nourishing, and plentiful for those who partake of it.

**More to Explore**

Torah, Vayikra 20:19; ibid. Devorim, 20:19; Talmud, Chulin 135a; ibid. Nedarim 32a; Ohr Hachaim, Vayikra 19:23; Likkutei Sichot, vol. 22, p. 329; Torat Menachem, vol. 7, p. 191; Hayom Yom, 4 Iyar; Igrot Kodesh of the Rebbe, vol. 5, p. 22; Yagdil Torah (periodical), no. 48.

# ימי הולדת

# *Birthdays*

Time is like a spiral, and when a specific day reappears each year, its unique spiritual energies are regenerated right along with it. The Divine emanation particular to each individual, revealed initially on the day we were born, returns every year to re-energize and strengthen our special spiritual attributes. Further, by crossing over into another year, God is showing us that we are needed by the world which remains incomplete without each of us.

The Midrash relates about many Sages who have rejoiced on their birthday, marking and celebrating it with a special feast. Indeed, over the centuries, leading Torah scholars, classic Kabbalists, and Chassidic masters have maintained this custom both publicly and privately. In Jewish tradition, a birthday is not merely a day for merriment, but first and foremost a spiritual event, a personal "Rosh Hashana" so to speak, granting the individual a personal opportunity for introspection, renewal, and spiritual realignment. It is a time to reflect on the year gone by, with its challenges and victories, and to resolve to improve in areas needing attention, starting with the "three pillars" of Torah, prayer, and charity.

It is customary to give generously to charity on your birthday (if it falls on Shabbat or a Jewish holiday, then give the day before and after), and to perform extra acts of loving-kindness. According to the Rebbe, in addition to enhancing their own service of God, the person celebrating a birthday should also utilize this special time to encourage others to do the same, thus amplifying and spreading the spiritual gifts inherent in this special day.

The Rebbe also encouraged those celebrating their birthday to study the chapter in the Book of Psalms (*"Tehillim"*) corresponding to their new age, along with its classic commentaries. This is in accordance with the custom introduced by the Alter Rebbe and attributed to the Baal Shem Tov, of reciting daily the chapter of Psalms corresponding to one's age. For example, a person entering his 25th year (i.e., the day of his 24th birthday) should recite Psalm 25 every day for the duration of that year.

It is also customary for men, including boys over the age of thirteen, to be called up to the Torah on the Shabbat before their birthday.

**More to Explore**

Midrash Sechel Tov 40:20; Ginze Yosef, chap. 4; Chida Lev Dovid, chap. 29; Shomer Emunim (end); Likkutei Torah, Nitzavim 47a; Ben Ish Chai Halachos, Year 1, Re'eh, par. 17; Sefer Hamaamorim, 5680, p. 338; Likkutei Sichot, vol. 2, p. 496; ibid. vol. 10, pp. 206-7; ibid. vol. 20, p. 399; ibid. vol. 24, pp. 179 and on; Torat Menachem, 5742, vol. 4, pp. 4179 and 4183; ibid. 5743, vol. 3, p. 1221 and 1223; Sichot Kodesh, Motzoei Vayetze 5739, chap. 6; ibid. 11 Nissan 5741, chap. 1; Hayom Yom, 11 Nissan; Gevurto Shel Torah (Rabbi Schochet, Toronto, 1983), pp. 69 and on. Yom Malkeinu (Rabbi M Laufer, Israel, 1984).

**Bottom Line**

On our birthday, our unique spiritual attributes are strengthened and renewed. It's a fitting time for reflection and commitment to continued self-improvement.

**Ponder/Action**

▸ Positive resolutions made on your birthday carry an extra spiritual boost that facilitates their fulfillment in the following days and months.

Bottom Line

A girl becomes obligated to fulfill Torah and mitzvot at the age of twelve due to her high level of maturity and spiritual sensitivity; hence the term *bat mitzvah* ("daughter of mitzvot").

Ponder/Action

▸ More than a material celebration, a *bat mitzvah* should be a momentous event with the spiritual bases of nurturing her Jewish identify and of launching a vibrant and fulfilling Jewish life.

# בת מצוה

# Bat Mitzvah

A girl becomes obligated to fulfill Torah and mitzvot at the age of twelve; hence the term *bat mitzvah* ("daughter of mitzvot"). It is self-understood that a person cannot be expected to fulfill certain duties and obligations before reaching a particular level of maturity. According to Jewish tradition, a Jewish girl attains such maturity at the age of twelve. Once a girl becomes *bat mitzvah*, she is obligated to perform many of the Torah's positive commandments and to respect certain of its prohibitions.

Females are exempt from mitzvot that carry a time contingency such as *tefillin*, *tzitzit*, *tallit*, etc., and elevate their spiritually sensitive, feminine souls through observing the mitzvot essential to Jewish living, such as lighting Shabbat candles, observing the kosher dietary laws, and putting into practice the many laws of Jewish family life. Each of these core mitzvot demonstrates the female ability to bring Godliness to all aspects of daily life. Shabbat transforms the weekday into a time of peace and sanctity; the kosher dietary laws reminds us that our sustenance comes from God and that even the mundane act of eating can be a Godly act; and the laws governing family life reflect how even bodily drives can be a vehicle for holiness.

In truth, preparation for a girl's *bat mitzvah* begins years before the actual date of the celebration. It is during the young, formative years leading up to the *bat mitzvah* that girls develop their own personal relationship with Judaism and God. During these years, a primary focus should be to support a young girl in nurturing her Jewish identity, studying the Torah and its mitzvot, including the Code of Jewish Law that addresses daily Jewish living, as well as reciting Jewish prayers each day.

Some *bat mitzvah* girls find it meaningful to "adopt" a specific mitzvah from the many performed by Jewish women and turn it into a "mitzvah project," researching it in depth and developing a personal connection to it. The mitzvah can involve others, such as a charity drive, or it can be more personal, e.g. daily prayer. A girl could also combine two mitzvot by, for example, preparing meals for the less fortunate in a demonstration of both charity and kosher dietary laws. Spiritually focused activities such as these help the *bat mitzvah* girl elevate a fleeting physical moment into an unforgettable launch of a vibrant and fulfilling Jewish life.

More to Explore

Talmud, Bava Metziah 59a; ibid. Niddah 45b; Likkutei Sichot, vol. 22, p. 387; Torat Menachem, vol. 22, p. 172; ibid. vol. 60, p. 138.

# בר מצוה

# *Bar Mitzvah*

A boy becomes obligated to fulfill Torah and mitzvot on the day of his thirteenth birthday; hence the term *bar mitzvah*, which in Hebrew means "son of mitzvot." At this time, he can also be counted as part of a *minyan* (religious quorum) of ten Jewish men required for prayer services and other religious ceremonies. Although the conferring of Jewish legal and moral responsibility occurs automatically on that day, it is nevertheless customary to celebrate the milestone with a festive meal together with family and friends, during which the *bar mitzvah* boy traditionally delivers words on a Torah topic.

Although boys are taught to practice mitzvot during their formative childhood years, the mitzvah of *tefillin*, which are phylacteries required to be worn by Jewish men for weekday morning prayer services, is only observed starting at age thirteen. For this reason, *tefillin* is a mark of honor for the *bar mitzvah* boy. Starting approximately sixty days before his thirteenth birthday, he practices wearing them during weekday morning prayers, to acquaint himself with the mechanics and meaning of the mitzvah.

During this training period, the boy recites the blessings over the donning of *tefillin*, but omits mentioning God's name in the blessing as he is not yet formally obligated in the mitzvah. On the day of his thirteenth birthday—if it falls on a weekday—he begins to recite the complete blessing when donning the *tefillin*.

The age of thirteen being chosen as a mark of adulthood is derived from the Torah. When Shimon and Levi, the sons of our Patriarch Jacob, rescued their sister, Dina, they were thirteen years old, and the Torah refers to them with the term *Ish*, which in Hebrew, means "adult."

Chassidut adds that on the *bar mitzvah* day, the boy's spiritual soul, constrained until now by his naturally infantile and self-centered drives, emerges from its state of suppression. It now becomes accessible to assist the young adult in surmounting the challenges posed by his natural instincts, thus helping him develop and refine his spiritual character. This internal shift is considered a spiritual redemption for the Godly soul, and is part of the reason for celebrating.

### Bottom Line

At the age of thirteen, a boy becomes an equal opportunity member in the Jewish nation and counts as part of a *minyan* (religious quorum) of ten Jewish men required for prayer services and other religious ceremonies. He also begins to put on *tefillin*.

### Ponder/Action

- At Mount Sinai, the Jewish nation unanimously declared, "We will do and we will hear" everything that God has said. In the same vein, the *bar mitzvah* boy is able demonstrate his acceptance of the Almighty's kingship by fulfilling Torah and mitzvot with sincerity and dedication.

**More to Explore**

Zohar, vol. 2, p. 98a; Zohar Chodosh, pp. 10c-d and 15d; Sefer HaMaamorim, 5653, p. 233; ibid. 5728, Vchozakto Vhoyito; ibid. 5728, Isa B'Midrash Tehillim; Likkutei Sichot, vol. 5, p. 410; ibid. vol. 15, p. 289; Torat Menachem, vol. 13, p. 352; ibid. vol. 16, p. 334; ibid. vol. 33, p. 285; ibid. vol. 50, p. 154; ibid. vol. 53, p. 260; Sichot Kodesh, 13 of Tammuz 5739, chap. 2; ibid. 5747, vol. 1, pp. 417-431; ibid. 5749, vol. 4, p. 55; Reshimot of the Rebbe, no. 59; Mishvochei HaRebbe, p. 169.

## Bottom Line

A match occurs when two souls who share the same root rediscover each other and unite spiritually and physically.

## Ponder/Action

▸ Whom we choose to marry has effects now and for all of eternity. Therefore, mature forethought and soul-searching, along with the guidance of a trusted mentor, are prerequisites for an enduring and fulfilling marriage.

▸ Finding one's soul-mate often involves the efforts of friends and family who can providentially suggest an appropriate match.

# שידוכים
# *Dating*

The Talmud relates that forty days before the creation of a child, a voice from heaven issues forth, "The daughter of [this person] is for the son of [that person]." From this we learn that our mate is ordained before we are even born. Yet, being born into separate families, and sometimes distant geographically as well, makes the destined discovery and union quite a feat. More difficult—the Talmudists say—than the splitting of the sea for the Jews as they fled Egypt. We know, however, that God finds ways to engineer events so that the couple meet and complete their oneness.

Traditionally, a *shidduch* (Hebrew for "match") is suggested and cultivated by a *shadchan* ("matchmaker"). The *shadchan* may be a friend of one or both families or someone who specializes in this role. After a suggestion appears suitable to both sides, the parties meet and spend meaningful time together to see if the other is a fitting potential marriage partner. Chemistry and a meeting of values and minds are key. If both are present, or at least the potential exists that they will emerge, the two prospective mates are advised to continue seeing each other over a reasonable period of time until they decide to either pursue marriage, or either party feels the fit is not for them.

In Chabad tradition, a couple would write to the Rebbe before becoming engaged, requesting his consent and blessing. Typically, the Rebbe would reply in the affirmative, often adding, "Surely they have resolved to build their home on the foundation of Torah and its commandments. The wedding should take place in a good and auspicious hour."

Many have turned to the Rebbe for advice on this topic. The following are some insights based on his guidance: Look for a mate who is God-fearing and has positive character traits. Be realistic—perfection doesn't exist in any one person. Don't accept or reject a *shidduch* based on a minor detail, including those irrelevant to the other's ability to participate in a healthy relationship. It is advisable that there be no more than a ten-year age difference between the two people, so there is a better chance they share common values and ideologies. It is unwise for either person to assume they can convince the other to make major religious or personality changes. If a child won't consider a *shidduch* suggestion from his or her parents, it is a good idea to ask one of their close friends to make the suggestion instead.

**More to Explore**

Talmud, Sotah 2a; Midrash Bereishit Rabbah 68:4; Mammorei Admur Hazoken, Mamorei Razal, p. 91; Torat Shmuel 5640, vol. 2 p. 595; Sichot Kodesh, 7 Tishrei 5752; Igrot Kodesh of the Rebbe, vol. 2, pp. 193-196; Heichal Menachem, vol. 3, p. 241; Hiskashrus (weekly), no. 873, p. 6; Kfar Chabad (weekly), no. 718, p. 34.; ibid. no. 767, p. 127; ibid. no. 860, p. 50.

# נישואין

# Marriage

According to Kabbalah, marriage represents the reunion of two soul-mates who were separated prior to their birth. Upon reuniting in a traditional Jewish marriage, a unique and infinite Godly energy exists between them. And this energy is the source of all the blessings the couple will need to build an enduring Jewish family. By living in harmony with Godly principles and continuing the chain of life by creating and raising offspring who walk the path of Torah, their marriage demonstrates the infinite capabilities of the Almighty.

It is certainly true that maintaining a successful and harmonious marriage involves constant work, commitment, and great dedication, Chassidut reminds us, though, that along the way we move toward our own ideal Godly potential. The Almighty plans each and every match for the optimal growth of each person, enabling us to find our truest self and experience personal growth and healing. It is thus vital to appreciate our spouse as key to our character refinement. Knowing this, stress and disagreements become opportunities for personal growth, instead of a cause of distance and division. From this perspective, relationship challenges are divinely crafted to smooth the rough edges of our personalities.

When we understand this idea and embrace normal relationship troubles as Divine stepping stones to be forded willingly and functionally, we become softer and kinder along the way. More importantly, with each challenge overcome, our union is strengthened in its spiritual perfection, and the love we share with our spouse becomes even deeper and more enduring.

Marriage is also outward focused, with its ability to create new life. Together with the third partner—God—the Giver of life, both spouses draw down and create new life in accordance with the Torah's laws of family purity. Here, as our children are guided and raised on the path of Torah, marriage evolves into an eternal, physical form, multiplying the spiritual light of both the husband and wife by adding to the very chain of life.

The Torah holds marriage as a sacrosanct and eternal bond. It also recognizes that there are times when a marriage fails despite one's best efforts, and provides for a Jewish divorce in certain irreconcilable situations as guided by expert rabbis.

**More to Explore**

Torat Shmuel 5637 and 5640; Sefer HaMaamorim, 5689, Lecho Dodi; ibid 5714, Lecho Dodi; Likkutei Sichot, vol. 19, p. 210; Torat Menachem, vol. 12, p. 200.

**Bottom Line**

Marriage represents the reunion of two soul-mates who were separated at their root before birth. When normal relationship troubles are embraced as Divine stepping stones key to each person's character refinement, both partners becomes softer and kinder, leading to a deeper and more enduring partnership.

**Ponder/Action**

▸ Marriage is a truly auspicious time in a person's life. Meeting one's soul-mate and embarking on the journey of marriage together brings powerful opportunities for true completeness.

Bottom Line

God provides sustenance for the entire world through His grace, kindness, and mercy. Yet, it is still the breadwinner's responsibility to do the necessary footwork to bring about His blessing by way of productive labor.

Ponder/Action

▸ To enhance your livelihood, business dealings should be done in strict conformance with Jewish law, and diligent attention should be given to meaningful daily prayer, reserving time for Torah study, careful observance of mitzvot, and contributing generously to charity.

# פרנסה

# *Livelihood*

Along with the joys and responsibilities of being a head-of-household comes the obligation to obtain livelihood to support one's family. This is also one of the obligations of a husband as stipulated in the *Ketubah*. Our Sages remind us in the first blessing of the Grace After a Meal, that God provides sustenance for the entire world through His grace, kindness, and mercy. Yet, it is still the breadwinner's responsibility to do the necessary footwork to realize and bring about God's blessing by way of productive labor. By adding a spiritual dimension to our work through heartfelt daily prayer, careful observance of mitzvot, making time for Torah study, and giving generously to charity, we also widen and solidify these channels.

Regarding trials and travails in finding a livelihood, our Sages tell us these are a "descent for the purpose of the ascent." This means, in ways best known to God, that struggles are for our ultimate benefit and growth. By nurturing our innate faith and trust that the One Who feeds and sustains all will provide us with an ample livelihood, we can approach its pursuit in a positive state of mind. It is this very joy, positivity, and pure trust in God that helps draw down material blessings.

By way of encouragement, our Sages remind us that life is like a turning wheel, which was explained by the Rebbe Rayatz as meaning that when a point on the wheel reaches the lowest degree, it is bound to turn upwards again. Yet, when things are going well, through God's abundance, we must be vigilant to maintain a healthy work/family balance so that family life is not weakened by the seeking of expansion and thereby even more riches.

On this topic, the Rebbe Rayatz reminded us that each year on Rosh Hashana, God ordains each person's livelihood for the coming year. Therefore it is shortsighted, even foolhardy, to become unhealthily enslaved to our work, because after we apply appropriate exertion in creating channels for gainful productivity, not a single extra penny will be netted above what was preordained for that year. Thus, he concluded, is it not far more rewarding to spend the extra energy and time nurturing our family and striving for the true, infinite spiritual gains stemming from dedicated Torah study and mitzvah observance?

**More to Explore**

Derech Mitzvosecha, Tiglachas Metzora, p. 106 (chap. 2); Likkutei Torah, Korach, p. 110; Torah Ohr, Noach, p. 16; Kuntres U'maayon, chap. 17; Likkutei Sichot, vol. 1, p. 62; ibid. vol. 3, p. 848; Torat Menachem, vol. 7, p. 138; ibid. vol. 12, p. 140; ibid. vol. 34, p. 222; ibid. vol. 40, p. 45; ibid. 5744, vol. 1, p. 171; Sichot Kodesh, Acharon Shel Pseach 5735 chap. 5; ibid. Shlach 5737 chap. 17; ibid. 11 Nissan 5738, chap. 23; ibid. Lag B'Omer 5740, chap. 3; Hayom Yom, 16 Adar II; ibid. 4 Menachem Av.

# ניצול הכשרונות

# Applying Talents

Every person has unique talents and abilities—some people can invent and build things, others can teach and enlighten, heal the ill and wounded, and so on. The Talmud declares that nothing was created in vain, meaning that the thread of intrinsic purposefulness that runs through all of creation includes each and every one of us with all our varied capabilities. For instance, in building the Tabernacle in the Sinai desert during our peoples' sojourn to the Land of Israel, the Jewish people contributed in accordance with their means and abilities. While some could contribute gold, silver, precious gems and expensive fabrics, everyone—regardless of their material means—played a part in some way by lending their talents.

In Jewish thought, the Jewish nation is compared to a body. Just as every part of the body contributes to the whole, so too, every member of the Jewish nation has a unique set of qualities that advance its unity and purpose. The Jewish peoples' mission of sanctifying the world is more fully realized when everybody utilizes their God-given abilities for the good of society.

Indeed, the Alter Rebbe taught that a core foundation of Godly service is the use of our inborn strengths, characteristics, and emotions to this end. Furthermore, an individual's role should be matched to his or her specific skills. Simply put, if one can culture pearls or polish gems but works instead at baking bread, even though baking bread is a vital and necessary craft, he is considered to have deserted his true service because his higher abilities were not fully put to use.

On this theme, the Rebbe Rashab taught that just as we must not deceive ourselves regarding our weaknesses, neither should we underestimate our personal strengths and abilities. Just as being aware of our weaknesses affects productivity as a necessary first step in their rectification, awareness of our capabilities is the first step toward mastering them for maximum usefulness. Another blessed byproduct is our own personal fulfillment and satisfaction. By working to discover and develop our strengths, we become more complete and truly become part of creation through the goodness we offer the world. As expressed in the concluding statement of the Ethics of our Fathers: "All that the Holy One, blessed be He, created in the world, He created solely for His glory." Directing our talents properly moves the world closer to its perfection and being a worthy dwelling-place for the Almighty.

### Bottom Line

Every person has unique talents and abilities. The thread of intrinsic purposefulness that runs through all of creation includes each and every one of us, and the Jewish peoples' mission of sanctifying the world is more fully realized when everyone utilizes their God-given talents for the good of society.

### Ponder/Action

▸ Your talents are waiting for you to discover and actualize. Choose work that utilizes your highest talents and one adds spiritual light to the world and directly benefits the people and community you care about most. The world needs your gifts!

**More to Explore**

Shemot 35:1-29; Talmud, Sanhendrin 37a and 38a; Pirkei Avot 6:11; Likkutei Torah, Nitzavim (beginning); Likkutei Sichot, vol. 16 p. 456; vol. 28 p. 47 and on; Torat Menachem, vol. 55, p. 318; ibid. vol. 27, p. 173; Likutei Dibburim (English), vol. 1, p. 319; Sichot Kodesh, Purim 5732, chap. 6; Hayom Yom, 26 Cheshvan; ibid. 25 Nissan.

Bottom Line

Body and soul work in unison and reflect each other. When a person is ill, he need to seek not only a physical cure, but also reconnect to the Source of life through careful observance of Torah and mitzvot.

Ponder/Action

▸ The body and soul are intertwined; thus, a person's actions have a profound impact on both. The potential for healing oneself is, to a certain extent, in an individual's own hands.

# חולי

# *Illness*

Every human body is composed of 248 limbs and 365 veins or sinews, interpreted by Kabbalah as spiritually corresponding to the Torah's 248 positive commandments and 365 prohibitive commandments. As such, body and soul work in unison, affecting each other. An illness in the body, God forbid, can reflect a lack of balance between its spiritual and physical parts—a "clogging" of the Godly soul's life-giving channels due to some deficiency in Torah observance. As such, a cure must include both medical care and spiritual realignment, the latter involving the mindful reconnection to Torah observance. As the Talmud prescribes, if one has a headache or a sore throat, he should study Torah, for through Torah flows the vital energy that nourishes and sustains life for the Jewish people.

Indeed, many great Torah Sages throughout Jewish history have practiced this two-pronged approach to medicine. These include Maimonides and Nachmonidies. Nachmonides, for example, wrote that a person with an illness should turn to a spiritual consultant for guidance in strengthening his Torah observance in order to aid in a full restoration to health.

In the spiritual dimension, Chassidut explains that certain traits within a person's soul can precipitate an internal "spiritual" illness that may manifest as apathy or a dullness to the spiritual. This is often instigated by the evil inclination which convinces a person to mindlessly pursue his physical desires and ignore the spiritual. Milder forms of soul sickness can result from indulging in permissible activities merely to satiate physical cravings and not solely in order to serve God. For example, a person can enjoy fine food and drink in honor of Shabbat, but doing so solely for physical pleasure places his spiritual and physical health at risk. If the soul illness is so severe that a person barely feels any influence from their Godly soul, this could be due to engaging in behaviors forbidden outright by the Torah, such as not carefully observing Shabbat, Kosher dietary laws, laws of modesty, family purity, and so on.

Cures for both physical and spiritual illnesses can be powerfully influenced by true repentance (*"teshuvah"*), prayer (*"tefillah"*), regular Torah study (*"limud torah"*), charity (*"tzedakah"*), and renewed observance of those and other mitzvot.

More to Explore

Talmud, Rosh Hashana 21b; ibid. Eruvin 54a; Talmud Yerushalmi 14:3; The Ramban and Eben Ezra, Shemot 21:19; Ramban, Vayikra 26:4; Shaarei Kedusha, pt. 1, Shaar 1; Tanya, pt. 1, chap. 7-8; pt. 3, chap. 6; Ohr HaTorah on Shir Hashirim, vol. 1, pp. 208 and on. Sefer HaMaamorim, 5660, pp. 97 and 103-104; ibid. 5678, p. 273 (bottom); ibid. 5722, Gedola Hachnosas Orchim; Torat Menachem, vol. 33, p. 249; Sichot Kodesh, 22nd of Elul 5722, chap. 4; Tzav 5740, chap. 37; Igrot Kodesh of the Rebbe, vol. 4, p. 444; Yagdil Torah, vol. 4, p. 279; see also "Healthy in Body Mind & Spirit," by Sholom B. Wineberg.

# זקנה

# Old Age

Throughout the Torah and Talmud, we can find that "old" is synonymous with "wise," and that living to a ripe old age is considered one of the greatest blessings bestowed by God upon man. Judaism's repeated call for the young to respect the elderly and value their sagacity underscores their true importance. Indeed, the world has much to learn and gain from its senior members, rather than to view them as a drag on society and its resources. At the same time, the golden-aged need to embrace their role as noble guides to the young and reflect this in their attitudes, teaching and actions. Thus, it is no surprise that in Judaism there is no concept of retirement, for the mission of each Jew to serve his Master continues until their very last breath.

According to the Torah, a person's value is not solely measured by the output from his physical labor, but also by the positive spiritual influence he has on himself and on his environment. After all, God created man to be His partner in creation, making life on earth purer, brighter, and holier. Therefore, the spiritual maturity of the aged more than compensates for their lessened physical strength. In fact, their insight and deepened spirituality becomes their greatest asset, which continues to grow with each passing day. This ongoing spiritual development not only invigorates the body, enabling the person to lead a productive existence for as long as the Almighty grants the gift of life, but it supplants boredom, futility, and despair. Thus, rather than putting the years of perceived "real" work behind, passively settling down to a non-productive, or less-productive, lifestyle to enjoy the fruits of youth's difficult labors, bear in mind that the very fact that God has granted one a single additional day means there is still something specific to be achieved in this world in order for him to fulfill his mission in life. In the words of the Talmud, "Today is the time to do; tomorrow, to reap the reward." Tomorrow, our Sages note, refers to the "World to Come" (i.e., Paradise) after one has completed his mission on earth.

This is not to deny that in later years a person's physical abilities may wane, often affecting his or her positive attitude and desire to be productive. Various illnesses can also take a large toll on body and mind, God forbid. But rather than being a source of despair and surrender, these natural events can be viewed as a challenge and opportunity to explore and develop new ways to express and improve oneself and one's surroundings, leading to even greater fulfillment and service of God.

**More to Explore**

Talmud, Kiddushin 33a; ibid. Eruvin 22a; Sichot Kodesh 11 Nissan, 5732; Eikev, 20 Menachem Av 5740; ibid. Re'eh, 5740; see also essay "Torah, The Beauty of the Elderly," by Sichos in English.

### Bottom Line

Torah celebrates the wisdom of the aged and teaches that a person's value is not solely measured by the output from his physical labor, but also by the positive spiritual influence he has on himself and on his environment. Thus, the golden-aged are urged to recognize the value of their accumulated wisdom and to embrace their role as noble guides to the younger generation as reflected in their attitudes, teaching and actions.

### Ponder/Action

- The later years of life represent an excellent opportunity for intensified Torah study, community service, and mentoring the younger generation.

# פטירה ועולם האמת

# Death & Afterlife

Life is a priceless gift from God, one which Judaism instructs us to cherish, celebrate and do our utmost to prolong. In the Torah's view, every second of life, from the moment of conception through a person's final day in this world, is of infinite importance and value. As the Jewish soul—the life-force of a person—is eternal, the culmination of life on earth does not represent an end, but instead a beginning. This is a spiritual existence built upon all the good thoughts, deeds, and actions performed throughout one's life. Thus, we pray that our lives be filled with days that are meaningful, healthy, and truly complete in the eyes of the Almighty, so that when our time is up, we return to Him with ample spiritual dividends.

While the soul is bound to the physical body, it is compelled to be involved with mundane activities foreign to its lofty spiritual nature. Yet, this seeming disadvantage is also an advantage, because during the soul's time in this world, it can actively participate in observing Torah and mitzvot, elevating not only itself and the body, but also the physical world around it, something impossible for it to accomplish while in Heaven. Once the soul returns to the world of pure spirit, it enjoys the fruits of its struggles and growth during its sojourn on earth. Thus, the soul's departure from the physical realm represents an immeasurable ascent for the person. This is the reason why, in describing the period following one's physical death, the Rebbe preferred the term "Higher-life" over "Afterlife."

Kabbalah teaches that even though the soul is elevated to Heaven, it retains all its faculties, memories, and knowledge gathered while on earth, and it reacts to the conduct and feelings of the relatives it left behind. It shares in their joys and sorrows, constantly praying and interceding on their behalf. The soul also continues to benefit from the Torah and mitzvot performed in its memory, which help it ascend to greater celestial heights.

Contemplating the moment when our soul will ascend and stand before God is understandably fraught with tremendous awe, trepidation, and uncertainty. Are we ready to meet our Maker? Did we lead our life in concert with our soul's mission? Were our days sufficiently filled with spirituality? This type of accounting encourages us to reflect upon and align our spiritual focus and life pursuits, and then to make any necessary improvements.

### Bottom Line

Life is precious and should be prolonged as much as possible. Death is a continuation of life but in the world of pure spirit. The Jewish soul dwells eternally in Heaven, enjoying the fruits of the Torah and mitzvot performed during its sojourn on earth.

### Ponder/Action

▸ Having a unique Godly spark within us is inspiration to undertake and accomplish great things while we are here. It also serves as motivation for us to learn Torah, pray, give charity, and perform mitzvot for the benefit of those who have already departed.

### More to Explore

Likkutei Sichot, vol. 5, p. 103; Sichot Kodesh, 20 Menachem Av, 5742 (Sicha 2); Torat Menachem, vol. 57, p. 241; Menachem Tzion, vol. 2, pp. 479 and on.

# לויה

# Funeral

A Jewish funeral is distinguished by its simplicity and solemnity. Its general format harkens back to Biblical times and has not changed in over four thousand years. In Judaism, we demonstrate respect for life by how we treat the deceased. The mitzvah of accompanying the deceased to its final resting place (in Hebrew, *l'vaya*) is so great, that it supersedes all other mitzvot, including Torah study. According to Jewish law, a Jewish funeral should ideally be held on the day of passing, and in the case of unavoidable circumstances, (e.g. time needed to arrange for proper burial, arrival of close family members, etc.), no later than three days after.

Receiving a proper Jewish funeral is so important that many Jewish people mandate it in their wills. Indeed, it is a moral obligation for each individual and those who will care for them after they die to ensure that all Jewish laws and traditions are carefully followed when the time comes. It is thus vital to ensure that one's own funeral, and that of one's loved ones, are done in accordance with Jewish law and tradition.

In accordance with Jewish law, a Jewish funeral is preceded with a preparatory *tahara*, which is a private ritual washing and dressing of the deceased by the local Jewish Burial Society (*"Chevra Kaddisha"*). Men attend to men and women to women. The funeral itself consists of paying respects (*"kavod"*) which includes gathering at the chapel or gravesite to recite psalms (*"Tehillim"*) and speak of the merits of the deceased, and accompanying the casket to its final resting place (*"leviah"*). *Kriah* (the rending of garments in grief) is performed by mourners prior to the burial, guided by a knowledgeable rabbi. This is followed by burial in a Jewish cemetery (*"kevurah"*) and the recitation of Kaddish and other prayers by mourners, after which the mourners are consoled (*"nechama"*). A tradition-filled mourning period follows the funeral (see, *"Mourning"*, p. 110).

In Judaism there are many laws and traditions regarding various end-of-life issues, conduct during a person's final moments of life, the moment of death, preparation for burial, burial in a Jewish cemetery, and the mourning period that follows. It is thus crucial that a knowledgeable rabbi is consulted for guidance at each stage.

The Rebbe points out that family members of the deceased following the path of Torah and mitzvot on a daily basis, not only benefit themselves but also vitally benefit the soul of the deceased, and to a much greater extent than giving the finest public eulogies at their funeral.

**More to Explore**

Rambam, Hilchos Avel, chap. 14:1; Rebbe's Igros, vol. 16, p. 213; see also "Jewish Mourner's Companion," by Rabbi Zalman Goldstein (Jewish Learning Group).

### Bottom Line

In Judaism, we demonstrate respect for life by how we treat death. The traditions of a Jewish funeral harkens back to Biblical times. There are many laws regarding conduct during a person's final moments of life; preparation for their burial; burial in a Jewish cemetery; and the mourning period that follows. A knowledgeable rabbi must be consulted for guidance.

### Ponder/Action

▸ A Jewish burial is of paramount importance to the eternal peace of the soul of the deceased. It is a great mitzvah that a person's funeral, and that of his loved ones, are done in accordance with Jewish law and tradition.

### Bottom Line

The mourning period is a time for reflection, when the living "take to heart" and internalize the worthy character traits and exemplary conduct of the departed.

### Ponder/Action

▸ Comforting a mourner is beneficial for the soul of the departed, as well as a reminder to those offering comfort about the fleeting nature of life and thus an awakening to what truly matters in life—a life filled with Torah and mitzvot.

# אבילות
# Mourning

The Torah recognizes the natural feeling of grief and bereavement resulting from the loss of a loved one and has provided a set of regulations providing a comforting framework for mourning, which allows sadness to be vented and eases the family's adjustment to their loss. The pain of an individual is also connected to pain of the community, as all Jewish people constitute a single body. Thus, in Jewish tradition, the mourning process includes a healing communal component so that a person does not suffer the loss alone and helps the community grieve as well. At the same time, the Torah sets limits pertaining to the length of mourning and its expression, including constraining mourning to *shiva* (Hebrew for "Seven"; i.e., the first seven days), *shloshim* (Hebrew for "thirty"; the first thirty days), and the *yahrtzeit* (Yiddish for "anniversary").

Traditionally, the mourning period flows through several stages, gradually easing the grieving process. General mourning commences once the burial is complete and the grave is closed. Mourning is at its highest intensity at this time and during the first three days of *Shiva*. Mourners gather to mourn, pray, and be consoled by visitors during the seven days of *Shiva*. Between the end of *Shiva* and until *shloshim*, some mourning constraints are reduced, and are even further reduced once the thirtieth day is reached. Many visit the grave of the deceased on this day. From *shloshim* until the *yahrtzeit*, many of the restrictions of the first thirty days are removed, but several are maintained during the entire first year. It is important to consult a knowledgeable rabbi for guidance, since each period of mourning has many detailed observances.

Mourning a loved one in accordance with Jewish law and tradition is the ultimate gift we can give to our dear departed, providing the soul with the greatest possible comfort and joy. It is a mitzvah that benefits both the mourner and the deceased, because the person following the Jewish way of mourning is eased through the pain of the loss while becoming sensitive to the cycle of life and importance of each living moment. At the same time, the person mourned is benefited by entering Heaven easily, the loved one's soul fortified by the mourner's recitation of Kaddish during the mourning period and on each *yahrtzeit*, the study of Torah and performance of mitzvot to honor the soul in Heaven, and the attunement of the descendants' earthly life to the life path of the departed soul, which is constantly ascending to higher spiritual realms.

**More to Explore**

Igrot Kodesh of the Rebbe, 5 Taamuz, 5743; see also "Jewish Mourner's Companion," by Rabbi Zalman Goldstein (Jewish Learning Group).

# מציבה
# Tombstone

Marking the location of a grave with a traditional tombstone (in Hebrew, *matzeiva*) is a very ancient Jewish tradition and a fitting way to honor the deceased. While the soul of the departed ascends and remains in its Heavenly abode, a trace of it remains at the body's final resting place, maintaining a connection with the soul above. This is one of the reasons people visit the resting place of their beloved departed—to receive comfort from being close to the deceased, to offer prayers to God, and to beseech the soul in Heaven to pray for the living.

In Jewish thought, a tombstone is not erected to remind people that the person is no longer with us, but rather to signify that the person and all that he or she stood for is still very much alive and affecting the world. This is especially true if visiting the grave inspires us to emulate the positive qualities of the deceased and improve our own relationship with God. In this way, the spirit and tangible effects of the soul of the deceased continue to bring merit to itself and those affected by it.

A Jewish tombstone is usually made from stone or granite and is placed at the head of the grave, with the plot outlined with a low-lying frame. The headstone traditionally displays information about the person, including his or her Hebrew name and father's name, the Hebrew date of passing, and a brief description of the person's positive qualities and accomplishments in the realm of Jewish life. One reason for writing the deceased's honorable deeds on the tombstone is to inspire those who pass by and read it to improve their ways. Positive actions born from their memory bless the soul in Heaven and invite God's mercy upon the person performing them. If the deceased had relatives who died and whose burial site is unknown, their names are also inscribed on the tombstone.

It is the Chabad custom that lettering on the tombstone be engraved, not raised, in Hebrew. The text should follow the standard set by other tombstones in the same cemetery. If one's lineage traces back to a great Torah personality and sage, this is noted. If the person was a Chassid or connected in any way to one of the Chabad Rebbes, this is noted as well. The tombstone text should be reviewed by the local Jewish Burial Society and/or rabbi. It is erected as soon as possible after *Shiva* (i.e., on the 8th day after burial). In Chabad, there is no special ceremony associated with its "unveiling."

**More to Explore**

Menachem Tzion, vol. 2, p. 344; Y'Mei Bereishit, p. 322; Igrot Kodesh of the Rebbe, vol. 11, p. 3; vol. 13, p. 94; vol. 20, p. 113; see "Toldos Reb Yitzchok Eizik of Homil," p. 105 (by Rabbi Yochonon Gurary).

### Bottom Line

The essence of the soul of a departed lingers at the body's burial site. Visiting a grave brings connection with the deceased person resting there. Tombstones are not erected merely to remind us that the person is no longer with us, but rather signify that the person and all that they stood for is still very much alive and affecting the world.

### Ponder/Action

▸ When visiting a deceased person's resting place, think about the good the departed stood for. Find ways to emulate and build upon that goodness in your own life.

# תחיית המתים

# Resurrection

It is a core Jewish belief that during the time of the ultimate, upcoming redemption ushered in by Messiah (see, *"Moshiach," p. 39*), there will be a revival of the dead (in Hebrew, *t'chiyat hameitim*). From this we learn that death, seemingly so final, is really only a form of sleep from which we will eventually awaken, and the resurrection of the dead demonstrates that the soul and body were never fully apart. Judaism believes that the world is constantly marching toward this messianic era, and the Rebbe fervently taught that we are at the cusp of this historic transformation.

According to tradition, at the time of resurrection, every Jewish person who ever lived, as well as all righteous gentiles, will be brought back to life to bask in the eternal light of God. Each body will be regenerated from its *luz* bone, traditionally defined as the bone at the top of the spinal column, where the knot of the head's *tefillin* rests, and all souls will return to re-animate the same bodies in which they fulfilled God's mitzvot.

According to Chassidut, a lesson for our spiritual service can be derived from the concept of the resurrection: God's Will may be fulfilled through intellect alone, without involving emotions, though at this level it is like the "deceased"—cold and frigid. God's Will can also be fulfilled through a blending of an individual's natural intelligence, which lends knowledge of God, and a deep emotional connection to the Almighty, resulting in a person's being moved and empowered by his or her love of God to awaken and invigorate ("resurrect") their spiritual service. Also, by learning Torah and observing its mitzvot we infuse the physical matter surrounding us with spiritual life, another form of "resurrection." As put forth by the Sages of the Talmud, the righteous are "alive" even after death, while the wicked are considered "dead," even during their lifetime. Throughout their lives the wicked attach great importance to the physical, which is of itself limited and short-lived; however, the righteous prioritize the spiritual and thereby elevate their physical life to an eternal Godly dimension.

On yet another level, a Jew's task is to "resurrect," i.e., to educate others and assist fellow Jews in transforming their manner of spiritual service from rote fulfillment and/or apathy to healthy vitality and passion, blending the cold "deadness" of the mind with an enduring fire of the heart and the everlasting life of Godliness.

### Bottom Line

During the time of the upcoming redemption through the Messiah, there will be a revival of the dead. Every Jewish person who ever lived, as well as all righteous gentiles, will be brought back to life to bask in the eternal light of God. Until then, a Jew's task is to "resurrect" and enliven his own spiritual service, as well as to educate and help fellow Jews transform their own, by blending the cold "deadness" of the mind with the enduring fire of the heart, and the everlasting life of Godliness.

### Ponder/Action

- When we performs a mitzvah, we revitalize the sacred spark in the physical object. This brings new life and vitality to the spark, "resurrecting," so to say, the physical to a holy realm.

### More to Explore

Prophets, Yishayau 26:19; Zohar vol. 1, pp. 69a and 137a; ibid. vol. 2, p. 28b; Talmud, Berochot 18:a-b; Sanhedrin 90a; Rambam, Hilchot Teshuvah 3:6; Bereshit Rabba 28:3; Tanya, pt. 1, chap. 37 and 49; ibid. pt. 4, chap. 17; Derech Mitzvosecha, Tzizit; Sefer Hamaamorim, 5680, p. 63; Likkutei Sichot, vol. 17, p. 344 and on; ibid. vol. 18, p. 248; Torat Menachem, vol. 316, p. 190; Menachem Tzion, vol. 2, p. 388; Hayom Yom, 11 Sivan.

# גלגול נשמות

# Reincarnation

The concept of reincarnation is discussed primarily in Kabbalah. It is also mentioned in the commentary of the illustrious Talmudist, the Maharsha (acronym for Rabbi Shmuel Eidels). The Hebrew word for reincarnation, *gilgul*, has the same numerical value as the Hebrew word *chessed* (kindness). This hints that although the process of reincarnation may be painful for the soul—for the new body may hinder its task yet again—reincarnation is ultimately a kindness for the soul, allowing it to attain its intended perfection.

The soul of the first man, Adam, was composed of all future souls. The soul of our patriarch Jacob was comprised of 70 parts which were subdivided into the 600,000 souls of Israel. These 600,000 were then subdivided further into another 600,000. Through the process of reincarnation, the myriad pieces of the "original" soul become elevated, bringing it eternal wholeness and completion.

Kabbalah teaches that every soul that descends into this world has a specific Divine purpose. Reincarnation means that the soul is sent down again, into a specific set of circumstances tailored to provide it another opportunity to perform the commandments, or to complete the task that it did not fulfill in a previous incarnation, and/or to rectify a sin. At times, souls may descend to perform additional tasks. This process can occur up to three times (i.e., three lifecycles).

The Kabbalists explain that only the parts of the soul not elevated by the first incarnation are reincarnated. The portion of the soul elevated by its Torah learning and mitzvah observance remains in Heaven where it receives its reward. Furthermore, all the good the soul has collected through its various journeys remains eternal and can never be uprooted. The bad, however, lacking the eternal quality of the light of Godliness, falls away forever through the soul's growth and renewal during its subsequent earthly trials and travails.

Chassidut adds that in addition to fulfilling all the other mitzvot, every soul has a unique mitzvah it must exclusively "specialize" in and conquer during its sojourn on earth, perhaps to rectify a deficiency from a previous incarnation. Thus, when we encounter exceptional challenges in fulfilling a specific mitzvah, it may be an indication that this is the one needing special attention.

**More to Explore**

Zohar, vol. 2, p. 100a; Sefer HaGilgulim, ch. 4; Shaar HaGilgulim, Introduction 11:16; Maharsha, Eruvin 18b and Moed Katan 15b; Maamorei Admur Hazoken 5568, p. 118; Sefer HaMaamorim, 5731, Podo Bsholom; Torat Menachem, vol. 32, p. 207; ibid. 5742, vol. 2 p. 1114; Sichot Kodesh 2nd Day of Shavuot 5736, chap. 7; ibid. Yud Tes Kislev 5738, chap. 18; Menachem Tzion, vol. 2, p. 387.

**Bottom Line**

Reincarnation is a process during which the soul descends again into this world to complete the mission it was assigned, but failed to fulfill, during a previous life.

**Ponder/Action**

▸ The Alter Rebbe received the following teaching from the tzaddik Reb Mordechai, who had heard it from the *Baal Shem Tov*: A soul may descend to this world and live seventy or eighty years in order to do a Jew a material favor—and certainly a spiritual one.

**Bottom Line**

Visiting the resting place of a tzaddik connects one's soul to that of the tzaddik, who in turn helps the person to accomplish his spiritual mission, while blessing him for his material and spiritual needs.

**Ponder/Action**

▸ Studying the Torah teachings of a tzaddik and carrying out his directives connects a person with the tzaddik on a deep level and elevates the person's spiritual being.

# ציון של צדיק

# A Tzaddik's Resting Place

The sacred act of visiting the resting place of a great Torah sage and tzaddik is known in the Talmud and in Midrash as *"Hishtatchut"* (prostration), and it is considered a great merit to pray there, for it is revered as a pure, hallowed place where prayer is readily accepted. Indeed, it has been a custom since the earliest times of Jewish history to pray at the grave of a tzaddik. Joseph, the son of our Patriarch Jacob stopped at *Kever Rachel*, which was his mother's resting place, to pray there for mercy as he was being led to Egypt as a slave. The Talmud also states that when Moses sent spies to the Land of Israel, Caleb traveled to the resting place of our Patriarchs in Chevron to pray for a successful mission.

This concept can be understood on numerous levels. For example, by visiting the grave of a *Nasi*, the spiritual leader of the generation, we can connect the highest level of our own soul (*"yechidah"*) to that of the tzaddik. This connection lives on in the days that follow the visit, affecting the visitor's thoughts, speech, and actions, inspiring and invigorating their service of the Almighty. Additionally, the Kabbalists state that on a certain spiritual level, the graves of the righteous in the diaspora are connected to the Land of Israel. Just as God's Presence dwells more readily in the Holy Land, it similarly rests more abundantly at the grave of a tzaddik. Here, the most elevated essence of a person's soul connects to the spirit of God, similar to the connection formed when visiting the Holy Temple in Jerusalem.

After the passing of the Rebbe Rayatz, the Rebbe urged Chassidim to keep writing to the Rayatz for blessings, declaring that the Rebbe would find a way from above to communicate his answer to his flock. Indeed, praying at the gravesite of a spiritual leader bridges us to a different dimension, because despite the leader's physical absence, he remains dedicated to his mission from on high and continues to intercede on behalf of those in his care. As the Zohar declares, a tzaddik who passes away is present in all worlds even more so than during his lifetime.

In addition to visiting a tzaddik's resting place during times of need, it is customary to pray there on the *yahrtzeit* (anniversary) of his passing, and during the days leading to the High Holidays. Some also visit on the day before the start of a new Hebrew month (*Rosh Chodesh*) and on the fifteenth day of each Hebrew month.

**More to Explore**

Tamud, Sotah 34b; Zohar, vol. 3, p. 71b; Tanya, pt. 4, chap. 27-28; Sefer Hamaamorim, 5564, p. 101; ibid. 5730, Lehovin Inyan Hilula (and footnotes); Likkutei Sichot, vol. 6, p. 283; Torat Menachem, vol. 2, p. 105; ibid. vol. 11, p. 30; ibid. vol. 13, p. 17; ibid. vol. 49, p. 6; Sichot Kodesh, Simchat Torah 5723, chap. 8; ibid. Evening prior the 24 Tevet 5723, chap. 4; ibid. Acharei 5727, chap. 2.

# יומא דהילולא

# A Tzaddik's Yahrtzeit

The day of the passing of a tzaddik is called a *Yom HaHilula* (literally interpreted, "day of celebration"). What's the cause for celebration on such a solemn occasion? The Alter Rebbe writes that the life of a tzaddik is not merely a life of the flesh, but a spiritual life filled with faith, awe, and love of God. Our Sages teach that on the day of a tzaddik's passing everything he accomplished during his lifetime is revealed spiritually both in the physical world and in the upper spiritual realms. As a result, the tzaddik's accrued merits cause ample blessings and salvations to flow from Above, especially for those connected to the tzaddik, his teachings, and his positive activities. This process continues on each subsequent *yahrtzeit* ("anniversary date") with the spiritual revelations cycling higher and higher on each passing year.

The *Yom Hilula* of a Rebbe and *"nasi"* (i.e, the spiritual leader of the generation) is unique in that it affects the entire generation. It is a day of holiness that also elicits profound Heavenly compassion. In Chabad, a *Yom HaHilula* is a propitious time to make good resolutions. The day is traditionally observed by writing a prayer-request (*"Pidyon Nefesh"*) and reading it at the resting place of the Rebbe. If one cannot go in person, it can be sent with a messenger, or electronically, to be read or placed on his resting place.

Praying at a holy person's resting place helps people internalize the person's vision, message and values, leading to practical positive change in their own lives. Studying the Rebbe's teachings and participating in a *farbengen* (Chassidic gathering) on his *yahrtzeit* is also compared to personally handing the Rebbe a *Pidyon Nefesh*. Other observances include lighting a 24-hour candle on the evening leading into the *yahrtzeit* that remains lit all day, reflective of the soul which is compared to a flame.

Reciting the *"Maaneh Lashon,"* which is a series of prayers, psalms, and readings structured to be recited at the graves of tzaddikim; studying portions of the Mishnah that are traditionally learned on a *yahrtzeit*, as well as studying the tzaddik's teachings; giving charity in support of causes dear to the tzaddik; committing to increase and enhance the performance of mitzvot all serve to honor the tzaddik's memory and create spiritual vessels for ourselves and our loved ones to receive God's ample blessings while perpetuating the legacy of the tzaddik.

**More to Explore**

Talmud, Soteh 34b; Tanya, Iggeret Hakodesh 27; Maamorei Admur Hoemtzo'i - Kuntresim, pp. 19 and on; Torat Menachem, vol. 36, p. 15; Sichot Kodesh, Shlach 5710; Responsa Minchas Elazar, pt. 1, chap. 68; see also "Whispers Between Worlds," by the Lubavitcher Rebbe.

### Bottom Line

On the date of the passing of a tzaddik, everything he accomplished during his lifetime is revealed spiritually in our physical world and in the upper spiritual realms, bringing ample blessings and salvation from Above, especially for those connected to the tzaddik, his teachings, and his positive activities.

### Ponder/Action

▸ The day of a tzaddik's passing is a time for self-evaluation and connection to the tzaddik. It is an auspicious day for making good resolutions.

SECTION SEVEN

# The Jewish Home

Bottom Line

The Jewish home is a place where the family grows and is nurtured not just physically, but also spiritually. Like the Temple in Jerusalem, it should radiate a spiritual aura that elevates the family and the entire community.

Ponder/Action

▶ Parents and older siblings should use the time they spend with their children and younger siblings to implant their desire to build a Jewish home that reflects the holiness found within their own.

# הבית היהודי
# The Jewish Home

Built upon a foundation of ageless values and traditions, the Jewish home is both a haven and learning place, an environment where families can grow together and provide mutual support for each other's spiritual wellbeing. As our Sages note, in the Torah, God commanded Moses, "Make me a sanctuary and I will dwell among them." Our Sages point out that the verse says, "I will dwell among *them*," and not "I will dwell within *it*," meaning that each and every Jewish home dedicated to fulfilling the will of God has the potential of being a miniature sanctuary for the Almighty.

In Kabbalistic terms, the four pillars of the family reflect the four letters of the primary name of God: The father represents the *yud*—the beginning. The mother represents the *hei*—corresponding to her role in the development and education of her children. The letter *vov* represents the son(s), and the second letter *hei*, the daughter(s).

At the heart and center of a Jewish home is the Jewish woman. Her efforts reach beyond influencing and guiding her children and observing and teaching the three mitzvot specific to women—observance of the kosher dietary laws, laws of family purity, and Shabbat and Jewish holiday candle-lighting—to her daughters. Her role extends to keeping the home kosher (food and environment), carefully supervising the Jewish education of her children, maintaining the home's blessing by having kosher mezuzot on necessary doorways, placing charity boxes in the kitchen and other places around the home, and ensuring that the house is filled with sacred Jewish books and other holy Jewish materials.

The Rebbe added that Chassidic virtuous practices fill a Jewish home with light and a Chassidic *niggun* (melody) fortifies hope and trust while bringing joy to all. In addition, daily Torah study is crucial for everyone, creating an atmosphere of holiness and piety.

Finally, just as the Holy Temple was uplifted on Shabbat, the religious tone of the Jewish home is enhanced on this special day, with the entire family sitting at the Shabbat table during the Friday night and Shabbat afternoon meals, sharing insights on the weekly Torah portion or on Shabbat prayers, responding *"Amen"* to each other's blessings, and singing Jewish songs.

**More to Explore**

Torah, Teruma 25:8; Likkutei Sichot, vol. 12 p. 250; Torat Menachem, vol. 23, p. 189; ibid. 5752, vol. 1 p. 45; Sichot Kodesh, Eikev 5733, chap. 9; ibid. Haazinu 5735, chap. 4; Hayom Yom, 4 Cheshvan; ibid. 22 Tammuz; Kfar Chabad (weekly), supplement no. 1137, pp. 14 and on;

# בחירת קהילה

# Choosing a Community

A person's character and behavior are strongly influenced by friends and associates, which is why living in a Jewish environment is vital for one's wellbeing and successful childrearing. Our Sages advised that our home should be established in a community that offers adequate support systems for Jewish living, including a kosher mikvah (ritualarium), a synagogue, Jewish educational facilities, and at least several other Torah-observant Jewish families to offer mutual encouragement, support, and wisdom. In an atmosphere of Torah and mitzvot there is healthy life.

Since ancient times, Jewish life has revolved around the home and its effect within the community, such that each foster and give meaning, connection, and holiness to the other. The role of the Jewish home in educating and nurturing the individual is often intertwined with that of the community in supporting and encouraging the practice of Judaism.

While Judaism certainly recognizes individual spirituality, its communal character is also strongly emphasized. Indeed, our Talmudic Sages taught that each Jew is bound up with every other, meaning that every Jewish person, regardless of his or her current level of religious observance, is key to completing the whole of the Jewish people. In other words, no Jew is a solitary figure who can live "off-the-grid," so to speak, because every Jewish person's physical and spiritual wellbeing affects the condition of the entire Jewish nation. Therefore, careful thought and deliberation should be applied in making choices about where and how to live.

Chassidut interprets the Sages' teaching about the connectedness of all Jews as more than just a call for physical unity and mutual responsibility among Jews, but the conferring of a moral responsibility on each individual to support the spiritual well-being of others at whatever level possible. Putting this into practice means becoming involved in Jewish outreach and educating others, and most importantly, setting a positive personal example.

Relating this to the choice of our living environment, we must not only take into account what is materially advantageous, but also the characteristics of an area that will foster our spiritual growth, and will allow us to contribute reciprocally to the spiritual wellbeing of the community.

**More to Explore**

Talmud, Shavuot 39a; Torat Menachem, 5746, vol. 1, pp. 521-522; Igrot Kodesh of the Rebbe, vol. 15, p. 354; ibid. vol. 25, p. 41; ibid. vol. 20, p. 302; Hayom Yom, 11 Tevet.

**Bottom Line**

Environment and associates strongly affect a person's character. Live among Torah observant Jews so that you can fortify yourself and learn from their ways. This is particularly crucial when raising children.

**Ponder/Action**

▸ A couple should choose their community as carefully as they chose each other for marriage.

## Bottom Line

The mezuzah connects the Jew, his property, and the entire world with God. It is a reminder of our close connection to God and to our Jewish heritage, signifying reverence for Jewish values and conferring constant protection by the Almighty.

## Ponder/Action

▶ Get some kosher mezuzot from a God-fearing scribe for the doorposts of your home and office. If you already have mezuzot, have an expert scribe check them to ensure that they are kosher and are correctly affixed at the right places.

# מזוזה

# Mezuzah

The mezuzah is a small parchment scroll upon which the first two passages of the *Shema* (core verses from the Torah encapsulating the monotheistic essence of Judaism) are handwritten in traditional form by a God-fearing scribe (in Hebrew, *sofer*). On the reverse side of the mezuzah is written one of the sacred names of God (שד"י), which is also an acronym for Hebrew words that mean, "Guardian of the doorways of Israel." Once completed, the mezuzah is rolled up and placed in a protective wrap or case and is affixed to the outside and inside doorposts of Jewish homes and offices (exceptions are doors leading to bathrooms and very small closets).

It is customary to touch the mezuzah upon entering or leaving a room—some also kiss the fingertips that touched the mezuzah as a sign of affection— and to teach children to do the same upon rising every morning and before going to sleep at night.

The mezuzah is a reminder of a person's close connection to God and their Jewish heritage, and signifies a reverence for Jewish values and the ongoing protection by the Almighty. The mezuzah's presence also inspires residents and visitors to fulfill the mitzvot of the Torah and protects them from temptation. Its blessings accompanies those who receive them wherever they go. As our Sages relate, just as the Holy Temple in Jerusalem radiated peace and sanctity that protected and refined the entire world, so does one's mezuzot. Thus, even when people are away from their home and office, the mezuzot on those doorposts continue to confer their spiritual inspiration and Divine protection.

The laws of preparing and writing a kosher mezuzah are numerous and very detailed. Each letter in the mezuzah must be properly formed; a single crack in the parchment or in a letter, or an omission of any sort, can invalidate the entire scroll. Therefore, extra vigilance is required to ensure that your mezuzot are obtained from a God-fearing scribe. In addition, mezuzot should be checked by a scribe at least twice in seven years (some do so every twelve months) for possible damage from water, sunlight, etc. The Rebbe would often encourage people who had experienced illness or other misfortunes to have their mezuzot checked and repaired or replaced if necessary.

### More to Explore

Likkutei Sichot, vol. 13, pp. 212 and 214; ibid. vol. 19, p. 121; Torat Menachem, vol. 57, p. 261; ibid. 5742, vol. 1, p. 283; ibid. 5747, vol. 2, p. 647; ibid. 5751, vol. 1, pp. 154 and 271; ibid 5751, vol. 2, p. 97; Sichot Kodesh, Acharon Shel Pesach 5722, Sicha 12; ibid. Matot-Maasai 5732, chap. 6; ibid. Behar-Bechukosai 5734, Sicha 1; ibid. Matot Maasai 5734, Sicha 1; ibid. 15 Shevat 5734, Sicha 3 and 5; 20th Menachem Av 5734, Sicha 6; ibid. 15 Tammuz 5735, Sicha 2; ibid. Chukas-Balak 5736, Sicha 4; ibid Simchat Torah 5737, Sicha 8.

# כשרות

# Kosher Dietary Laws

The Hebrew word "kosher" means fit and proper. In the context of food, it refers to food that meets specific conditions established by the Torah. For example, not all mammals, fowl, fish, and other living creatures may be eaten by a Jew. In the case of animals, those considered kosher must chew their cud and have split hooves, be carefully slaughtered, deveined, and prepared in accordance with Jewish law.

Other kosher laws mandate the separation of meat and milk during their preparation and consumption (i.e., separate cooking and eating utensils are used), with a waiting period required between eating food from either category. Even a trace of a non-kosher substance can render foods, utensils, and preparation surfaces not kosher. This is why all processed foods, including eating establishments, require kosher certification by a known, reliable rabbinic supervision agency.

Regarding the Torah's kosher dietary laws, Kabbalah explains that on a deeper level, eating and drinking not only provides sustenance for the body, but affect a person spiritually, profoundly influencing his or her character. Kosher food strengthens our faith and connection to God and is therefore one of the core pillars of a Jewish home.

Chassidut derives many lessons in life from the laws of kosher. For example, the requirement for animals to have split hooves and chew their cud can be related to our individual spiritual service. For just as hooves separate the animal from the ground, so, too, the Torah encourages us to create a holy space between our higher selves and the mundane world at our feet. However, Chassidut explains, this doesn't mean that a person should be entirely cut off from the world. The "split" in the hoof represents the creation of a healthy space for the spiritual and practical to coexist and function, while our true spiritual self remains above and set apart.

There is another lesson from kosher animals, such as cows which chew their food, swallow, bring it back up, and chew it again until the food is ready for further digestion. In a spiritual analogy we are advised to carefully weigh, or "chew" over, decisions that can affect our spirituality and our service of God, such as where to live, study, and work, as well as who to marry and where to send our children to school. For like the food we eat, the decisions we make in these key areas have long-lasting spiritual and physical implications.

**More to Explore**

Likkutei Sichot, vol. 1, p. 224; ibid. vol. 13, p. 260; Sichot Kodesh, 6 Tishrei 5740, chapt. 40; Torat Menachem, 5744 vol. 1, p. 130; ibid. 5751, vol. 1, pp. 45 and 201; ibid. 5751, vol. 2, p. 262; Kfar Chabad (weekly), no. 797 (Eng. sec., p. 14); see "Going Kosher in 30 Days," by Zalman Goldstein (Jewish Learning Group).

**Bottom Line**

Food and drink need to meet specific conditions established by the Torah before they can be consumed by a Jew. On a deeper level, eating and drinking not only provide sustenance for the body, but affect a person spiritually. Kosher food strengthens our faith and connection to God, and is therefore one of the core pillars of Jewish life.

**Ponder/Action**

▸ The laws of kosher reinforce that "we are what we eat." When there is a deficiency in observance of kosher dietary laws, it is compared to one who partially preserves the health of the body—eventually, the degree of neglect will become evident physically and spiritually.

# האשה היהודית

# The Jewish Woman

The Jewish woman identifies closely with the Divine presence and has her own uniqueness, mission, and special qualities and capabilities endowed by the Almighty for elevating herself and the world around her in the manner of our Matriarchs, Sarah, Rivka, Rachel, and Leah. The Jewish woman is at once a facilitator and a nurturer, creating an environment that determines the character and atmosphere of the entire home, fostering the tangible and intangible growth of her family, such as those relating to self-esteem, development of talents, and spirituality and family traditions. She is also a "connector," able to nurture and connect herself and others with the spiritual, awakening an innate love of God, love of Torah, and love of fellow Jews.

Our Sages tell us that our ancestors were redeemed from ancient Egypt in the merit of righteous Jewish women who never despaired of God's redemption during their suffering at the hands of the Egyptians. They remained steadfast in their faith, raising a generation of children who later witnessed God's miraculous salvation. So, too, it will be owing to the righteous Jewish women today who fulfill their vital mission as the *akeret habayit*, the mainstay and bedrock of the Jewish home, with joy and dedication, that the Jewish people will be redeemed once again through *Moshiach*.

By Jewish women actively participating in strengthening the three "pillars" of every Jewish home—observance of the kosher dietary laws, family purity, and Shabbat and holiday candle-lighting—and by fostering knowledge of Torah and mitzvot on a daily basis, they vitally ensure the continuity of the Jewish People and fulfillment of its mission to create an abode for the Almighty.

Regarding the distinct gender roles in Jewish life, our Sages remind us that it is God after all—not us—Who establishes how one becomes sanctified and how one sanctifies. Thus, the distinct roles ascribed by the Torah for men and woman are tailored to each gender's essential nature. In the Divine plan, men and women have specific and diverse missions that work in harmony. Both serve the same ultimate mission of carrying out God's will in the manner set forth for each of them in accordance with Torah and authentic Jewish law.

### Bottom Line

Jewish women have their own unique identity and mission and are innately able to connect themselves and others with the spiritual. They have the capacity to create an environment fostering growth and awakening every Jew's innate love of God, love of Torah, and love of fellow Jews. Their active participation in strengthening the spirituality of their home is crucial for the continuity of the Jewish People.

### Ponder/Action

▸ Jewish woman are the spiritual and physical founders of new generations. Through their effort, the Jewish people will merit to greet *Moshiach*.

### More to Explore

Talmud, Sotah 11b; Likkutei Sichot, vol. 8, p. 320; ibid. vol. 20, p. 228; Sefer HaSichot 5752, vol. 2, p. 354; ibid. 27 Iyar 5737; Torat Menachem, vol. 41, p. 156; ibid. vol. 56, p. 198; Sichot Kodesh, 27 Iyar 5737; Igrot Kodesh of the Rebbe, vol. 20, p. 226; ibid. vol. 23, p. 209.

# צניעות

# Modesty

A cornerstone of Jewish faith is conducting our lives with dignity and modesty (in Hebrew, *tzniut*). As members of the Kingdom of Priests and a holy nation, the protective values of *tzniut*, which apply to men and women, each in their own way, affect both how others see us, and how we see ourselves. From the way we dress, speak, and act, to our innermost thoughts, feelings, and desires, living with *tzniut* helps us align our outer and inner worlds, bringing unity and consistency to our spiritual, emotional, and physical realms. Thoughtful adherence to its laws and values helps establish healthy boundaries, generate true self-respect, and provide enduring inner-confidence.

In a society that is often self-centered and values the superficial over underlying truths, we are reminded by King David in the Book of Psalms that, "The honor of the king's daughter rests within." Her existence is safeguarded, not cheapened. Her refined personality, intelligence and talents are, ultimately, her true identity.

Chassidut explains that the Torah's concept of *tzniut* does not advocate complete repression or rejection of the physical and sensual, but describes protective boundaries for their healthy and vibrant expression. As with all powerful natural forces, the bond between male and female requires great care and responsibility.

Modest dress for Jewish women means that any clothing worn is refined and dignified, not drawing undo attention. The neckline is covered to the collarbone, sleeves cover the elbows, and skirts cover the knees. Married women also cover their hair. Similarly, dressing appropriately applies to men as well, as does ongoing conscientious restraint of their natural masculine impulses. Further, since a Jew's essence is Godly, and the Almighty is present everywhere and at all times, *tzniut* is observed both publicly and when alone, even in the most private of places.

The Midrash relates that one of the traditions the Jewish people preserved during the years of exile in ancient Egypt was they did not alter their uniquely Jewish dress. Instead, they remained true to their principles even during times of immense difficulty. This dedication was part of the fortitude that enabled their redemption. From this we learn that adhering to the laws of *tzniut* preserves the strength of the Jewish people as a whole, ultimately leading to our true and final redemption.

**More to Explore**

Tehillim 5:14; Shulchan Aruch, chap. 2; Likkutei Sichot, vol. 8, pp. 223 and on (incl. footnote 28); Torat Menachem, vol. 37, p. 153; Igrot Kodesh of the Rebbe, vol. 26 pp. 324 and on; Kfar Chabad (weekly), no. 1513, p. 52.

**Bottom Line**

The Jewish laws of modesty help align our outer and inner worlds, bringing unity and consistency to our physical, emotional, and spiritual qualities. They do not espouse repression or rejection of the physical and sensual, but describe protective boundaries for their healthy and vibrant expression.

**Ponder/Action**

▸ Modesty is not only reflected in how we dress, but also by our innermost thoughts, feelings, and desires, as demonstrated in our thoughts, words and actions.

# מקוה

# Mikvah

The *mikvah* ("ritualarium") is a pool of water sourced from a river, stream, or rain, which spiritually refines the person who immerses in it, bestowing purity and holiness. Mikvahs are found in most cities around the world that have Jewish populations and are tastefully appointed with an emphasis on personal consideration and privacy. Both men and women use a mikvah, although at different times and for distinct reasons.

The Torah commands married women to immerse in a mikvah after their monthly menstruation period, thereby enabling husband and wife to renew their physical relationship in a sanctified manner. According to Kabbalistic and Chassidic custom, men are encouraged to immerse in a mikvah every morning, in order to spiritually attune themselves for prayer and the service of God.

From a Chassidic view, total immersion in a mikvah, such that not even a hair remains outside the water, symbolizes a state of nullification before our Creator, and a new beginning, or "rebirth," upon subsequent emergence from its waters. Further, Chassidut compares the Torah to life-giving waters, thus entering the mikvah signifies entering into the words of Torah and enveloping ourselves in its life-giving force.

The utilization of the mikvah as a gateway to purity began with the first man, Adam, who, the Midrash recounts, immersed himself in a river that flowed from the Garden of Eden in his effort to repent and return to his original purity. Additionally, before receiving the Torah at Sinai, the Jewish people were commanded by God to prepare for the revelation by immersing themselves in the waters of the "Well of Miriam."

Other examples include the immersion of the High Priest Aaron and his sons in a mikvah before being inducted into the priesthood; and during Temple times, the required immersion of priests, or any Jew wishing to enter the House of God. Indeed, since time immemorial, the mikvah has been so central to the Jewish people that their observance of this sacred and private mitzvah has been steadfast throughout history, even during times of religious persecution and danger.

Our Sages taught that careful observance of the laws of mikvah, so central to the Torah's laws of Family Purity (in Hebrew, *Taharat Hamispacha*), elicits abundant blessings for one's entire family, including blessings for children, good health, and prosperity.

**More to Explore**

Rambam, Hilchos Mikva'ot (end); Likkutei Torah, Tovo, p. 43b; Torat Menachem, vol. 9, pp. 167-169; ibid. vol. 18, p. 163-164; ibid. vol. 24, p. 228; ibid. vol. 40, p. 303; ibid. 5745, vol. 2, p. 995; Sichot Kodesh 5703, p. 85; Menachem Tzion, vol. 2, beginning with p. 365; Igrot Kodesh of the Rebbe, vol. 1, p. 259; ibid. vol. 20, p. 93.

### Bottom Line

Immersing in a mikvah brings purity and holiness. Both men and women use a mikvah, although at different times and for distinct reasons. The Torah commands married women to immerse in a mikvah after their monthly menstruation period, and according to Kabbalistic and Chassidic custom, men are encouraged to immerse in a mikvah every morning to spiritually attune themselves for prayer and the service of God.

### Ponder/Action

▸ After becoming ritually pure, a person leaves the mikvah and reenters the world to engage with and elevate it. In the same way, we must leave our "holy corner" and go into the world around us to create a dwelling place for God.

# שלום בית

# Marital Harmony

While a physical home can be built with a hammer and nails, an everlasting Jewish home is built with wisdom, tact, goodwill and peace. In addition to actively infusing our home with Jewish values, including Torah study and mitzvah observance, maintaining tranquility in marriage and in the Jewish home (in Hebrew, *shalom bayit*) ensures that the home remains properly grounded and draws abundant blessings from the Almighty.

According to the Torah, every Jewish home is a dwelling place for the Divine presence. The Hebrew word for man (*"ish"*) and woman (*"isha"*) share the letters that comprise the Hebrew word *"aish,"* which means fire. Though warm and intense, fire cannot burn on its own. It can also burn out of control. However, in the Hebrew word for man their is also the letter *"yud,"* and for the woman the letter *"hei."* Those two letters represent God's name. Thus, our Sages stated, that when husband and wife merit, the sacred letters of the Almighty's name dwells among them. When a Jewish marriage places God in the center, its fire becomes one that is sacred, nourishing, and everlasting. Devoted to a higher ideal, the couple automatically possesses a powerful unifying quality.

Marital issues and tensions are common during the early years and stages of marriage, especially as each partner begins to see the human faults and foibles of the other. Knowing that this is something all couples go through can help newlyweds get through it constructively, provided each approach their challenges with wisdom, maturity, and a desire to improve in the process. Lasting marital harmony is achieved when both partners exert themselves on behalf of the Jewish home they are building together. This requires continual communication, cooperation, and above all, a deep resolve to making the marriage flourish.

On a spiritual realm, there is a need to bring about "marital harmony" between our body and soul, helping each harness its individual strengths toward the service of God. When two seeming opposites, such as the physical body and the spiritual soul, align in harmony and work toward one Godly purpose, nothing can stand in the way of their success. The same can be said for marriage. Working toward this level of self-awareness and alignment within ourselves and within our marriage contributes not only to overall positive physical health, but also to the overall health and success of one's marriage and home.

**More to Explore**

Sefer HaSichot 5704, p. 100; Igrot Kodesh of the Rebbe, vol. 4, p. 422; ibid. vol. 5, p. 61 and 225; ibid. vol. 6, pp. 143 and 156; ibid. vol. 10, p. 80.

### Bottom Line

An everlasting Jewish home is built with wisdom, tact, goodwill and peace. In addition to actively infusing our home with Jewish values, maintaining tranquility in our marriage and in the Jewish home ensures they both remain on firm ground and draw abundant blessings from Above. On a spiritual realm, there is a need for us to bring about "marital harmony" between our body and soul, helping them harness their individual strengths toward the service of God.

### Ponder/Action

▸ If there are serious issues with marital harmony, mezuzot and *tefillin* should also be checked by a qualified scribe to ensure they are kosher, and efforts should be made to improve the observance of the Kosher dietary laws in the home; the laws related to family purity; the taking of challah; and timely lighting of Shabbat and holiday Candles.

# פריה ורביה

# *Having Children*

To be fruitful and multiply is the first mitzvah in the Torah, underscoring its importance and centrality to Jewish life. Having children is one of the greatest blessings possible, giving rise to some of life's most meaningful moments (in Hebrew, *nachas*) and deep personal fulfillment. Indeed, to bring a holy Jewish soul into the world, initiate a child into the Jewish faith, educate children in Torah and mitzvot, and watch them develop and someday become parents themselves is a singular, everlasting legacy.

The Talmud states there are three partners in the creation of a human being: the father, mother, and God. Unlike all our other interactions in the world, bearing children allows us to be partners in God's infinite power of creation, with each such experience drawing vast blessings into all the other areas of our lives. Judaism asserts that with the arrival of each child comes a new, increased flow of blessings for the material, financial, and spiritual stability of the home, and not just for the parents, but for the entire family.

A couple's normal concerns about providing for their offspring are understood by the third Partner as well, and thus God grants children only when there is potential for them to lead a life filled with meaning and purpose. By placing our trust in God and welcoming each soul that is given to us while putting forth our best efforts, we are assured that the necessary material and spiritual resources for raising each child will be graced upon us by the Almighty.

For those thinking of delaying having children for "life-planning" reasons, such as for the benefit of a career, or the "good of the planet," (not including for emotional or physical health-related reasons, for which rabbinic guidance is required), the Rebbe cautioned that these individuals may find that as they head into their well-planned life, things may turn out differently than expected. In their middle and later years, they may find themselves feeling lonely, despite their business successes. Others may face an inability to have children at the time they want or increased chances of complications, God forbid. The Rebbe thus strongly urged couples to realize that the time is now; the blessings await.

For couples facing infertility issues, the Rebbe encouraged enhancing observance of the laws of Family Purity (*taharat hamishpacha*) alongside any pursuit of medical intervention as permitted by Jewish law.

### More to Explore

Bereishit 1:28; Kiddushin 30a; Sichot Kodesh, Noso 5740; ibid. 17 Sivan 5740; ibid. Shelach, chap. 71; ibid. Korach, chap. 64; Likkutei Sichot, vol. 20, p. 428, et al; see also "Essay on Family Planning" by Sichos in English.

### Bottom Line

To bring a holy Jewish soul into the world, initiate a child into the Jewish faith, educate children in Torah and mitzvot, and watch them develop and someday become parent themselves is a singular, everlasting legacy. With the arrival of each child comes a new flow of blessings, not only for the parents, but for their entire family. The time is now; the blessings await.

### Ponder/Action

▸ We exist because our parents gave us the gift of life. Our parents exist because they received the gift of life from their parents. Back it reaches over countless generations. Will we repay their gifts, adding links to the chain and continuing the legacy of creation?

# חינוך
# Education

King Solomon wrote: "Train and educate a child according to his path, so that when he gets older he will not turn away from it." Guiding one's household in the path of the Torah (in Hebrew, *chinuch*) is one of the most important jobs in the world. The Torah obligates a father to teach his sons Torah, and the mother, too, profoundly influences the children by transmitting Jewish morals and values in her uniquely feminine way. Indeed, since time immemorial, Jewish parents have dutifully educated their children, imparting everlasting Jewish values to the next generation.

In Jewish writings, a child is compared to a young tree. Even the smallest influences at the earliest stages of a sapling's growth produces real consequences down the road. The same is true with the Jewish education and training of children. Further, it is not only what children are taught, but even more what they see at home and in their surroundings, that leaves an everlasting impression.

The education of Jewish children starts from the earliest moments of conception and never really ends. While still in the womb, the fetus is already affected by the mother's thoughts and conduct. Later as an infant, the child absorbs all that he or she sees and hears, from the lullabies sung, to the pictures hung around their crib, from the stories read to them, to the food and drink given. Nothing is inconsequential, and everything has an everlasting effect. In Jewish tradition, as soon as a child begins to talk, he or she is taught to recite the blessings on various foods, along with some basic Jewish prayers. When a boy turns three, he is given his first haircut (see, "*Upshernish,*" p. 98), leaving sidelocks ("*payot*"), and is taught to wear a *kippah* and *tzitzit*. Beginning at the age of three many teach their daughters to light Shabbat and holiday candles (with the help of an adult). Thus, children are off to a robust Jewish education starting in their most formative years. As mentioned above, a Jewish education continues throughout a person's lifetime, and certainly doesn't end at the age of Bat or Bar Mitzvah.

The Rebbe Rashab proclaimed that just as wearing *tefillin* (phylacteries) every weekday is a mitzvah commanded for every man, regardless of his current standing in Torah, it is likewise an absolute duty for every parent to spend at least thirty minutes a day thinking about the Torah education of children, and to do everything in their power—and beyond their power—to inspire them to follow the path upon which they are being guided. And we are also assured that sincere efforts in this regard which are pursued wisely and with friendship will certainly bear positive fruit.

**More to Explore**

Likkutei Sichot, vol. 25, p. 309; Torat Menachem, vol. 55, p. 101; ibid. vol. 56, p. 279; Sichot Kodesh, Miketz 5734, chap. 1; ibid. 12 Tammuz 5737, chap. 10; ibid. 6 Tishrei 5743, chap. 3; Hayom Yom, 11 Tishrei; ibid. 22 Tevet.

**Bottom Line**

Children should be given everything necessary for their spiritual development. Doing so has an eternal effect on them and on the generations that come from them.

**Ponder/Action**

▸ We sometimes underestimate the capacity of children to absorb certain aspects of the world around them. Soothing touches, sights, sounds, and smells affect both a child's body and soul.

## Bottom Line

Torah study and religious instruction which are fundamental to the Jewish nation, are the core functions of a yeshiva. From preschool through the end of high school and beyond, the yeshiva's immersive environment serves as a supportive continuation and extension of the Jewish education being given at home, playing a vital role in growth and maturity.

## Ponder/Action

▸ For children in today's world, education in a yeshiva is absolutely necessary to guide them on the correct path in life. This not only benefits them but the generations ahead that they will affect. As the Talmud states, "He who saves a single life is considered to have saved an entire world."

# ישיבה

# *Yeshiva*

A Jewish school, or yeshiva (in Hebrew, sitting; a place where one sits and learns), has many functions, but at its core is where Jewish children are taught the written and oral law of the Torah and are educated about the love and fear of the Almighty, as well as His boundless love for those who serve Him. The concept of the yeshiva originated with our Patriarchs who were constantly studying, as related in the Talmud. According to the Torah, before Jacob went down to Egypt, he sent his son Judah ahead to prepare a yeshiva where they would study Torah. These accounts demonstrate that Torah study and religious instruction are fundamental to the Jewish nation.

The immersive environment of the yeshiva nurtures and prepares children for studying on their own throughout the lives. It also fosters personal growth and maturity by providing a healthy environment for establishing positive friendships, many of which last a lifetime. It serves as a supportive continuation and extension of the home, where the child is already being taught basic blessings, prayers, and verses of Torah. In this day and age, it is advisable for Jewish children to attend a Jewish nursery and kindergarten until the age of six or seven, when they are ready for a Jewish school.

A yeshiva's curriculum should be focused on instilling sanctity through daily connection with the Almighty. This is accomplished by fostering a strong emphasis on instructing and encouraging the fulfillment of mitzvot on a practical level, helping children understand that God and spirituality is a true and real part of their everyday lives. Additionally, in Chassidic view, a dean or teacher's role is not only to teach Jewish law or pages of the Talmud, but more significantly, to introduce and build in students a basic fear and awe of God, and a love for every Jew, including a desire to demonstrate the ways of Torah within the world at large.

The study regimen in Chabad yeshivas is based on the course of study established by the Rebbe Rashab when he founded the *Tomchei Temimim* network of yeshivot. Nowadays, the general focus of the curriculum for boys and girls is on Jewish prayer and Torah study, which includes (depending on the students' age), Torah, Mishnah, Talmud, the Code of Jewish Law, and works of Chabad Chassidic philosophy. Also conveyed are practical skills necessary to lead a meaningful and productive Jewish life. As students mature, boys are directed to a more rigorous course in Talmud and Jewish law, and girls are instructed in specific skills and information they will need to become proud and productive Jewish women.

**More to Explore**

Talmud, Yuma 28b; Rashi, Vayigash 46:28; Likkutei Sichot, vol. 16, p. 145; Torat Menachem, vol. 7, p. 283; ibid. vol. 50, p. 43; Sichot Kodesh, ibid. Shavuot, 5734, chap. 5 [end]; ibid. Purim 5735, chap. 4.

# דוגמא אישית

# *Setting an Example*

Instilling a healthy moral compass and building respectable character traits in children is accomplished in various ways. The most common approach is to present and explain a concept orally and then answer any questions. Another technique—far more powerful and effective—is to vividly demonstrate what's being taught and becoming a living example for others to learn from based on our carefully considered choices and behavior. Creating such an example or visualization for others to learn from is what the Talmud means when it says that the most effective way to internalize a Jewish law or teaching is by seeing it in action.

Thus, whether at home, school, camp, or any place between, children absorb what they see. Witnessing the words and actions of parents, teachers and other authority figures can easily become "the final word" in their eyes, with lasting positive or, God forbid, negative effects.

When those in an influential role personally follows the guidelines they are imparting, the child will come to accept and respect their instruction. For example, when a child sees his father and mother observe the commandment to honor their own parents, we can expect that this child will learn and do likewise. The same goes for all other matters, big and small.

This type of teaching is notably different from that of a doctor, for example, who may lecture his patients about healthy practices, yet not feel obliged to conduct his own personal life according to these very parameters. Jewish people, however, are bound to an entirely different set of obligations from that of the rest of the world, and regardless of the role we play in society, our daily conduct carries consequences and profoundly influences those around us.

Since children naturally long for people to admire and emulate, we must remember to look inward and focus on being a fitting example of the Torah values we are trying to impart. Further, we must be mindfully vigilant regarding the people, places, and ideas which we allow our children to be exposed and thus become influenced by. Ultimately, being a respectable role model for the children in our care not only benefits them and their future offspring, but also challenges us to be and become our best selves.

**More to Explore**

Talmud, Bava Basra 130b; Likkutei Sichot, vol. 14 p. 284; Torat Menachem, vol. 45, p. 254; Hiskashrus (weekly) no. 441, p. 10; Igrot Kodesh of the Rebbe, vol. 22, p. 343; ibid. vol. 23, p. 6; Sichot Kodesh, Simchat Torah 5726, chap. 6; ibid. 19 Kislev 5726, Sicha 21; ibid. 10 Shevat 5733, chap. 2 (end); ibid. Vayero 5737, chap. 19; ibid. 13 Sivan 5738, chap. 19; ibid. Korach 5738, chap. 22; ibid. 13 Tammuz 5739, chap. 2; ibid. 20 Menachem Av 5741, chap. 25.

**Bottom Line**

By far the best way to impart moral values to children is by setting a personal example. This is what the Talmud means when it says that the most effective way to internalize a Jewish law or teaching is by seeing it in action. As children naturally long for people to admire and emulate, we must be introspective and aware of the example we are setting, as well mindfully vigilant regarding the people, places, and ideas to which we allow our children to be exposed and thus influenced by.

**Ponder/Action**

- Teaching or coaching can certainly have a positive effect on a child. However, over the long term, being genuine and consistent with our own values may provide the greatest impact.

**Bottom Line**

Our Patriarch Abraham forged a path of kindness and hospitality for his descendants to follow, so that no stranger would ever go uncared for. Inviting Jewish guests truly fulfills the mitzvah of loving your fellow Jew and models for our children the age-old Jewish values of kindness and sharing with others.

**Ponder/Action**

▸ Doing something for another Jewish person often yields more for the giver than for the recipient.

# הכנסת אורחים

# *Hospitality*

Unmistakable with his open desert tent, ready with a hot meal and bed to rest for any weary traveler, followed in the morning by a spiritual boost and gracious farewell, our Patriarch Abraham forged a path of kindness and hospitality that has continued through the ages. Following Abraham's selfless demonstration, Jewish people throughout history provided assurance that no stranger would ever go uncared for in their midst.

Inviting Jewish guests into our homes for a meal and/or providing them with a place to sleep, is a loving continuation of this tradition. In addition, Jewish hospitality (in Hebrew, *hachnassat orchim*) provides invaluable opportunities for us to model Judaism's ageless values of kindness and generosity for our children. Such acts truly fulfill the mitzvah of loving your fellow Jew, especially when performed for people we have never met before.

Our Sages teach that when we act altruistically toward a fellow Jew, God sends down twice as much kindness upon us and our family. Even beyond the Almighty's blessing, enjoying a meal with guests, especially on Shabbat and Jewish holidays, helps forge deep bonds between fellow Jews leaves a lasting, positive impression of our rich heritage and values.

Those looking for opportunities to fulfill this mitzvah can find guests by word-of-mouth, in the synagogue following services, or by volunteering their homes to Jewish organizations that place Jewish students or visitors. For some, hosting people they have never known or met may be a real challenge, but be assured that it gets easier with practice. You can begin modestly and build from there, perhaps by inviting a guest for dinner, and with time—maybe months or even years later—you might reach a point where you can "host another ten" without batting an eye. No matter the number of guests, you soon learn that doing something for someone just because they are a fellow Jew yields more for the giver than for the recipient.

On a spiritual level, Chassidut teaches that every Jewish soul is a "guest" in this world, distant from its heavenly abode. The Hebrew word for guest, *"orach,"* also means "paths" and "ways." The Jew has a two-path mission during his lifetime: drawing down Godliness into this world and elevating this world to a Godly standard, both of which reunite the soul with its source.

**More to Explore**

Talmud, Peah 1:1; ibid. Shabbos 119a; Rambam, Hilchos Avel 14:2; Ohr Hatorah, Bamidbar, vol. 4, p. 275; Sefer HaMaamorim, 5745, Vhiskadishtem; Likkutei Sichot, vol. 1, p. 68; ibid. vol. 5, p. 324; Torat Menachem, vol. 7, p. 278; ibid. vol. 29, p. 19; ibid. vol. 34, p. 311; ibid. 5750, vol. 1 p. 107; Sichot Kodesh, Yud Shevat 5731, chap. 1; ibid. Behar-Bchuksai 5740, chap. 12; ibid. 12 Iyar 5744; see also "The Shabbat Primer," by Nechoma Greisman.

# ניסיונות

# Challenges

The trials and tribulations encountered in life are called, in Hebrew, *"nisyonot"* which mean "experiences" or "tests." The interrelated meaning of experience and test is key to understanding our troubles more constructively. On the surface, difficulties seem very real, their existence undeniable; yet the Sages of the Talmud declare that everything God does is not only good, but also in our best interest. How can we reconcile difficult challenges and even suffering with the Almighty's ever-flowing goodness?

Chassidut explains that everything we personally see and experience in this world is but a very small sliver of a large puzzle that was specifically tailored for our personal growth. The grand picture is beyond our vision, remaining hidden in the spiritual realms. It is thus understandably impossible for us, limited and finite creatures, to grasp the puzzle's ultimate design. Therefore, to effectively deal with challenges in this world, we must place them in their proper perspective. As Jews, we believe and trust that God, the benevolent Creator of heaven and earth, Who is present within all its physical and spiritual realms, knows best how the seemingly fragmented bits and pieces of our life, its ups and downs, successes and failures, weave a unique tapestry.

From this perspective, difficulties are best overcome and their positive contribution to our lives discovered when they are met with resilience and a deep awareness that we can ultimately choose how we react to them, despite how threatening they may seem. With this approach, despondency becomes hope and despair turns into a directed pursuit of practical solutions. At the end, the obstacles themselves help draw out the inner-strength needed to surmount them. And once we do, we not only emerge as a stronger person, but we perfect and elevate a portion of the world along the way.

An analogy for this is the Torah's obligation for Jews to observe its negative mitzvot (the "Do Not's"). In refraining from the forbidden, the restraint itself elevates the world in time and space. It is the positive response to the challenges posed by the negative mitzvot that lifts us above them, revealing a great inner-strength that allows us to overcome any hurdle. The power of a positive outlook was summed up by the Tzemach Tzedek in the Yiddish adage, *"tracht gut, vet zein gut,"* meaning "Think good, and it will be good." Having a good dose of trust and confidence that God, the ultimate source of Good, will make things right, brings about the very positive outcome we seek.

**More to Explore**

**Talmud, Berachot 60b; Likkutei Torah, Parshas R'eh, p. 19b; Derech Mitzvosecha, pp. 370-372; Sefer HaMaamorim, 5708, pp. 94 and on; Likkutei Sichot, vol. 20, pp. 286 and 292; ibid. vol. 24, p. 40; Torat Menachem, vol. 25, p. 157; Sichot Kodesh, Erev Shavuot 5740, Sicha 1.**

### Bottom Line

Everything we see and experience in this world, including our trials and tribulations, is but a very small sliver of a large puzzle specifically tailored by the Almighty for our personal growth. Facing challenge with a positive outlook and absolute trust that God, the ultimate Good, will make things right, actually brings about the positive outcome we seek.

### Ponder/Action

▸ "Think good, and it will be good" is not just a cute phrase. By thinking positively, even when all seems hopeless, we actually create powerful conduits that draw down God's blessings which leads to a positive outcome.

## Bottom Line

When a child or young adult displays disinterest in Torah study or Jewish observances, medical and psychological reasons should first be ruled out. Then, loving efforts of family, friends, and professionals should be employed to draw the child back with an abundance of love.

## Ponder/Action

▸ A warm embrace, kind word, and loving concern are infinitely more powerful than closed doors, a cold shoulder, or a caustic reprimand. Perhaps this is precisely because the former is that much more difficult to do.

# נושרים מדרך התורה

# *Drifting Children*

From time immemorial, parents and grandparents have taught their children to have a fear and awe of God and have invested their heart and soul directing them on the proper path of Torah. Enrolling children in Jewish schools gave further assurance that their children would gain the Torah knowledge and skills needed to lead a richly fulfilling Jewish life. Indeed, seemingly before we are able to turn around, children graduate and begin building their own Jewish homes, continuing the process with their own offspring.

Sometimes, however, things don't proceed as neatly. For a variety of reasons, some children may show a lack of interest in what they are being taught or associate with the wrong crowd and fall under their undesirable influence. Over time, they may find themselves drifting away from their family's values and, God forbid, Torah observance. Pain, blame, and confusion often befall the family and home.

While most parents recognize that some children are easier to raise than others, their children's differences usually fall within a spectrum. Occasionally, however, a child comes along who challenges the family's norms and threatens its equilibrium. In such cases, all can seem hopelessly lost. After medical causes are ruled out, this type of disconnect may rise due to a discordance between the child's emotions and intellect, generating pain from a deep lack of inner harmony. On a deep soul level, the child refuses to accept the status quo until this anguishing dissonance is resolved. Whether brought about by confusing religious messages from parents or other authority figures, ongoing discord in the home or at school, or some other traumatic experience, their inner conflict causes them to be dissatisfied with their lot, which aggravates and accelerates a downward spiral.

Hope, however, should never be lost. In many cases, a child's inner conflict can be resolved through the loving efforts of family, friends, and outside help, such as a neighborhood rabbi, mentor, therapist, or youth counselor, who can help the child reconnect with the values of their parents and ancestors. Experience has shown that an understanding and loving approach—versus criticism, reprimand, and coldness—yields the best chance for healing and lasting spiritual and physical unity. Strengthening our own Torah study and Jewish observance, increasing meaningful prayer and acts of charity, and maintaining a loving atmosphere in the home, are key to inviting God's healing and blessings for them and the entire family.

### More to Explore

Torat Menachem, vol. 20, p. 114; ibid. 5744, vol. 3, p. 1808; ibid. 5745, vol. 3, p. 1946; Sichot Kodesh, Shavuot 5734, chap. 5; ibid. Purim 5735, chap. 4; ibid. Lag B'omer 5738, chap. 23; Nelcho B'orchosov (1996), p. 194.

# נכות

# Disabilities

When referring to people with various developmental disabilities, the Rebbe preferred to use the terms "special" and "exceptional" rather than "handicapped" and "disabled," the latter words suggesting some type of inferiority. This positive mindset, the Rebbe taught, is key to their rehabilitation and care. He explained that according to the teachings of Kabbalah and Chassidut, God has endowed these individuals with powers above and beyond the capacity of an ordinary person, enabling them to overcome obstacles that an ordinary person cannot.

The Rebbe advised those interacting with special needs individuals, especially social workers and teachers, to approach their care with the basic premise that the individual's situation can be improved, regardless of negative pronouncements or dire prognoses of specialists in the field. Science and medicine are constantly advancing, potentially offering new therapies and cures. Caregivers who exude positivity and faith not only empower the individuals in their care, but provide support to other caregivers and even encouragement to scientists to persist with medical research to develop new methods of healing.

It is important that individuals with special needs also be verbally reassured and cared for in such a manner that instills confidence that they are not, God forbid, "cases," but experiencing issues considered temporary and readily improvable with a concerted effort. Obviously, this approach should be thoughtful and balanced, not raising false hopes or making far-fetched promises.

Additionally, individuals with special needs must not be seen as people with limited capabilities who thus should not be "burdened" with religious education or observances, God forbid. Rather, all of their religious needs must be properly served. Consider the irreparable damage if they sensed that they had been removed from experiencing Judaism as it should be, or if they eventually found out that they are Jewish but had been deprived of their Jewish identity and heritage. Conversely, when these individuals are included in Jewish education and religious observances—not just peripherally but in a regular and tangible way—for example, by actually performing mitzvot and observing customs and traditions, it will give them a deep sense of belonging and security. Such positive effects are also cultivated by caregivers putting time and effort into incorporating religious activity into the lives of those with special needs in their care.

**More to Explore**

Letter by the Rebbe, dated 22 Menachem Av 5739

### Bottom Line

People with special needs are endowed with powers above and beyond those of an ordinary person in overcoming obstacles. A positive mindset toward the disabled is key for their effective rehabilitation and care. Individuals with special needs should be included in Jewish education and religious observances in a regular and tangible way, as this further provides a deep sense of belonging and security.

### Ponder/Action

▸ People with special needs teach the world a deeper meaning of love, faith, devotion, and hope.

# *Health & Culture*

SECTION EIGHT

## Bottom Line

Holiness is as likely to be found in ordinary physical things, such as what we eat and drink, as anywhere else. By eating according to Torah law, we elevate all the lower domains, including earth, vegetation, and animal, and thus elevates the entire order of creation.

## Ponder/Action

▸ We are what we eat. When we eat kosher foods, our mind and character traits become more lucid and refined.

# אכילה
# Eating

The various laws relating to foods permitted for consumption appear in the same Torah section that addresses holiness and sanctification. Our Sages tell us that this proximity is intentional. Though food, items that are physical, being related to holiness, an ethereal quality, seems counterintuitive, the Torah places them in such proximity to suggest that there is, in fact, a connection. Holiness and spirituality are indeed to be found in ordinary physical things as anywhere else. Thus, as the noted commentator Rashi explains, the term "holy" implies self-restraint, and in this context, "being holy" means being in control of ourselves, which is also the path that leads to holiness.

To better convey how food and drink relate to the spiritual, our Sages explain that it is not the food itself that bestows life, but the life-sustaining spark of Godliness that sustains it. When a person eats bread, for example, the spiritual life-force in its bulk, fiber and nutrients impart their energy to his soul. The soul is then nourished by this Divine energy, which then sustains and animates the body. Thus, when a Jewish person makes a blessing and eats kosher food, and then uses the provided energy to perform a mitzvah, he elevates not only himself but all related physical domains, such as the earth and the inanimate, vegetation, and the animal kingdom. In this way, the whole order of creation is joined to its spiritual source in a more refined state, something no single physical component can accomplish on its own.

Eating "Jewishly" requires both self-awareness and self-control. For example, our choice of food and drink needs to be kosher, and the person's intent while eating should be not just to satisfy one's physical appetite, but to acquire strength for Torah study, prayer, and the performance of mitzvot. Eating even one kosher meal for the purpose of sanctity can elevate all previous (kosher) meals.

Chassidut draws a lesson from the activity of eating to illustrate the proper approach towards religious observance. No one would ever say, "I ate yesterday, so I don't need to eat again today." Similarly, we cannot be complacent with yesterday's Torah study and mitzvah performance. Just as our bodies require food regularly for its existence and strength, our soul hungers for spiritual nourishment, which is obtained through ongoing, thoughtful religious observance.

### More to Explore

Torah, Vayikra, 11:44; Etz Chayim, portal 49, beg. of chap. 4; Tanya chap. 7; Torat Shmuel, Mayim Rabim, ch.113; Sefer HaMaamorim Kuntreisim of the Rebbe Rayatz, vol. 2, p. 818; Sefer HaMaamorim, 5663, p. 60; ibid. 5713, Vehu Omed Aleihem; Sefer HaSichot, 5703, p. 145; Likkutei Sichot, vol. 10, p. 105; ibid. vol. 13, p. 260; Torat Menachem, vol. 2, p. 70; ibid. vol. 31, p. 44; ibid. vol. 59, p. 348; ibid. 5751 vol. 3, p. 398; Sichot Kodesh, Haazinu 5731; chap. 1; ibid. Mishpatim 5736, chap. 1 (end); ibid. Behar Bechukosai 5740, chap. 11; ibid. Tovo 5740, chap. 90; ibid. Korach 5741, chap. 10.

# שינה

# Sleep

Sleep is both a spiritual and physical state, and an important function in Divine service. When lying down, the head, heart, hands, and feet are on the same level, their natural hierarchy indistinguishable. Similarly, during a dream, our intellect is subdued, which is why a dream can contain impossible visions and conjure opposite extremes. During sleep, the subconscious emerges, enabling the soul's essential powers to ascend on high and unite with its spiritual source, at which time it gives an accounting of its accomplishments that day, absorbs revelations in Torah, and receives spiritual rejuvenation. Once returned to the body, the soul is refreshed and reinvigorated to resume its Divine service.

A principal in Jewish mysticism is that before we can access a higher spiritual level, there must be closure between one stage and the next. Sleep serves as this type of bridge, enabling a person to rise and grow in his or her Divine service. Without closure between one day and the next, the experience of renewal and ascension, of turning a fresh page, would be missing. This is why during bedtime prayers is an opportune time to consider any accomplishments of the day, as well reflect on areas where we may have fallen short, and resolve to improve our future conduct.

In spiritual terms, sleep is likened to a state during which Jewish people are lacking in active and passionate observance of Torah and mitzvot. The Midrash relates that when the Jews lived in Ancient Persia, under the rule of King Ahasuerus, a lack of Torah observance generated a type of "drowsiness" in the Heavens, leaving the Jewish nation vulnerable to the malicious plans of wicked Haman. When the Jews repented and returned to God, however, their actions "awakened" His providence, leading to their salvation through the miracle of Purim.

In Chassidic thought, the state of exile is viewed as sleep. Our metaphorical "eyes" are closed and we cannot see Godliness. Our senses are dulled, and we struggle to remain faithful in our Divine service. Nevertheless, we are reassured that, as with physical sleep, the Jew's essential power is most revealed in the shadows of exile. This power can nourish us during times of despair, comfort us in moments of doubt, and hold us together when we feel most broken. Further, in the same way that physical sleep ends and we awaken with a stronger, reunited body and soul, we pray for God to finally awaken us from the slumber of exile and restore the world's ultimate unity through the coming of *Moshiach* (the Messiah).

**More to Explore**

Torat Menachem, vol. 10, p. 69; ibid. vol. 18, p. 82; ibid. vol. 29, pp. 53-56; ibid. 5742, vol. 1, p. 257; ibid. Erev Simchat Torah 5717, chap. 3; ibid. 5750, vol. 4, p. 90; Sichot Kodesh, Purim 5700; ibid. Mamorim, Purim 5720, 5728, and 5744; ibid. Balak 5741, chap. 18 and on; Hayom Yom, 4 Tevet.

### Bottom Line

Sleeping is a process of renewal, an essential element of Divine service. During bedtime prayers before retiring for the night, we should pause to consider our accomplishments that day, as well as reflect on areas where we may have fallen short, and resolve to improve our future conduct.

### Ponder/Action

▸ Sleeping is an extension of what took place during the day. Therefore, we should be discerning about what we allow ourselves to think, hear, and see during the day. What we view or listen to before going to sleep also profoundly affects the quality of our spiritual rejuvenation.

## Bottom Line

The care and maintenance of our health, which includes a healthy diet, sufficient physical activity, adequate rest, and avoidance of foods and activities known to weaken the body and cause illness is an inseparable component of Divine service.

## Ponder/Action

▸ Examine your current health and hygiene practices for areas that can be improved, and resolve to address them right away.

# שמירת הבריאות

# *Health Maintenance*

Spiritual, physical, and mental health are inexorably intertwined and require balanced attention—lack of wellbeing in one has negative effects on the others. For example, weakness of the body detracts from mindful prayer, focused Torah study, and joyful performance of mitzvot, which consequently prevents the soul from being adequately nourished. Conversely, correcting a deficiency in the soul helps the body heal and become well (see, *"Illness,"* p. 106). The Torah itself commands scrupulous guarding of our health, and based on this commandment, Maimonides ruled that maintaining our health, which includes a healthy diet, sufficient physical activity, adequate rest, and avoidance of foods and activities known to weaken the body and cause illness, is an inseparable component of Divine service.

According to Judaism, we don't own our bodies—God does. We are but its custodian. As such, we must take our wellbeing seriously so that we are able to serve God fully. In this context, the Maggid of Mezeritch admonished his son, Avraham the Malach (Hebrew for "Angel"), so called because of his great piety and rigorous asceticism, that he must fastidiously guard his health, admonishing him that, "A small hole in the body causes a large hole in the soul." By this he meant that as lofty and holy as the soul may be, it cannot serve God fully unless it resides within a healthy body.

The Midrash relates a story about the Talmudic sage, Hillel, who on the way to the bathhouse exclaimed to his students that he was on the way to fulfill a commandment. Noticing their puzzlement he explained, "If civilian caretakers can derive so much pleasure and receive great honor in caring for the marble statues of kings and noblemen that decorate the great plazas, how much more so must we care for our own bodies which were created in the Divine image and form!"

From a deeper perspective, just as the health of the heart is dependent on organs and limbs functioning in unison, the Divine presence is dependent on the Jewish people (its "limbs") to reveal and draw it down into the world through the study of Torah and observance of its mitzvot. Indeed, the Alter Rebbe was quoted as saying that we have no conception of how precious the body of a Jew is to God, for it is through the body that His will is actualized in this world.

**More to Explore**

Torah, Devorim 4:15; Vayikra Rabbah 34:3; Rambam; Hilchot Deyot, ch. 4; Tanya, ch. 37; Torat Menachem, vol. 55, pp. 128-129; ibid. 5742, vol. 1, p. 312; ibid. 5751, vol. 3, p. 384; ibid. 5752, vol. 2, p. 304; Sichot Kodesh, 15 Tammuz 5716; ibid. Yud Shevat 5734, chap. 2; ibid. Miketz 5739, chap. 24 and 26; ibid. 17 Sivan 5740; ibid. 12 Tammuz 5741, chap. 22; Heichal Menachem, vol. 1, p. 223; ibid. vol. 3, p. 252; HaTamim, vol. 7, p. 29; see also "Healthy in Body Mind & Spirit," by Sholom B. Wineberg.

# שיפור עצמי

# Self-Improvement

Mankind's ability for self-improvement, to evolve and progress over the course of our lifetime, endows us with a unique advantage over most of creation, even over heavenly angels who remain fixed in their created state throughout their entire existence. In this context, the Torah compares a person to a tree, which continuously grows and develops throughout its life. Indeed, with dedicated and devoted work, each and every person is able to leap to an entirely new and infinitely higher level than from where they began.

This growth is achieved by nurturing our spiritual core through the study of Torah, mindful daily prayer, and joyful observance of mitzvot, all of which strengthen positive character traits such as responsibility, honesty, kindness, compassion, bringing a peaceful attunement to our world. These practices also diminish and subordinate our lesser instincts to the Divine soul, transforming negative traits like anger, laziness, depression, and others into vehicles for good.

Some people approach change beginning with the question, "What do I want out of life?" Transcendent transformation begins with the question, "What does life want out of me?" Confronting our weaknesses, making better choices throughout the day, and committing to forward growth in spite of setbacks characterize the path to greater fulfillment and self-actualization.

It is true that from the moment of birth, a human's natural and material instincts dominate; however, as the Torah teaches, and Chassidut emphasizes, all of us are gifted with the power to rise above—indeed, to dominate over—these instincts, as opposed to surrendering and allowing them to dictate our attitudes and behavior (see, *"Character Refinement,"* page 85; and *"Mind Over Emotions,"* page 86).

Working through character flaws is certainly tedious and challenging work, yet the Midrash offers a comforting statement: "The Holy One, blessed be He, said to Israel, 'My sons, open for Me an opening of repentance as tiny as the eye of a needle, and I will open for you an entrance large enough for wagons and carriages to pass through.'"

God is on our side, encouraging us and supplying us with the strength we need to improve our lives and reach, even surpass, our fullest potential.

**Bottom Line**

Mankind's ability for self-improvement is also its responsibility. While working through character flaws is tedious and challenging, God is on our side, encouraging us and giving us all the strength we need to improve our lives and reach our fullest potential.

**Ponder/Action**

▸ Every day give us plenty of opportunities for personal growth. It is our job to recognize them and use them as a means for positive personal transformation.

**More to Explore**

Shir HaShirim Rabba, 5:2; Talmud, Shabbat 105b; Sefer Hamaamorim, 5657, p. 39; Likkutei Sichot, vol. 4 p. 1114; ibid. vol. 6, p. 308; ibid. vol. 16, p. 530; Torat Menachem, 5748, 15 Shevat.

# רופאים

# Doctors

Healing ultimately emanates from God, yet the Torah informs us that God desires healing to come about through agents such as physicians and their prescribed medications and therapies. The Code of Jewish Law states that the Torah gave physicians permission to heal, adding that it is, in fact, a positive mitzvah for them to do so. Indeed, in the time of the great Rabbinical Judicial Court in the Holy Temple, when a medical issue arose, they turned to the medical experts of their time. Since the power to heal emanates from the Torah, the doctor's orders are equally beneficial to body and soul.

When physicians view themselves as instruments of the Almighty and humble emissaries of His cure, they become worthy channels of healing capable of intuiting what needs to be done, of course within the framework of Torah law and values. As such, a physician's role is solely one of healer, with no authority to declare ominous outcomes, God forbid, as ultimately all is in the hands of Heaven.

From the patients' perspective, the Rebbe advised that when health issues or ailments arise, patients should first and foremost place their firm trust in the Almighty, the ultimate healer of all flesh. At the same time, they must meticulously obey the doctor's orders in a spirit of confidence and joy, for in so doing they fulfill God's will, which itself generates additional blessings and pathways for healing.

The Rebbe also advised that when a person is faced with a choice between two physicians, one religiously observant but with less expertise, and the other not presently religiously observant but more qualified in the relevant field, the Torah rules that the greater expert should be selected for treatment. When two physicians disagree in opinion, the patient should seek a third opinion and follow the majority.

In highly-complex and delicate areas of medical care, such as fertility treatments, organ transplantation, and end-of-life matters, etc., it is crucial for doctors and patients to seek and follow the guidance of expert rabbis who are knowledgeable in these areas of Jewish law.

### Bottom Line

A physician serves as a channel for the delivery of healing from the Almighty. When physicians view themselves as instruments of God and humble emissaries of His cure, they become worthy of intuiting what needs to be done to bring about healing in accordance with Torah laws and values.

### Ponder/Action

▸ In addition to enlisting help from a physician, a person who is seriously ill should pray and enhance their fulfillment of Torah and mitzvot. This includes having a qualified scribe check all their mezuzot and *Tefillin* to make sure they are still kosher.

### More to Explore

Brochot 60A; Yoreh Deah 336:1; Likkutei Sichot, vol. 2, p. 529; Torat Menachem, vol. 22, p. 148; ibid. vol. 33, p. 193; ibid. vol. 48, p. 332; ibid. vol. 49, p. 428; ibid. 5744, vol. 3, p. 1589; ibid. 5745, vol. 1, p. 562; ibid. 5746, vol. 1, p. 172; ibid. 5746, vol. 3, p. 657; ibid. 5747, vol. 3, p. 338; Sichot Kodesh, Purim 5731, chap. 6; ibid. Simchat Torah 5736, chap. 5; ibid. 19 Kislev 5736, chap. 5; ibid. Simchat Torah 5737, chap. 8; ibid. 20 Kislev 5737, chap. 41; ibid. Simchat Torah 5739, chap. 11; Igrot Kodesh of the Rebbe, vol. 3, p. 39; ibid. vol. 3, p. 298; ibid. vol. 4, p. 444; ibid. vol. 11 p. 202; ibid. vol. 15, p. 39; see also "Healthy in Body Mind & Spirit," by Sholom B. Wineberg.

# תרופות
# Medicine

Medicine that helps the body heal itself is a gift from God. As previously mentioned (see, *"Illness,"* page 106), the consummate healing process includes both medical care and spiritual realignment, the latter involving a mindful evaluation of and re-dedication to Torah observance, for in order to thrive body and soul must work in harmonious unison. In this context, a distinction is made between healing through physical channels, such as medicine and other therapies, and that which comes from Above. A physical cure might entail pain, including undesirable side-effects on the way to being cured. Furthermore, there is no guarantee that all traces of the illness will be eliminated. Healing from Above, however, comes without pain or lingering remnants of the ailment.

In healing a bodily illness, there are generally two medical approaches: healing the specific organ or faculty directly; and/or strengthening the healthy organs and faculties surrounding the ailing part so they can assist with healing the compromised area. When these two approaches are applied to spiritual/soul illnesses, they parallel the two approaches in serving God—repentance and return (in Hebrew, *teshuvah*), and performing good deeds (in Hebrew, *maasim tovim*). The first deals head-on with the deed itself and includes remorse and regret, both of which naturally evoke emotional discomfort. The second creates an environment of intense positivity, which elevates the person from a state of inertia into a space of reinvigorated spiritual service, leaving no trace of negativity behind. Both these processes are necessary in the service of God. Another lesson from the world of medicine: A person can visit a doctor and receive a course of treatment, but unless he follows through with it, nothing is accomplished. Similarly, studying Torah and learning about mitzvot without implementing them leaves the soul and body wanting. The practiced deed is what is essential.

To many who have written to the Rebbe to seek his advice regarding medical matters, the Rebbe advised that in addition to seeking expert medical advice, a person should enhance an aspect of his or her Torah study and mitzvah observance, creating a spiritual vessel for healing. The Book of Psalms (*Tehillim*) should be recited. A qualified scribe should check the person's mezuzot and for a male, their *tefillin*, to make sure they are still kosher. There should also be increased vigilance regarding the kosher dietary laws. Finally, a charity box should be maintained at home and at work.

### Bottom Line

Medicine is a gift from God, helping the body to heal itself. Nevertheless, an ailing person needs to enhance their spiritual condition to aid the efficacy of the medicine. This is achieved by enhancing one's observance of Torah and mitzvot.

### Ponder/Action

▸ We need to know that the best remedy is "healing by prevention," part of which is enhancing our spiritual channels by staying connected to Torah and mitzvot.

**More to Explore**

Sefer HaMaamorim, 5653, p. 267; Likkutei Sichot, vol. 16, p. 518; Torat Menachem, 5742, vol. 3 p. 1224; ibid. 5749, vol. 2, p. 281; ibid. 5751, vol. 1, p. 335; ibid. Simchat Torah 5712, chap. 3; Sichot Kodesh, Bechuskosai 5741, chap. 63; ibid. Balak 5741, chap. 22; ibid. Vayikra 5731, chap. 4; ibid. 12 Tammuz 5733, chap. 5; ibid. Matot-Masai 5741, chap. 1; ibid. Bechuskosai 5741, chap. 63; Hayom Yom, 28 Menachem Av; Kfar Chabad (weekly) no. 1251; Aspaklaria, p. 29; see also "Healthy in Body Mind & Spirit," by Sholom B. Wineberg.

# פסיכולוגיה

# Psychology

People are born with different natures, temperaments, and even genetic deviations that can lead to numerous emotional and mental irregularities. In the foundational text of Chabad philosophy, the *Tanya*, the Alter Rebbe explains that one can find descriptions of the various layers of the human personality within Jewish mystical thought, as well as how they may conflict with each other and interfere with our healthy functioning and our service of God. He sets out clear and practical ways to overcome common psychological impediments such as depression, anxiety, feelings of inadequacy, and others. His approach, which became known as "Chabad," is that emotions and behavior are generally symptoms of what we allow into our mind and what is dwelt upon. He goes on to present a solution that consists of developing a mindset more in line with an individual's basic divine qualities, which eases inner conflict and allows for emergence of the person's innately true and positive character.

According to the Alter Rebbe, human beings are essentially good, and their fundamental drive and energy originates from a sacred, Godly soul that is perfectly good and wholesome. Thus, by fortifying our spirituality through Torah study and inspired observance of its mitzvot, we support the healing of many emotional and mental health issues that are closely linked to the soul. In addition, active involvement with others in a community helps produce stability, as well as peace of mind and soul.

Maimonides writes that although one may have natural inborn inclinations or propensities for certain behavior, none of these can force a person to act in any particular way and that free choice is always present. If an individual desires to do good, he has the power to do so. The free will bestowed by God is decisively all-powerful and this can—and should—be harnessed to overcome those traits that are damaging to ourselves and/or others. It is important to note, however, that the aforementioned concepts apply to surmounting common, normal-ranged obstacles. In cases of persistent mental illness or true psychosis, it is imperative to seek help from medical professionals in conjunction with obtaining guidance from one's spiritual advisor.

Some concepts in modern psychology are complementary with Torah, such that when applied with Torah guidance, a Jewish person's maladaptive attitudes and behaviors can be improved or corrected using certain evidenced-based therapies aligned with the individual's spiritual needs and obligations.

**More to Explore**

Rambam, Hilchot Teshuvah, 5:1; Sichot Kodesh, Purim, 5746; Igrot Kodesh of the Rebbe, vol. 24, p. 247; ibid. vol. 26, p. 158; see also "Healthy in Body Mind & Spirit," by Sholom B. Wineberg.

**Bottom Line**

Human beings are essentially good, and their fundamental drive and energy originates from a sacred, Godly soul. Thus, by fortifying our spirituality through Torah study and inspired observance of its mitzvot, we support the healing of many emotional and mental health issues that are closely linked to the soul. Nourishing our spirituality supports the healing of many emotional and mental health issues.

**Ponder/Action**

- Secular psychology and Torah have some concepts in common, such that with Torah guidance, a Jewish person's maladaptive attitudes and behaviors can be eased and even improved with the help of various evidence-based therapies.

# התבוננות

# Meditation

Meditating on God's greatness and kindness has its roots in the very beginning of Jewish heritage. When practiced in a manner consistent with Jewish law, meditation can increase the devotion of our service of the Almighty. This is one reason why our Patriarchs chose the profession of shepherding, finding the solitude conducive to contemplation and communion with God.

A popular Jewish form of meditation that builds spiritual sensitivity is contemplation of the intellectual profundity of an idea or concept that has been learned and mastered. The next-higher level is meditating before prayer on feeling the emotional energy of that concept. An even higher level is deep meditation during prayer on sensing the concept's inherent divinity.

Meditating on sacred concepts is an important skill for advancing in prayer and service of God, but its practice must be approached with caution. Many popular forms of meditation, especially those used in secular settings, are adopted from Far Eastern faith practices rooted in forbidden idol worship. This includes practices such as bowing, using incense, and performing many of the exercises found in the practice of Yoga. Therefore, one must be knowledgeable and practice great discretion when pursuing various forms of meditation.

Even meditation that is assuredly free of foreign religious trappings shouldn't be used indiscriminately. Most types of meditation promote isolation over involvement, and Judaism stresses that mankind is created to achieve, build, and be productive in the world. Withdrawal into oneself represents the opposite idea.

Thus, we find the directive in the Code of Jewish Law that prior to prayer, an individual should "meditate on God's greatness and man's inconsequentiality." This is to awaken and realign a person's latent spiritual sensitivities, leading to more effective transformation during prayer, which in turn affects the rest of the day. This meditation, however, has fixed times—prior to prayer—and a specific goal—to enhance one's spirituality.

If practicing meditation with coach or a healer, care must be taken that the professional guiding the meditation has precise knowledge of what form of meditations are permitted according to Jewish law.

### Bottom Line

The practice of meditation has its roots in the very beginning of Jewish heritage. Meditating on sacred concepts must be approached with caution, for many popular forms of meditation, especially those used in secular settings, are adopted from Far Eastern faith practices rooted in forbidden idol worship.

### Ponder/Action

▸ Those who practice meditation for stress-relief and other health issues should look for meditation free of attached values, avoiding those that border on idolatry.

### More to Explore

Hayom Yom, 20 Tammuz; see essay "Meditation" (by Sichos in English); see "Mind Over Matter" edited and translated by Dr. A. Gotfryd. Ph.D. (Jersualem 2000); Kfar Chabad (weekly) no. 900, p. 64; ibid no. 1251, p. 40; Ibid no. 1339, p. 37; see also "Healthy in Body Mind & Spirit," by Sholom B. Wineberg.

**Bottom Line**

We can gain spiritual lessons by studying appropriate artwork and applying these insights to our daily service of God.

**Ponder/Action**

▸ Artwork expresses emotions and visions that cannot be easily conveyed in words. The artist should ponder his ultimate message to the viewer, and the viewer should use discretion regarding the artwork and imagery he chooses for inspiration.

# אמנות
# Art

• • • • • •

A picture may be worth a thousand words; some works of art may be worth far more, since by studying them we can gain spiritual lessons applicable to our daily service of the Almighty. Indeed, the Rebbe Rashab once visited an art gallery and spent many hours examining its paintings, deriving lesson for the service of the Almighty. In essence, art is the ability of a person to outwardly express what he sees and what he feels internally, through media such as music, sculpture, painting, etc.. The talent of the artist represents a special blessing from the Almighty and it should be used in positive ways to advance ideas reflective of Torah and mitzvot, introducing and inspiring others to its many values. On a deeper level, an artist blessed with a keen perception of the inner essence of all things can convey the ethereal qualities within objects physical, material, or otherwise limited by time and space, transforming and elevating them to the spiritual realm. This echoes a key characteristic of a Jew's spiritual aspirations—to reveal and elevate the Godliness in the material world (see *"The Purpose of the Jew,"* page 77).

The editor of a periodical for young Jewish children once sought the Rebbe's guidance regarding illustrations to be used in the publication. The Rebbe gave several suggestions, the first of which was to refrain from depicting Torah stories and events, so young readers could imagine for themselves what the subject or event looked like. Another was to avoid drawing the faces of our Patriarchs, since we don't have clear images of what they truly looked like. When necessary, he advised, they should be drawn in profile. Other guidelines included not depicting people in an overly exaggerated style, e.g. hugely fat, disproportionately large nose, etc., and to steer away from images of non-kosher animals as much as possible (exceptions would be when depicting them in nature or when discussing kosher signs) in order to discourage children from forming attachments to their unholy influence.

Regarding art in a synagogue, the Rebbe advised that imagery on the ark of the creatures described in the Heavenly Chariot, or those that symbolize certain Jewish tribes can serve as lessons in serving the Almighty. He cautioned, however, that overly intense imagery on synagogue walls, or on the cantors' stand, can distract from prayer. Also, when the Two Tablets (the *"Luchot"*) are depicted they should be shown in their proper square form (i.e., not with the Roman-inspired half-round cupolas on top).

**More to Explore**

Likkutei Sichot, vol. 14, p. 233; ibid. vol. 25 p. 309; Torat Menachem, vol. 49, p. 362; Sichot Kodesh, 24 Tammuz 5736, chap. 4; Igrot Kodesh of the Rebbe Rayatz, vol. 3, p. 394; Igrot Kodesh of the Rebbe, vol. 4, p. 223; Hiskashrus, no. 134, pp. 10-13; ibid. no. 194, p. 10 and on; Kfar Chabad (weekly), no. 685, p. 26; ibid. no. 860, p. 45; ibid. no. 1072, Mishpocha section, p. 6.

# מוזיקה
# Music

Song and melody are a powerful force and are deeply integral to Jewish life. Regarding this, the Alter Rebbe wrote, "Words are the pen of the heart; music is the pen of the soul." Indeed, music has tremendous capacity to influence with its ability to enter a person's consciousness and touch the soul's very essence. The Torah relates that Moses led the Jewish people in song after the splitting of the sea; the Psalms of King David are filled with songs and praises to the Almighty; and during the time of the Holy Temple, the Levites sang a special "Song of the Day" accompanied by musical instruments.

The Sages of the Talmud encouraged vocalizing prayers by singing them aloud, stating *"kol m'orer hakavanah,"* meaning that vocalization evoke concentration. The Rebbe Rayatz commented that the Hebrew word *"kavanah"* is loosely related to the Aramaic word for "windows." Thus, he taught, our Sages are hinting that melody opens "windows" between our mind and heart, permitting each to inspire the other and transcend any obstructions, such as emotional numbness or spiritual apathy.

This is especially true of a Chassidic *niggun* (melody), which comes from and affects the deepest parts of the Jewish heart and soul. In the words of Rebbe Rayatz, "A Chassidic *niggun* fortifies hope and trust, generates joy, and brings one's home and family into a state of light." Joyous *niggunim* serve to raise a person above his or her limitations; solemn ones reach into the depths of a person's soul, inspiring repentance and a commitment towards personal improvement. Both types express a longing to lessen our attachment to the material and to move closer to God, followed by practical channeling of the spiritual energy gained into more righteous and loving daily conduct.

The Rebbe Rayatz once explained at a Chassidic gathering, that when someone sings a song composed, or even just cherished, by another person, the singer connects to that person's soul on a more profound level than what is possible through intellect alone. For this reason, during auspicious occasions, such as on important Jewish holidays, the Rebbe would instruct Chassidim to sing a *niggun* from each of the Chabad Rebbes. A corollary of Rebbe Rayatz's teaching is the crucial importance of being discerning about the music we choose to listen to, sing and play.

**More to Explore**

Talmud, Megillah 32a; Sefer Haniggunim, vol. 1, p. 13; Likkutei Sichot, vol. 24, p. 429; Torat Menachem, vol. 13, p. 11; ibid. vol. 35, p. 167; Sichot Kodesh, Devorim 5735, chap. 1-2; ibid. 13 Tishrei 5736, chap. 13; ibid. Purim 5736, chap. 9; Hayom Yom, 25 Tishrei.

**Bottom Line**

Music has a tremendous power to influence and create deep, soul-level connections. A Chassidic melody fortifies hope and trust, generates joy, and brings our home and family into a state of light. The powerful impact music can have teaches us the critical importance of using discernment regarding what we listen to, sing and play in our daily lives.

**Ponder/Action**

▸ Since music can affect the very essence of a person's heart and soul, we should endeavor to listen to music from holy sources.

# ידע כללי

# Secular Knowledge

The Midrash states, "If someone tells you there is wisdom in other nations, believe it." Yet there are major differences between the teachings of the secular world, known as *Chochmot Chitzoniut* (secular wisdom) and *Hanochat HaOlam* (assumptions of worldly views and behavior), and the guidance of Torah and Chassidut. Our Sages taught that the Torah is the blueprint of creation, which means that all the laws of nature and of social science originate with it. Thus, by studying Torah and thoroughly exploring the depths of each of its branches, an individual can have all the knowledge needed to fully function in God's world.

Secular ideas and philosophies can lead a person away from his or her genuine religious beliefs; thus, caution is advised for those who must be involved in these fields. As expressed by the Alter Rebbe in his classic work, *Tanya*, the study of secular sciences can defile the delicate intellectual faculties of the Godly soul. God's intellect, however, as it is expressed in the Torah, is intended to sanctify rather than merely satisfying human intellect. The reason is that, at its core, the focus of secular philosophy and training is on the external aspects of the subject of interest, and not the oneness of the Almighty. Secular studies also never acknowledge the existence of something superior to the human mind. When a Torah scholar acquires Divine wisdom, however, it is never separated from its Godly source. His understanding sanctifies and refines his character, while simultaneously drawing him closer to God.

The Rebbe Rashab once said that the success of a pursuit of knowledge depends on "where the middle point is placed from where the circle is drawn." If one sets his anchor firmly in God and the Torah, the resulting knowledge is more likely to be wholesome and complete, versus another person who draws a circle and then goes searching for a point within it. By studying Torah and the teachings of Chassidut, we learn an infinite perspective unconstrained by the framework of the human condition. This process nourishes faith and infuses a proper sense of humility towards the Almighty.

As far as studying secular subjects in order to earn a livelihood, one should do so only after he or she gains sufficient mastery in the areas of faith and Torah study. Likewise, the Rebbe passionately urged educators to delay the introduction of secular studies for their students until they have attained a solid grounding in proper Torah study and religious observance. Even then, their Torah studies must remain their primary focus.

### Bottom Line

Secular ideas and philosophies can lead a person away from his or her genuine religious beliefs; thus, caution is advised for those who must be involved in these fields. Conversely, by studying Torah and thoroughly exploring the depths of each of its branches, a person has all the knowledge needed to fully function in God's world.

### Ponder/Action

▸ Being mindful of the books and periodicals we read or bring into the home goes a long way in ensuring the spiritual wholesomeness and eternal sanctity of one's household.

### More to Explore

Breishit Rabba 1:1; Midrash Pesikta Rabbati, Eicha 2:13; Tanya chap. 8; Derech Mitzvosecha p. 104b; Torat Shalom, p. 244; Sefer HaMaamorim, 5737, Vayishma Yisro; Likkutei Sichot, vol. 2, p. 561; ibid vol. 12 p. 197; ibid vol. 15 p. 43; Torat Menachem, vol. 31, p. 224; ibid. vol. 50, p. 203; ibid. vol. 51, p. 330; ibid. vol. 56, pp. 358 on.

# מדע

# Science

Science reflects the human drive to understand the world, and Torah supports an individual in studying the wonders of the universe in the interest of improving one's service of the Almighty. Consider, for example, the study of the vast solar system, with the mystery of its planets and nebulae; and the intriguing world of biology and plant life, including the complexity of cells and molecules. Both introduce a person to the greatness of the Almighty, while potentially leading to discoveries that could assist mankind in areas such as energy, medicine, and conservation.

Science serves as a tool for searching for the truth about our world, and as scientific technology advances, we often find validation for the authenticity of the Torah and existence of God. For example, science is now researching the fundamental building blocks of numerous elements in chemistry, exploring the possibility that they all stem from one atomic nucleus. This implies a unity behind the diversity—an ultimate demonstration that everything stems from one God. Indeed, scientific progress over the past half-century alone has coaxed the physical world into revealing many of the truths it conceals.

In correspondence with scientists and others on the intersection of science and Torah, the Rebbe has often emphasized that the field of modern science cannot challenge the Torah or Jewish faith, because the Torah deals with absolute truths, whereas science by its very nature is constantly changing and adapting in light of varying hypotheses, deductions, probabilities, ongoing discoveries, and reclassification of phenomena. The knowledge gained is far from immutable, and claiming scientific findings as absolute truth is self-contradictory.

If scientific hypotheses are represented as facts, such as with their theory of evolution that involves scientists attempting to reconstruct the very distant past from data derived over a relatively short period of time, a few decades to a couple of centuries at most, and with far less information on which to base future predictions, this is, in itself, a gross and unscientific misrepresentation (see, for example, *"Age of the Universe,"* page 25). Regarding those who work in the field of science, the Rebbe instructed them to utilize their academic position to introduce Jews to Jewish faith and observance, beginning, of course, with themselves and with their own family.

### Bottom Line

Torah supports an individual in studying the wonders of the universe, in the interest of improving his service of the Almighty. With a correct eye, the more that scientific technology advances, the more it validates the authenticity of the Torah and existence of God.

### Ponder/Action

▸ Science stresses that every theory needs to be tested via a practical method and not just be accepted intellectually without supportive data. This is similar to the proper approach towards Torah and mitzvot, which need to be practiced in a physical sense and not limited only to a person's thoughts, feelings, or words.

**More to Explore**

Zohar, part 1, p. 117a; Torat Menachem, vol. 3 p. 366; ibid. vol. 36, p. 223; Album HaRebbe, vol. 1, p. 38; Kfar Chabad (weekly), no. 649, p. 20; ibid. no. 1402, p. 25; ibid. no. 1215, p. 21; see also "Mind Over Matter" edited and translated by Dr. A. Gotfryd. Ph.D. (Jersualem 2000).

# טכנולוגיה

# Technology

Over the last few decades we have witnessed incredible advances in technology, the application of which has allowed people to live longer, more healthily, and with greater comfort. The development of more productive and efficient farming and manufacturing processes has also led to reduction of hunger and famine in many parts of the world. One monumental step forward has been the utilization of technology to achieve instant global communication, offering people everywhere the ability to obtain and share knowledge, thereby empowering and unifying all. These astonishing technological accomplishments are a demonstration of the Godly forces manifest in nature given to mankind to assist them in civilizing and refining the world.

Our Sages declare that everything the Almighty created in the world was made solely for His glory. Thus, all of creation finds its ultimate fulfillment when used to serve Him. Furthermore, a principal teaching of Chabad Chassidut is that Divine providence applies to every element in creation, including all new technological advancements, like those in the fields of communications and computer technology, as well as the development of new tools for personal expression in art and music. Hence, in the view of Chabad Chassidut, technological progress is not to be shunned, but instead harnessed appropriately and responsibly towards the service of God.

Modern technology provides several lessons for improving our service of the Almighty. Just as a few keystrokes can have enormous, sometimes world-altering effects, a small effort to improve our sphere of influence can produce dramatic results for the good. Secondly, just as a person utilizing a computer doesn't have to comprehend its underlying circuitry to gain immediate benefit from its use, those who fulfill a mitzvah derive spiritual fulfillment simply by performing it, even if they don't necessarily understand its deeper meaning. Lastly, the way a computer provides information in microseconds, providing data that would otherwise require a long time to acquire manually, is similar to the way Torah can aid a person in making drastic, positive changes in him- or herself within micro-units of time. From an even broader perspective, the invisible forces powering the technologies we have come to know and depend on bolsters our faith in what is unseen and not clearly understood, and helps us to be more open to trusting in the intangible and sublime aspects of this world.

**Bottom Line**

Technological advances and accomplishments are a demonstration of the Godly forces manifest in nature, given to mankind to assist in civilizing and refining the world. All of creation, including technology, finds its ultimate fulfillment when used positively in the service of the Almighty. Technological progress must not be shunned, but instead harnessed appropriately and responsibly for the positive service of God.

**Ponder/Action**

▸ Tap into the global reach made possible through technology by setting a regular time to study Torah, and availing yourself of the thousands of classes and resources offered online, such as those on Chabad.org.

**More to Explore**

Likkutei Sichot, vol. 15 p. 42; ibid. vol. 20 p. 417; ibid. 12 Sivan 5740, chap. 1; Torat Menachem, vol. 53, pp. 472-475; ibid. 5742, vol. 1, p. 139; ibid. 5748, vol. 4 p. 178; Sichot Kodesh, Shlach 5735, chap. 20-21; ibid. Noso 5735, chap. 7; ibid. Nitzavim-Vayelech 5736, chap. 4 and 48; ibid. 5742, vol. 1, p. 139; Album HaRebbe, vol. 1, p. 340.

# Around the Year

# שבת

# Shabbat

The day of Shabbat marks the culmination of the six days of Creation. It is a day of peace, tranquility, and reconnection to our Jewish identity. It is a time when the distractions and demands of work are set aside so we are available to become one with our spiritual center. The Talmud tells us that, in fact, on Shabbat all Jews receive a *neshama yiteira*—a special additional "Shabbat soul." In keeping with the Torah's command to "remember" and "keep" the Shabbat, we remember it by proclaiming its sanctity during the recitation of *kiddush* at the Friday evening and Shabbat afternoon meals and *havdalah* at its conclusion, and we "keep" it by abstaining from work as codified in the Code of Jewish Law.

The laws guiding Shabbat observance help us tap its elevated spiritual state, so that for the duration of Shabbat our thoughts, speech, and actions are aligned with the sublimity and holiness of the day. From the lighting of the Shabbat candles before sunset on Friday evening, to the spirited prayers in the synagogue; from the delicious meals that nourish both body and soul, to the meaningful time spent with family and friends, Shabbat is the spiritual and physical anchor for the entire week. By studying and carefully observing its laws, we are rewarded with its many spiritual and physical blessings.

Taken on a deeper level, during the week, while engaged in a task, we invest our intellect and emotions into the project. When it is completed, these capacities are "withdrawn," returning to the bounds of our soul in an elevated state. On a deeper level, there is a similar return and elevation of our numerous focused actions over the week, culminating on Shabbat. On this day, we experience a more intense and profound level of spiritual and physical delight, for the cumulative elevation within our souls is more fully revealed.

In the same vein, the process of creation is reenacted every week by God, as He invests His essence into renewing and elevating the Divine energy of the world. This process is perfected by sunset on Friday. At that time God "withdraws" His creative force into Himself and "rests," so to speak. Out of His delight in His "handiwork," three unique emanations of pleasure flow into the world over the course of the day of Shabbat, reflected in the three traditional Shabbat meals enjoyed on Friday evening, Shabbat afternoon and late afternoon.

### Bottom Line

Shabbat is a unique spiritual experience. It is a day of peace, tranquility, and awareness of our Jewish identity, enabling us to become one with our spiritual center without the distractions and demands of our work.

### Ponder/Action

▸ Shabbat is an auspicious time to experience both physical and spiritual pleasure. Help make it happen for yourself and your family!

### More to Explore

Talmud, Beitza 16a; Likkutei Torah, Shir Hashirim, p. 25a; Siddur Tefilos Mikol Hashana, Shaar HaShabbat, pp. 169 and on; Torat Shmuel, 5628, p. 6; Sefer HaMaamorim, 5562, vol. 2, p. 481; ibid. 5663, p. 61; ibid. 5713, Vehu Omed Aleihem 5713; Reshimot of the Rebbe, no. 15, chapt. 15, p. 54; Torat Menachem 5744, vol. 4, pp. 2547-2550; Rebbe's Pesach Message, 11 Nissan, 5745; Rebbe's letter, 18 Elul, 5743.

# ראש חודש

# *Rosh Chodesh*

The Jewish calendar follows the lunar cycle, with each month beginning at the birth of the new moon. The first day of each month is called *Rosh Chodesh* (Hebrew for "head of the month"). Just as the head of the body regulates life throughout body, *Rosh Chodesh* "regulates," or sets the rhythm for the upcoming days in the new month. The day also symbolizes the *Geula* (final Redemption), for like the moon waning, but then waxing, so too will the Jewish nation be restored to its full glory with *Moshiach*.

The eve of *Rosh Chodesh*, as well as the fifteenth day (middle) of the Hebrew month, are auspicious days for prayer and blessings. It is customary for Jewish people to gather to share words of Torah, to bless each other that their prayers should be fulfilled, and to make good resolutions for the upcoming month in matters of Torah and mitzvot. Giving extra charity on this day is also fitting, as our Sages tell us that charity hastens the ultimate Redemption. It is also customary to study several verses from the chapter of the Book of Psalms (*"Tehillim"*) corresponding to our age (e.g. at age thirteen, a person studies verses from the upcoming chapter fourteen), along with the commentaries of Rashi and Metzudat Dovid. We should endeavor to complete the study of the appropriate chapter in time for our next birthday, and then begin with the next one.

The Shabbat before Rosh Chodesh is known as *Shabbat Mevarchim* (Hebrew for the "Shabbat that blesses [the new month]"), and a special blessing is recited for the upcoming month. It is a Chabad custom to recite the entire Book of Psalms on this day. Regarding the recitation of Psalms in general, the Tzemach Tzedek once said that if we only knew the power of saying its words, we would say them continuously.

Chassidic teachings reveal several lessons based on the cycle of the moon: Just as the moon's job is to reflect the sun's light onto the earth, so is it every Jew's responsibility to reflect the light of God in the world. Just as God provides the moon with all that it needs to accomplish its task, every Jew is given unique abilities to draw down the Almighty's blessings into his surroundings. Also, from the cyclic pattern of the moon we can draw a comforting and encouraging lesson: Though we may experience periods of "waning" in our Torah learning or observance we should never despair and give up, for before long there will be the inevitable "waxing" period, when we become inspired and empowered to grow spiritually, reaching greater heights than ever before.

**More to Explore**

Prophets, Shmuel 1, 20:19; Rashi on Talmud, Megilah 22b; Pirkei D'Rebbe Eliezer, chap. 45; Taz on Orach Chaim, chap. 417:1; Ohr HaTorah of the Tzemach Tzedek, Pekudei, p. 1985; Torat Menachem, 5742, vol. 2, pp. 640 and 1077; ibid. 5743 vol. 2, p. 976; ibid. 5745, vol. 3, p. 2683; ibid. 5748 vol. 1, pp. 104 and on; ibid. 5750, vol. 3, p. 382; Igrot Kodesh of the Rayatz, vol. 5, p. 240.

**Bottom Line**

The first day of each month is called *Rosh Chodesh* (i.e., head of the month). Just as the head of the body regulates life throughout body, *Rosh Chodesh* "regulates,"or sets the rhythm for the upcoming days in the new month. It is an auspicious day for prayer and the recitation of Psalms.

**Ponder/Action**

▸ Make good resolutions on Rosh Chodesh to be maintained throughout the next month and beyond.

Bottom Line

On Rosh Hashana, every Jew has the opportunity to anoint the Almighty once again and receive blessings for the new year.

Ponder/Action

▸ Cherish each moment of the holiday, committing yourself to God and His commandments through devoted prayer and listening to the sounding of the *shofar*, and by encouraging others to do the same.

# ראש השנה
# Rosh Hashana

The holiday of Rosh Hashana, celebrated on the first and second days of the Hebrew month of *Tishrei*, is filled with momentous events of global and personal impact. It celebrates the unique relationship God established with humanity and reasserts its mutual dependence—our reliance upon God for our very life and sustenance, as well as God's self-constrained dependence upon us to make His presence known and felt in this world. Rosh Hashana also marks the anniversary of the creation of Mankind. As such, it is an annual day of judgment by God for all people, when the heavenly court decrees the fortunes of each person in the areas of life, health, and sustenance for the upcoming year, and it is on this day that Jewish people pray for all of humanity.

Kabbalah teaches that the continued existence of the universe depends upon the reawakening and renewal of the Divine desire for a world. Thus, during the sounding of the *shofar* (ram's horn) on Rosh Hashana, the Jewish nation coronates and proclaims God as King of the Universe, accepting upon themselves His kingship. The cry of the *shofar* is also a call to repentance (in Hebrew, *Teshuvah*), serving as the first of the "Ten Days of Repentance" that lead up to Yom Kippur, the Day of Atonement.

On the eve of Rosh Hashana, the Divine energy that sustained the world for the passing year returns to its source and is elevated in the spiritual realms. At the sounding of the *shofar* on Rosh Hashana, God bestows energy from a higher spiritual source to energize the world for the upcoming year. On the soul level, we renew our dedication to the Almighty by reaffirming our commitment to Torah and mitzvot. This is reflected in the three notes of the *shofar* sounding, *terua*, *tekia*, and *shvarim*. These symbolize a broken and heartfelt call from the depths of our souls, which cannot be articulated with words.

Some Rosh Hashanah observances include candle-lighting, the recitation of special prayers in the synagogue, making *kiddush*, eating a piece of apple dipped in honey to symbolize our desire for a sweet new year, delighting in other special foods symbolic of the new year's blessings, and most importantly, listening to the sounding of the *shofar*. A special prayer called *tashlich* is also recited near a body of water (i.e., an ocean, river, stream, or pond) in evocation of the verse, "And You shall cast their sins into the depths of the sea."

More to Explore

Sefer Hamaamorim, 5656, pp. 244 and 263; ibid. 5666 (beginning); Likkutei Sichot, vol. 4, pp. 1144-1148; ibid. vol. 19, p. 291.

# צום גדליה

# The Fast of Gedaliah

The Fast of Gedaliah occurs on the third day of the Hebrew month of *Tishrei*. It commemorates the assassination on the holy day of Rosh Hashana of Gedaliah, son of Achikam, a Jewish governor in the Land of Israel. He was appointed by Nebuchadnezzar to supervise the land of Judah after the Babylonians destroyed the Holy Temple and exiled its Jews in 3338 (423 BCE). Because a public fast day could not be called on a holy day such as Rosh Hashana, it was postponed until the next weekday.

Under Babylonian rule, the remaining Jews in the Holy Land rallied around Gedaliah, raising hopes of maintaining a Jewish settlement in the land despite the surrounding destruction. However, a Jew by the name of Yishmael ben Netaniah, jealous of Gedaliah's position of power, traitorously murdered him. Following this, the few remaining Jews fled to Egypt fearing the wrath of the Babylonians, leaving Israel devoid of Jewish leadership. Their exile had become complete.

Our Sages explain that communal fasting to commemorate such events serves as a reminder of our nation's past misdeeds, leading us to examine our own conduct and to repent. Indeed, on this day, healthy adults abstain from food and drink from dawn to nightfall, and special prayers are added to the morning and afternoon services.

The Fast of Gedaliah occurs during the special ten-day period known as the "Ten Days of Repentance" (in Hebrew, *Aseret Yimei Teshuvah*). Beginning on Rosh Hashanah and culminating on Yom Kippur, these days are especially favorable for self-reflection and repentance, and special additions reflecting heightened spiritual awareness are included in daily prayers. Of course, repentance and calling out to God are always timely, but they are particularly auspicious during these ten days, when we are promised that our prayers and efforts are immediately accepted.

The Baal Shem Tov instituted the custom of reciting three additional chapters from the Book of Psalms each day, beginning from the first of the month of *Elul* and finishing on Yom Kippur. The chapters recited during this period includes the following verse, particularly meaningful and appropriate for this time period: "He will call Me and I shall answer him; I am with him in distress; I shall rescue him and I shall honor him."

### Bottom Line

The Fast of Gedaliah commemorates the assassination of Gedaliah, son of Achikam, a Jewish governor appointed by Nebuchadnezzar to supervise the land of Judah after the Babylonians destroyed the Holy Temple. Communal fasting serves as a reminder of our nation's past misdeeds, leading us to examine our own conduct and to repent.

### Ponder/Action

▸ *Gedaliah* was slain by a fellow Jew. The best way to correct the negative spiritual effect of this heinous act is to increase in our observance of the mitzvah of loving a fellow Jew.

### More to Explore

Prophets, Yirmiyahu, chap. 40-43; Tehillim, chap. 91; Rambam, Laws of Fasts, chap. 5; ibid. Mishneh Torah, Laws of Teshuvah, 2:6; Torat Menachem, 5742, vol. 1, p. 17; ibid. 5743, vol. 1, p. 37; ibid. 5744, vol. 1, pp. 65-73; ibid. 5745, vol. 1, pp. 78-83; ibid. 5747, vol. 1, p. 49; ibid. 5748, vol. 1, p. 89 and on; ibid. 5749, vol. 1, p. 17; ibid. 5750, vol. 1, pp. 28-33; ibid. vol. 4, p. 303; ibid. 5751, vol. 1, pp. 31, 33, 35, 38, and 40; Sichot Kodesh, Tzom Gedalia 5741, chap. 1-9.

**Bottom Line**

Yom Kippur reveals the essential connection between every Jew and the Almighty.

**Ponder/Action**

▸ Following the spiritual elevation of Yom Kippur, we become sensitized to matters previously unrecognized by us as sinful. The inner work we do to prepare for and respond to our new spiritual awareness helps us soar spiritually during the year to come.

# יום הכפורים

# *Yom Kippur*

Yom Kippur, the Day of Atonement, is the holiest day of the Jewish calendar. It is observed on the tenth day of the Hebrew month of *Tishrei*. It is a day on which transgressions between ourselves and our Creator are forgiven, and a day when we are likened to angels, sustained solely by God. Even though Yom Kippur is a most solemn day, filled with fasting, tears, and prayer, there is an undertone of jubilance as we bask in the spirituality of the day, confident that God will forgive our sins and ready us for a year of life, health, and happiness.

Drawing the focus away from our physical needs, the Torah cites five activities that are prohibited on Yom Kippur: eating, drinking, washing/anointing, wearing leather shoes, and having marital relations. These restrictions are also reflective of our being compared on this day to angels, who have no physical needs.

The day is spent in the synagogue, where we devote ourselves to repentance and prayer. Yom Kippur is the only day of the year that has five prayer services, which, as explained in Kabbalah, correspond to elevating one of the five levels of the Jewish soul: *nefesh*, *ruach*, *neshama*, *chaya*, and *yechida*. Atonement is achieved by revealing the core essence of the Jewish soul, which is so pure that even sin cannot defile it.

In Chassidic teachings there are two approaches, or types, of repentance: *Teshuvah Tata-a* ("lower repentance") and *Teshuvah Ila-a* ("higher repentance"). The first deals with sin on its simple, earthly level, with acknowledgment and regret; the second nullifies the sin at its root and restores the soul's attachment to the Creator achieved through the study of Torah and performance of acts of kindness. The inner work begun on Rosh Hashana, followed by the introspection and growth during the "Ten Days of Repentance, " culminating in heightened self-awareness and devotion on Yom Kippur, assure that we fulfill both levels.

The concluding prayer service of Yom Kippur, called *Neilah* (Hebrew for "closing" or "sealing"), is an intensely spiritual time, during which the essence of the Jewish people is united with the essence of God. During this service, extraordinary spiritual leaps are possible as we receive supernatural strength to succeed in our service of God in the coming year.

**More to Explore**

Tanya, Iggeret Hakodesh, chap. 10; Likkutei Torah, Vayikra 29a, and Pinchas (end); Torat Shmuel, 5636, vol. 2, p. 311; Sefer HaMaamorim, 5666, p. 108; Likkutei Sichot, vol. 4, pp. 1360, 1149, and 1151; Erev Yom Kippur 5747; ibid. Ha'azinu 5742; Torat Menachem, 5745, vol. 1, p. 159 (bottom); ibid. 5747, vol. 1, p. 114; ibid. 5745, vol. 1, p. 159 (bottom); Hayom Yom, 9 Tishrei.

# סוכות
# Sukkot

The holiday of Sukkot, which begins on the fifteenth day of the Hebrew month of *Tishrei*, is known for its temporary booths or huts (in Hebrew, *sukkot*) covered with natural branches. These specially constructed *sukkot* commemorate the protective clouds of glory that enveloped the Jewish people during their journey from bondage in Egypt to the Land of Israel. During this seven-day holiday, all meals are eaten in the *sukkah*, leaving the security of our homes, and, in so doing, reaffirm our trust in the ongoing providence and kindness of God.

From a Chassidic viewpoint, in the same way that the *sukkah* envelops a Jew, the Almighty fully embraces the Jewish people with His holiness and love. In addition, the holiday of Sukkot reflects the unity of the Jewish nation, as our Sages teach us that all Jews are worthy to sit in the same *sukkah*. It is also traditionally a holiday of joy, when the Jewish people celebrated the gathering of their harvest. We rejoice with the Almighty, and in turn, the Almighty rejoices with us.

Another mitzvah unique to *Sukkot* is taking, binding, and waving together the four species: *etrog* ("citron"), *hadas* ("myrtle"), *lulav* ("date palm"), *aravah* ("willow"). Our Sages teach that the four species represent four different kinds of Jews: the *etrog* has both a good taste and scent, representing the Jew who excels in both studying Torah and fulfilling its commandments; the *hadas* has a good scent but no taste, representing the Jew who excels in fulfilling the commandments, but does not study Torah; the *lulav* has a good taste but no scent, representing the Jew who excels in studying Torah, but does not fulfill its commandments; and the *aravah* has neither taste nor scent, representing the Jew who neither excels in Torah, nor excels in fulfilling its commandments.

Binding these four species together on *Sukkot* is symbolic of our uniting all segments of the Jewish nation. In this context, each of the four species signify unity as expressed by how and when they grow: the *etrog* can be found on the tree year-round, thus uniting all four seasons (i.e., all four types of Jews mentioned above). The leaves of the *hadas* grow in clusters of three, all of which stem from the same point on the branch (i.e., we all share the same origin). The *lulav* is a branch with many leaves that are bound to one another, signifying separate elements that are nonetheless still connected. Finally, *aravah* plants grow closely together, demonstrating natural unity.

**More to Explore**

Likkutei Torah, Shemini Azteres, p. 84a-b; Siddur Tefilos Mikol Hashana, Shaar HaSukkot and Shaar HaLulov; Sefer HaMaamorim, 5637, Hemshech Vkocho, chap. 87 and 93; ibid. 5733, 13 of Tishrei; Likkutei Sichot, vol. 4, p. 1159.

### Bottom Line

Sukkot is a holiday during which we are commanded to rejoice in recognition of the eternal, loving bond between the Jewish people and the Almighty. This joy is incorporated throughout the year through the study of Torah and the fulfillment of its commandments.

### Ponder/Action

▸ Invite Jews to fulfill the mitzvot of Sukkot, thereby uniting all Jews and hastening the time when, as we say in our *sukkot* prayers, the Almighty "will spread over Israel His all-encompassing *Sukkah* of Peace."

# שמחת תורה

# *Simchat Torah*

The holiday of Shemini Atzeret, which includes Simchat Torah, immediately follows the seven-day holiday of Sukkot, and is a festival unto itself. It celebrates the special relationship between God and the Jewish people, and is the time when the annual Torah-reading cycle concludes and begins anew. Through the community's jubilant singing and dancing with the Torah in the synagogue, the radiant Festival of Joy caps the solemn High Holiday season with spirit and confidence.

According to Chassidut, all the revelations and spiritual advancements generated from our service during the High Holidays are absorbed by our soul during this festival, serving as a source of energy and spiritual enthusiasm throughout the coming year. The holiday also serves as a "second chance" to secure blessings for the New Year. As the Rebbe taught, the mode of Rosh Hashana is one of elevation—our proclamation of God as King of the universe and our acceptance of His kingship; the focus of Shemini Atzeret, however, is drawing down the energies from On High. What is accomplished on Rosh Hashana with solemn supplication, submission, and deep introspection, can be accomplished on Shmini Atzeret through unbridled joy and jubilation. As our Sages assert—joy breaks through all barriers.

While Shemini Atzeret is typically translated as the "Eighth Day of Assembly," *atzeret* also means "to hold back." The Midrash explains that the feeling of this holiday is analogous to a king who invited his children to a feast for a number of days, and when the time came for them to depart, said to them: "My children! Please, stay one more day; it is difficult for me to part with you!" Shemini Atzeret amplifies God's expression of love for the Jewish people.

On Simchat Torah, the final portion of the Torah is read, followed by a reading from the first portion at the beginning of the Torah. This reflects the ongoing upward spiral of growth that characterizes the religious life of a Jew.

The tradition of *hakafot* ("to circle")—when the congregation dances around the reading table holding the Torahs—symbolizes the essential unity of the Jewish people. Just as a circle has no beginning and no end, no top and no bottom, dancing on Shemini Atzeret and Simchat Torah demonstrates the bonding of the Jewish people with each other, with the Torah, and with the Almighty.

### Bottom Line

The festival of Shmini Atzeret and Simchat Torah is the time when we absorb the spiritual richness generated from our service during of the month of *Tishrei*. And what may have been lacking in service on Rosh Hashana can be accomplished through joy on this holiday.

### Ponder/Action

- We can accomplish more through the "feet" (i.e., dancing; concrete action) than through the "head" (i.e., cold intellectual analysis).

**More to Explore**

Likkutei Torah, Shemini Atzeret, p. 88d; Sefer HaMaamorim, 5711, p. 79; ibid. 5713, Lehovin Inyan Simchat Torah; Sefer HaMaamorim Melukat of the Rebbe, vol. 1; 5747, Kuntres Shmini Atzeret and Simchat Torah; ibid. vol. 2, p. 140; Torat Menachem, vol. 13, p. 67; Sefer HaSichot 5704, p. 31; Likkutei Sichot, vol. 4, pp. 1168 and on; Hayom Yom, 22 Tishrei.

# חנוכה

# Chanukah

The eight-day holiday of Chanukah begins on the twenty-fifth day of the Hebrew month of *Kislev* and commemorates the miraculous spiritual and military victories of the Jewish people over their Greek-Syrian oppressors and their Hellenist supporters in the Land of Israel, around the 2nd century BCE. It also celebrates the wondrous event that occurred when the Jews restored and rededicated the second Holy Temple, but could find little pure oil with which to light the menorah. A single cruse of uncontaminated oil that was found, enough to last just one day, miraculously burned for eight days until new oil could be prepared under conditions of ritual purity. Ever since then, the Jewish people light a menorah on the eight days of Chanukah to celebrate and recall these events.

The core conflict between the Greek rulers and the traditional Jewish establishment centered, in essence, on the source and sanctity of the Torah and its commandments. The Greeks' agenda was to make the Jewish people forget and violate the ways of the Torah, insisting that Godliness must be severed from the mundane world. As the Midrash puts it, the Greeks demanded that the Jewish people affirm that they had no share in the God of Israel, God forbid. Simply put, it was a war against God. Unfortunately, temptation and pressure to assimilate was too powerful to resist and many Jewish people became mired in reckless fraternizing with the Greeks, which lead to studying their culture and eventually publicly profaning Shabbat and Jewish holy days, eating non-kosher food, and neglecting the laws of family purity. This lead to the spiritual destruction of the Holy Temple, merciless war, needless death, and ultimately, slavery in exile. It was only through the self-sacrifice and profound dedication of the small band of religiously faithful freedom fighters known as the "Maccabees," that the miracle of Chanukah came about.

Chassidut illuminates that just as the Chanukah candles are kindled after sunset when darkness begins to fall, we shouldn't feel forlorn in any "spiritual darkness" that might surround us. Also, just as another light on the menorah is added each night, we too should always be increasing our religious observance. Further, just as the lights of the Menorah illuminate the "outside," we also should "light up" the world by sharing the practice of Torah and mitzvot with our fellow Jews. Lastly, there is forever a drop of "pure oil" deep in the heart of every Jew, which, when kindled, is able to grow into a flame powerful enough to break through any and all natural limitations.

### More to Explore

Bereishit Rabba, chap. 16; Shulchan Aruch, Laws of Chanukah; Ohr Hatorah, Bereishit, vol. 5, p. 959; Sefer HaMaamorim, 5701, p. 63; ibid. 5670, p. 104; Hayom Yom, 29 Kislev; ibid. 2 Tevet.

### Bottom Line

Chanukah commemorates the miraculous spiritual and military victories of the Jewish people over their Greek-Syrian oppressors and their Hellenist supporters and celebrates the restoration and rededication the second Temple in Jerusalem.

### Ponder/Action

▸ The menorah is customarily lit at the door post of our front door to publicize the miracle of Chanukah. This teaches us that we should never be satisfied with merely illuminating our own home. Our "light" must extend beyond ourselves and contribute to illuminating the entire world.

### Bottom Line

This fast day recalls the siege of Jerusalem by the Babylonian ruler Nebuchadnezzar, marking the beginning of the events that lead to the destruction of the Holy Temple nearly three years later. It is also the *yahrzeit* of Ezra the Scribe, a great Jewish leader who led a spiritual revival in the Land of Israel following the Babylonian exile.

### Ponder/Action

▸ The calamitous events that begun on the 10th of Tevet should serve as a reminder of the importance of Jewish unity which can vanquish—instead of nourish—evil, and draw down God's blessings upon the world.

# צום עשרה בטבת

# The Fast of the 10th of Tevet

The tenth day of the Hebrew month of *Tevet* is a public fast day, recalling the siege of Jerusalem by the Babylonian ruler Nebuchadnezzar during the era of the Jewish King Tzidkiyahu (circa 425 BCE). This date marks the beginning of all the misfortunes associated with the loss of the Holy Temple, including its eventual destruction on the ninth of the Hebrew month of Av ("*Tisha B'Av*") nearly three years later. This is one reason why the fast of the 10th of Tevet has a stringency that does not apply to other minor public fasts, namely, were the date to fall on Shabbat, fasting would be required, even though fasting is normally prohibited on Shabbat. The same is true when Yom Kippur, whose fast is biblically mandated, falls on Shabbat. (Currently, the Jewish calendar is arranged so that the 10th of Tevet never falls on Shabbat.)

During those painful times, the Prophets continually urged the Jewish people to repent and turn to God so that Jerusalem would be spared from destruction, but the people not only ignored their pleas but also mocked the Prophets as being out of touch with the times.

When Jerusalem fell under siege by the Babylonian armies, the Jews, faced with the actualization of the prophets' words, still had the opportunity to halt the wheels of destruction by turning to God and eliciting His protection through repenting and bolstering unity among themselves. Sadly, however, this opportunity was squandered as well. Their shortsighted defiance of the Prophets' exhortations ultimately led to the calamitous destruction of Jerusalem and the exile of the Jewish people.

Another historic event occurring in close proximity to this day was the passing of Ezra the Scribe on the ninth of Tevet (313 BCE). A rousing and inspirational leader, Ezra led the Jewish people out their Babylonian exile and back to the Land of Israel. He oversaw the building of the second Holy Temple and significantly elevated the religious education and practices of the Jewish people. As head of the Men of the Great Assembly (the "*Sanhedrin*"), he canonized the twenty-four books of the Holy Scriptures and enacted many religious laws and customs, including fixed daily prayers, thereby anchoring authentic Judaism for all times.

Between these two events, we can appreciate the power of opportunity wasted versus seized. On the 10th of *Tevet* we embrace the eternal Truth, resolving to fulfill the potential of the day and every day thereafter, by reflecting on repentance, speaking words of Torah, performing mitzvot, and acting in ways that fortify Jewish unity.

**More to Explore**

Likkutei Sichot, vol. 20, pp. 354, 518, 528; ibid. vol. 25, pp. 267, 447, 449, 464, 470.

# ט"ו בשבט

# *Tu B'Shvat*

The fifteenth day of the Hebrew month of *Shvat*, known as *"Tu B'Shvat"* (the Hebrew letters *"tet"* and *"vov"* of *"tu"* numerically equal fifteen), marks the beginning of a new year for trees. It is the season in which the earliest-blooming trees in the Land of Israel begin a new fruit-bearing cycle. Although there is no fruit on the trees at this time of year, new sap begins flowing to nourish the trees. We commemorate this day by eating fruits for which the Torah praises the Land of Israel, such as grapes, figs, pomegranates, olives, and dates.

The ultimate purpose of a fruit-bearing tree, comprised as it is of roots, trunk, branches, and leaves, is to produce fruit. Other ways it benefits us is by the shade it creates and the oxygen it releases. Its roots, though hidden underground, serve as the foundation and source of strength for the entire tree. The trunk, branches, and leaves grow if the tree is nurtured, and at the right time, its life-sustaining fruit emerges. Chassidut teaches that this is a metaphor for every Jew's spiritual makeup: The "roots" that anchor us and provide strength to persevere in the face of adversity is our unshakable faith, which grounds the Jewish soul. As a person grows spiritually, it is this faith that continues to bind him to the Almighty, the Source of life. The tree's trunk, branches, and leaves signify our Torah study, fulfillment of mitzvot and good deeds. And just as a tree ultimately bears fruit, a Jew is fruitful when he has provided the foundation for his children and those in his environment to discover the path of Torah and fulfill its commandments. Lastly, just as fruit is sweet and enjoyable, a Jew's mitzvot and charitable deeds "sweeten" his surroundings and benefit everyone around it.

The Talmud records the story of a man who was traveling through the desert feeling hungry, thirsty, and tired. He came upon a tree bearing luscious fruit and affording plenty of shade, with a spring of water beneath it. He ate of the fruit, drank some of the refreshing water, and rested beneath the shade. When he was about to leave, he turned to the tree and said: "Tree, O tree, with what should I bless you? Should I bless you that your fruit be sweet? Your fruit is already sweet! Should I bless you that your shade be plentiful? Your shade is plentiful! That a spring of water should run beneath you? A spring of water runs beneath you! There is one thing with which I can bless you, and that is, may it be God's will that all the trees planted from your seeds should be like you!" Indeed, may it be God's will that *our* fruit, our children, students, and acquaintances shall benefit and grow from our positive example.

**More to Explore**

Torah, Devorim 20:19; Talmud, Taanit 5b; Likkutei Sichot, vol. 4 p. 1114; ibid. vol. 6, p. 308; ibid. vol. 16, p. 530; Torat Menachem 5750, vol. 2, pp. 252-256.

### Bottom Line

*Tu B'Shvat* marks a new season. It is a time of renewal and reevaluation. Since the Torah compares man to a tree, this day should serve to inspire us to take additional steps toward personal growth.

### Ponder/Action

- We must nurture and maintain sturdy roots (i.e., strong belief), while growing a substantial trunk, branches, and leaves (i.e., Torah study, fulfilling commandments, and doing good deeds) that will ultimately produce fruit (i.e., affecting and teaching others).

# תענית אסתר

# The Fast of Esther

The fast of Esther is observed on the thirteenth day of the Hebrew month of *Adar*. On this day, the Jewish people of ancient Persia united and stood up against their enemies, successfully saving themselves from annihilation. They rested and celebrated on the following day, which is remembered and marked by the holiday of Purim.

The Rebbe explained that the reason the fast is named after Esther is that on the day of battle, the Jews wanted to fast to evoke God's mercy and blessing for success on the battlefield, but they couldn't do so because they needed to maintain their strength to confront and vanquish the enemy. Instead, they vowed to fast on another day. Queen Esther, however, sitting in the relative safety of the palace, did not have to physically participate in the battle and was therefore able to fast.

Another reason given by other commentaries is that the fast is in remembrance of Queen Esther's request to Mordechai to have the Jewish people fast on her behalf, to evoke God's mercy before she entered the chambers of King Achashverosh.

The fast of Esther is the only fast day commemorating an event that took place outside the Land of Israel, demonstrating that even in exile, the Jewish people can successfully call forth God's compassion and blessing through fasting and prayer.

Another meaningful lesson that can be gleaned from this event is that even though the Jews had the full support of King Achashverosh to defend themselves, they still vowed to fast and pray to God, recognizing that they were still in the Almighty's hands and that it is but with His grace and assistance that victory can be had, even in assured situations. This is a reminder for us to always seek God's blessing, even when circumstances appear to be in our favor.

Lastly, the naming of this fast for Esther highlights the special role of women in the redemption of the Jewish people. Our Sages teach that in the merit of righteous women the Jews were redeemed from Egypt, and also from later exiles. This includes the last and final redemption from the present exile, with the arrival of *Moshiach*, may it arrive speedily in our days.

**Bottom Line**

The Fast of Esther is observed right before Purim. It commemorates the fast that the Jewish people of ancient Persia undertook to evoke God's mercy and blessing to be victorious in standing up against their enemies in battle. It reminds us to turn to God in prayer, even when success may seem assured due to natural factors.

**Ponder/Action**

- The Fast of Esther is an auspicious day for us to transform the negative into goodness through the study of Torah, prayer, and charity—the three pillars upon which the world stands.

**More to Explore**

Likkutei Sichot, vol. 6, pp. 371-2; ibid. vol. 17, p. 67; Torat Menachem, vol. 59, p. 407; ibid. 5742, vol. 2, p. 930; ibid. 5744, vol. 2, pp. 1170-2; ibid. 5745, vol. 2, p. 1375; ibid. 5746, vol. 2, pp. 695-697; ibid. 5749, vol. 2, pp. 439 and 460; ibid. 5751, vol. 2, p. 332; Sichot Kodesh, Taanis Esther 5740, chap. 4 and 9; ibid. 5741, chap. 1.

# פורים

# Purim

The holiday of Purim is celebrated on the fourteenth day of the Hebrew month of *Adar*, commemorating the deliverance of the Jewish people in ancient Persia from Haman's annihilation plot (circa 356 BCE). The fascinating story is recounted in the Book of Esther (*"Megillat Esther"*), which is read twice on Purim. In addition to this reading, our Sages instituted several other mitzvot to be observed, all of which express and affirm the unity of the Jewish nation. These mitzvot include sending gifts of two kinds of food to at least one person (*"Mishloach Manot"*), giving charity to at least two poor people (*"Matanot L'Evyonim"*), and having a Purim feast during which one drinks *"ad delo yoda,"* which means "until one doesn't know" the difference between 'cursed is Haman' and 'blessed is Mordechai.'

In the story of Purim, the Jewish leader Mordechai refused to bow before the King of Persia's Jew-hating advisor, Haman. This affront infuriated Haman, who then convinced the king to order the extermination of all Jews on a date chosen by lottery. Following Mordechai and Queen Esther's instructions, the Jewish nation repented and merited the miracle of Purim (*pur*, in Persian, means lottery), during which the Jews defended themselves and Haman and his cohorts were obliterated.

During that fateful period, when the Jewish people were under the threat of total annihilation, they still collectively refused to renounce their faith. The potent Godly essence in their souls was stirred, showing itself in a resolve to defend their Jewish beliefs to the point that they were willing to sacrifice their lives. Even Jews who had assimilated into Persian culture and become lax in their religious observance reaffirmed their devotion to God. Mordechai's public and proud loyalty to his Jewish observance demonstrated to the Jewish people of his day, as well as to all Jews since, that we should always feel pride as a member of the Jewish nation and to conduct ourselves likewise wherever we may be. Indeed, the holiday of Purim is a day that forever provides inspiration "from above," bestowing upon all Jews a supernatural strength to reinvigorate of our beliefs and religious observance.

In the same vein, Kabbalah teaches that Purim is closely connected with Yom Kippur. On both of these days we connect with the Almighty on a level "above and beyond" reason. On Yom Kippur, this connection is achieved through fasting, and on Purim it is achieved through joyously drinking wine and eating a festive meal, and of course, observing the other traditions of the holiday.

**More to Explore**

Torah Ohr - Purim, pp. 120d and 121; Shaarei Ohra, p. 182; Sefer HaMaamorim, 5669, p. 156; Sefer HaSichot 5705, p. 72; Likkutei Sichot, vol. 4 p. 1277; ibid. vol. 6, p. 189; ibid. vol. 11 pp. 323 and 336; Torat Menachem, vol. 36, pp. 208 and 212; ibid. vol. 52, p. 117; Sichot Kodesh, Purim 5749 and 5750.

**Bottom Line**

Mordechai, the leader of the Jewish people at the time of the events surrounding Purim, remained loyal to his Jewish beliefs and proudly conducted himself so publicly. Likewise, every Jewish person should always feel pride as a member of the Jewish nation and to conduct himself or herself likewise, wherever one may be.

**Ponder/Action**

▸ Participate in the observances of the holiday of Purim. Attend a local reading of the Megillah, and involve your children in the festivities.

# פסח

# Passover

The holiday of Passover ("*Pesach*") is observed on the fifteenth day of the Hebrew month of *Nissan* and commemorates the deliverance of the Jewish nation from their bondage in ancient Egypt (circa 1312 BCE). From midday on the day leading into Pesach, until the conclusion of the eight-day festival, we may not own, consume, or benefit from any food and drink that contain *chometz* (leavened grain). On the first two nights, we make a festive Seder meal at which we eat *matzah* (unleavened flat-bread), *marror* (bitter herbs), drink four cups of wine, read the Haggadah, recounting the story of the Exodus, and enjoy a festive meal.

Our Sages state that in every generation and on every single day a person is obliged to regard himself as if he himself had left Egypt. How are we to understand this? Chassidut explains that we can compare the Egyptian exile to the way the animal soul restricts the Godly soul to the point that the latter appears diminished and obscured. In this context, the daily "exodus" refers to the Divine soul breaking out of the limitations imposed on it by the body, and aligning itself and its surroundings—including the animal soul itself—with Godliness. This is accomplished by engaging in Torah and mitzvot, particularly when reciting the prayer of *Shema*, which reflects the acceptance of the yoke of Heaven.

A lesson can also be learned from the matzah eaten on Pesach. As the Torah recounts, when the Jewish nation left Egypt they ate matzah, a simple mix of wheat and water. The simplicity of matzah reflects the pure, essential faith deeply ingrained in every Jewish soul, as opposed to *chometz*, which is "puffed up," representing arrogance. It was this simple faith that allowed the Jewish people to follow Moses into the formidable desert. In this light, matzah is both food of faith and food of healing, fortifying the Jewish soul while nourishing the body.

According to Kabbalah, the eighth and final day of Pesach is a time when all spiritual revelations of Pesach are revealed and incorporated into the soul. This is closely parallel to the era of *Moshiach* (the Messiah; the final redemption from exile) when the spiritual emanations generated through Torah learning and performance of mitzvot during our long and dark exile is revealed in this world (see, "*Moshiach,*" p. 39). In this context, the Baal Shem Tov named the final meal of the last day of Pesach, "*Moshiach's Seuda*" (in Hebrew, the meal of *Moshiach*). At this meal in particular, we reinforce our belief in the coming of *Moshiach*.

### More to Explore

First days, Tanya chap. 47; Likkutei Torah, Tzav, pp. 12c-13c-d; Torah Ohr, Shemot, p. 57a; Shaar HoEmuna, Rabbi DovBer of Lubavitch; Sefer HaMaamorim, 5734, B'chol Dor; Likkutei Sichot, vol. 7, pp. 272–278; ibid. vol. 12, p. 155; ibid. vol. 17, p. 72; Torat Menachem, vol. 33, p. 338; ibid. 5742, vol. 3, p. 1441; Sichot Kodesh, Shve'i Shel Pesach 5748; Hayom Yom, 25 Tevet; ibid. 4 Shevat; ibid. 15 Nissan; ibid. 23 Nissan.

### Bottom Line

On Pesach, we relive the process of going from slavery to liberation. Spiritually, this represents the ability for one to escape the powerful grip of the animal soul, which is primarily consumed with bodily pleasures. On the last day of Pesach each Jewish soul receives a taste of the era of *Moshiach*.

### Ponder/Action

- From the liberation experienced on Pesach, we have the ability to rise in all matters beyond limitations. Going beyond our comfort level in matters of increasing religious observance represents a heightened level of "exodus from Egypt," yet it is within the reach of every person.

# ספירת העומר

# *Sefirat HaOmer*

The time of *Sefirat HaOmer* (Hebrew for "the counting of the Omer") spans the forty-nine days between the second night of Passover *("Pesach")* and the eve of the holiday *Shavuot*. The Hebrew word *omer* refers to the barley-offering brought in the Holy Temple on the second day of Passover. The counting of the *omer* on each evening commemorates the excited anticipation of the Jews for the receiving of the Torah at Mount Sinai and their spiritual preparation for it over the seven weeks between the Exodus from Egypt.

Kabbalah explains that each day of this forty-nine-day period corresponds to a facet of the seven archetypal attributes of the human experience: *Chesed* ("loving kindness"), *Gevurah* ("justice and discipline"), *Tiferet* ("harmony"; "compassion"), *Netzach* ("endurance"), *Hod* ("humility"), *Yesod* ("bonding"), and *Malchut* ("sovereignty"; "leadership").

During the *Sefira* period, we are given an opportunity to examine and refine one of these traits as it relates to all the others (i.e., seven into seven). For example, on day one of the omer counting our focus is drawn to the aspect of *Chesed* in *Chesed*, examining the generous aspect of love; day two focuses on *Gevurah* in *Chesed*, examining the disciplined, balanced side of love, and so on. This alternating type of inner work allows us to arrive at Shavuot and "re-receive" the Torah on a deeper level, from a place of emotional peace and complete internal harmony.

The Rebbe Rayatz elaborated on this point, stating that when we learn a new lesson in life, it shouldn't simply remain in the abstract but should be absorbed and incorporated into our character. As such, the work done during *Sefirat HaOmer* should be integrated and expressed in our emotions and behavior, as we are given extra power during this period to tap the intellect's knowledge and ability to train and control our less-reasoned attitudes and emotions. By doing so, we ultimately arrive at a place where we can navigate life's gifts and challenges with our mind in full control of our emotions.

The Rebbe encouraged the practice of studying the Talmudic tractate of *Sotah* (which has forty-nine pages) during the *Sefirat HaOmer* period. He stated that our commitment to study it during these days, as well as encouraging others to do the same, brings salvation to the person and to the entire world.

**More to Explore**

Aggadah, quoted in Rabbeinu Nissim, end of Pesachim; Sefer HaSichot 5704, p. 116; Torat Menachem, vol. 1, p. 96; ibid. 11 Iyar 5749; Igrot Kodesh of the Rebbe, vol. 4, p. 269; Hayom Yom, 7 Nissan; ibid. 10 Nissan; ibid. 24 Nissan; ibid. 11 Iyar.

**Bottom Line**

The period of *Sefirat HaOmer* is an opportune time to examine our character traits and make improvements in our personal lives, so that we arrive at the holiday of Shavuot and "re-receive" the Torah on a deeper level, from a place of emotional peace and complete inner harmony.

**Ponder/Action**

- Time is very precious. It needs to be counted, evaluated, and filled with positivity.

# פסח שני

# *Pesach Sheini*

Following the Exodus from Egypt, the Jewish people were commanded by God to observe the holiday of Passover (*"Pesach"*) on the fifteenth of the Hebrew month of *Nissan* and to bring a Pesach offering as they had done on the eve before leaving Egypt. For the Jews who were ritually unclean and thus unable to offer this sacrifice on the designated date, as well as for those who willfully transgressed God's will and skipped the Pascal offering, God established *Pesach Sheini*, a second Passover, on the fourteenth of the Hebrew month of *Iyar*, granting these individuals an opportunity to fulfill the mitzvah. Today, it is customary to eat some *matzah* to mark and commemorate the special day.

This second Passover originated from the clamoring of a small group of Jews who were unable to participate in that year's Pesach observances due to ritual impurity. They begged not to be deprived from presenting God's offering. As a result of their pure and self-initiated plea, expressed from their depth of yearning for attachment to God—a yearning that only their distant state could have evoked—God opened this new channel of repair and restoration, which exists to this day.

By establishing *Pesach Sheini*, God demonstrated that the concept of "It's never too late!" applies to matters of Torah and mitzvot as well. The ability to put things right is always there, waiting to be embraced, even for those who find themselves "ritually impure," i.e., lacking in Torah observance, due to lack of education, other circumstances beyond their control, or even willfully. *Pesach Sheini* is there to teach that no Jew is ever a "lost cause" and that it doesn't matter how far a person has strayed, or where he or she is holding spiritually today—there is always a chance to repair and reconnect.

This concept also applies to circumstances not even as spiritually dissonant as being "ritually impure," but wherein a person is still somehow encumbered in his ideal service of God. *Pesach Sheini* teaches that here, too, a person should never despair. The path to spiritual rebirth and growth is always open.

The establishment of *Pesach Sheini* demonstrates the awesome power latent within every Jewish person. When a Jew resolves to connect with God, opportunities are given, doors are opened, and hearts are inspired with help from Above. Not coincidently, *Sefirat HaOmer* (the counting of the *omer*—see previous page) runs through the same month as *Pesach Sheini*, as both share themes of self-improvement and self-refinement.

**More to Explore**

Sefer HaMaamorim, 5738, Lehovin Inyan Pesach Sheini; Likkutei Sichot, vol. 12, p. 216; Sichot Kodesh, Pesach Sheini 5744 and 5749; Hayom Yom, 14 Iyar.

**Bottom Line**

*Pesach Sheni* teaches us that one can always hop back onto the wagon and resume one's relationship with the Almighty.

**Ponder/Action**

- Reflect on the past day, week, and month to find areas of potential inner-growth and do something positive about it. As the famous Sage, Rabbi Akiva, stated, "One who seeks to purify himself, he is helped along from Above."

# ל"ג בעומר

# *Lag BaOmer*

The Torah commands the Jewish people to count the forty-nine days between the second evening of Passover *("Pesach")* and the eve of *Shavuot* in preparation for receiving the Torah on the fiftieth day (see, *"Shavuot,"* on the following page). This counting period is called *"Sefirat HaOmer"* (Hebrew for, "counting of the Omer"). *Lag BaOmer* refers to the thirty-third day of this counting period (the letter *lamed* has a value of thirty and the letter *gimmel* has the value of three).

During the time of the great sage Rabbi Akiva (circa 50–135 CE), a plague struck and some 24,000 of his students died. On the *Lag BaOmer*, the plague ceased. Undaunted, Rabbi Akiva resumed teaching, starting over with just five students. One of them was Rabbi Shimon Bar Yocha'i, called the *Rashbi*, who was the first to publicly teach the mystical dimension of the Torah, and who authored the earliest and most renowned of all the books relating to Kabbalah.

Many years later, Rabbi Shimon Bar Yocha'i passed away on the day of *Lag BaOmer*. Before his soul departed, he instructed his students to mark the day of his passing as a time of joy. He referred to it as his "day of festivity," comparing it to a spiritual wedding day, during which his soul could finally leave the body and unite with the Creator. Ever since, Jewish communities around the world celebrate *Lag BaOmer* as a day of joy and celebration, commemorating the life and righteousness of the Rashbi.

Children playing in fields with imitation bows and arrows, parents giving their three-year-old boy an *Upsherenish* ("first haircut"), and the lighting of bonfires, are all part of the traditions associated with this day. In some circles it is customary to eat carobs on *Lag BaOmer*. This commemorates the lifesaving carob tree that miraculously grew at the entrance of the cave where Rabbi Shimon and his son hid from the Roman regime for several years, providing them with ready nourishment.

The Rebbes of Chabad considered the day of *Lag BaOmer* an auspicious one, and many wonders were witnessed at that time, particularly the blessing of children upon barren couples. People waited all year long for the revelations that took place in the Rebbe's court on *Lag BaOmer*.

In more recent times, at the call of the Rebbe, Jewish communities around the world organize communal parades on *Lag BaOmer* to promote Jewish pride and unity. At Chabad headquarters in Brooklyn, New York, the Rebbe attended the parades and spoke before the thousands of men, women, and children assembled, afterwards watching those gathered march by.

**More to Explore**

Sefer Hamaamorim, 5666, p. 219; Likkutei Sichot, vol. 32, pp. 254 and on; Hayom Yom, 18 Iyar.

**Bottom Line**

*Lag BaOmer* is an auspicious day to rededicate oneself to Torah, mitzvot, and the study of Chassidut.

**Ponder/Action**

▸ Participate in a *Lag BaOmer* event in your community. If there isn't one, make a gathering for your family and friends, share stories of the *Rashbi*, and devote additional time to learning the mystical aspects of the Torah.

Bottom Line

After the Giving of the Torah, the Jewish people were given the privilege and ability to draw Godliness into the world through the study of Torah and observing its mitzvot.

Ponder/Action

▸ Every time we fulfill a mitzvah, we establish an additional cherished connection to the Almighty.

# שבועות

# *Shavuot*

On the sixth day of the Hebrew month of *Sivan*, we celebrate the two-day holiday of *Shavuot*, commemorating God's Giving of the Torah on Mount Sinai over 3,300 years ago (see, "*The Giving of the Torah,*" p. 32). On this day we renew our acceptance of God's Torah, as God once again entrusts us with it. On the first day of *Shavuot* it is customary for men, women, and children (including infants) to hear the reading of the Ten Commandments in the synagogue and to experience the "giving of the Torah" anew. In Hebrew, the word *shavuot* means "weeks," referring to the completion of the seven-week counting period leading up to it. It also means "vows," referring to the vow that God made on this day of His everlasting devotion to the Jewish people and their vow in return to always be loyal to Him. Indeed, our Sages have compared the epochal event to a "wedding" between God and the Jewish people.

The Midrash states that before God gave the Torah to the Jewish people, He demanded guarantors that would ensure the Torah will always be cherished and observed. He rejected all their prospects until they said, "Our children will be our guarantors; they will cherish and observe the Torah." God immediately accepted and agreed to give the Torah. We can glean a lesson about ourselves by observing children. Our knowledge and wisdom can, at times, also be limited, and when this is the case it would be wise to accept what we are taught by those who know more than we do. This was the same belief shown by the Jewish people in preparing to receive the Torah, as they declared, "*naaseh v'nishma*" ("We will do and we will hear"). In this way, they expressed a full commitment to following the will of God, without any exceptions, trusting that deeper understanding would come later. This level of commitment is reflected in our daily spiritual service in which we don't delay observing the mitzvot that are required of us. First we do, the rest will follow.

According to Kabbalah, the millions of Jewish people who witnessed the events at Mount Sinai experienced one of the highest levels of spiritual revelation and their souls were profoundly affected as a result. They also gained a distinct advantage in terms of spiritual service over our Patriarchs, whose fulfillment of mitzvot prior to the Giving of the Torah on Mount Sinai did not transfer the latent spirituality found within mitzvot's into the physicality of the world. Since the Giving of the Torah, however, any Jew who studies Torah and performs mitzvot draws Godliness into the world, permeating and elevating the physical realm as well.

**More to Explore**

Midrash Rabba, Shir Hashirim 1:4; Likkutei Torah, Bamdibar, p. 14a; Torat Shmuel 5629, p. 252; Sefer HaMaamorim, 5655, p. 186; ibid. 5656, p. 386; ibid. 5715 and 5736, Lehovin Inyan Matan Torah; ibid. 5743 and 5745, Bsho'ah Shehikdimu; Sefer HaSichot Kodesh, 5704, p. 127; Likkutei Sichot, vol. 4, p. 1026; ibid. vol. 8, p. 23; ibid. vol. 13, p. 135; ibid. vol. 23, p. 32; Sichot Kodesh, First Day Shavuot 5749.

# צום שבעה עשר בתמוז

# *The Fast of the 17th of Tammuz*

The seventeenth day of the Hebrew month of *Tammuz* is a public fast day, recalling five tragedies that took place on this day in Jewish history. It is also the start of a three-week mourning period for the destruction of Jerusalem and its two Holy Temples. According to the Talmud, it was on this day that 1) Moses broke the Two Tablets when he saw the Jewish people worshiping the Golden Calf; 2) During the Babylonian siege of Jerusalem, the Jews were forced to cease offering the daily sacrifices; 3) Apostomos (according to some historians, a general during the Roman occupation of Israel) burned the holy Torah; 4) An idol was placed in the Holy Temple; and 5) The Romans breached the walls of Jerusalem after a lengthy siege, which led to the destruction of the second Temple the following month. The Jerusalem Talmud maintains that this is also the date that the Babylonians breached the walls of Jerusalem on their way to destroying the first Holy Temple.

Our Sages taught that if there is any generation in which the Holy Temple is not rebuilt, is as if it had been destroyed in that generation. The fast day is an opportune time to confront and reflect on this sobering point. Maimonides writes that on a fast day, it behooves us to learn about the day's tragedies and extract their lessons, as well as reflect on our own behavior and to repent. On this day, we are empowered to spiritually repair the cause of these catastrophes so that we will merit the complete and ultimate Redemption and the rebuilding of our Holy Temple in Jerusalem (see, "*Moshiach*," p. 39).

Regarding the Two Tablets that Moses brought down from Mount Sinai, the Rebbe taught several lessons: The Torah states that the words of God were engraved upon them. The act of engraving makes the letters an integral part of the stone. Likewise, when a Jew studies Torah, its ideas must become "engraved" within him, flowing freely from one's intellect down through all of one's various character traits. Additionally, just as engraving inexorably fuses words with a material, Godliness is forever "engraved" in the Jewish soul and always there, ready to be called upon. Finally, Moses broke the Tablets in order to minimize the punishment of the Jewish people. We, too, should follow Moses's example by increasing our love and concern for all of our fellow Jews. Regarding breaching the walls of Jerusalem, we should take care that there is no "crack" in our own personal "spiritual walls," allowing negativity to enter and overrun our lives, God forbid.

**More to Explore**

Torah, Shemot 32:16; Talmud, Taanit 26b; Talmud Yerushalmi, Yoma 1a; Rambam, Misnhe Torah, Hilchot Taaniyot 5:1; Likkutei Sichot, vol. 18, p. 313; ibid. vol. 23, pp. 275, 277, 279, 281; Torat Menachem, 5742, vol. 4, p. 1870; ibid. 5748, vol. 3, p. 543; ibid. vol. 4, pp. 25 and 28; ibid. 5750, vol. 4, p. 32; Sichot Kodesh, Shlach 5739, chap. 38; ibid. Shlach 5740, chap. 9.

**Bottom Line**

The 17th of *Tammuz* marks the breaching of the walls of Jerusalem. Every Jew has a protective wall within his soul that protects him spiritually. We need to be cautious in order to prevent unholy influences from tampering with and breaching this wall. Even the smallest crack can weaken the entire structure.

**Ponder/Action**

- When the Jewish people are careful to observe the Torah, the world is as it should be, with evil having no footing.

## Bottom Line

The fast of *Tisha B'av* is the saddest day on the Jewish calendar. So many tragedies have befallen the Jewish people on this date it seems that this day was set aside by God for misery and suffering. Yet there is a beacon of light. *Tisha B'av* is ultimately a day of hope. The intense, dark energy of the day will ultimately be converted to even more powerful positivity with the coming of *Moshiach*.

## Ponder/Action

▸ Darkness is only the absence of light. Even a small light banishes much darkness. Our Sages state that due to unwarranted hatred, the Holy Temple was destroyed; thus, due to unwarranted love among Jews, the Holy Temple will be rebuilt.

# צום תשעה באב

# *The Fast of Tisha B'av*

The day of *Tisha B'av* (the ninth day of the Hebrew month of *Av*) is a public fast day. It is the saddest day on the Jewish calendar. So many tragedies have befallen the Jewish people on this date that it seems that this day was set aside by God for misery and suffering. As part of our mourning for the horrific events that occurred on this day, we abstain from many pleasurable activities from nightfall on the 8th of *Av* until after nightfall the following day.

The severity of the day is reflected in the restrictive laws of the fast, which exceed even the restrictions of the fast of Yom Kippur. In addition to not eating or drinking, refraining from washing/anointing, not wearing leather shoes, and abstaining from marital relations, we forgo chairs, instead sitting on the floor, or on a low stool. In the synagogue, the curtain is removed from the ark and lights are dimmed in the sanctuary; lamentations and elegies are read; the *tallit* and *tefillin* are not worn until the afternoon services; and one may not study Torah, which brings joy, other than sections that discuss the destruction of the Temples or other somber topics.

Some of the tragedies recalled include the demoralizing report by the spies dispatched by Moses to scout the Land of Israel, frightening the Jewish people and leading to God ordering the generation to wander in the desert for forty years and decreeing that only their children would enter the land of Israel. Both the first and second Holy Temples were destroyed, beginning the physical exile and spiritual displacement in which we still find ourselves today; Jerusalem was plowed over; the city of Betar fell along with more than half a million Jews; in the year 1290, King Edward I expelled the Jews from England; in 1492, King Ferdinand and Queen Isabella expelled the Jews of Spain; in 1914, Germany entered World War I, the aftermath of which led to the Holocaust; and in 1941, the SS formally received approval from the Nazi Party for "The Final Solution."

Given all this, and more, the tzaddik, Rabbi Levi Yitzchok of Barditchov, succinctly expressed, "On Yom Kippur, one is prohibited from eating. On *Tisha B'Av*, how *can* anyone eat?!" However, there is yet a beacon of light, as darkness is only the absence of light. We are promised that the intense, dark energy of Tisha B'av will ultimately be converted to even more powerful positivity. As the Talmud relates, *Moshiach* was symbolically born at the very moment the Temple was set aflame and the exile began.

**More to Explore**

Sefer Sefer HaMaamorim, 5731, Eicho; ibid. 5744, Balaylo, chap. 5; Likkutei Sichot, vol. 14, p. 186; ibid. vol. 18, p. 313; Torat Menachem, vol. 57, p. 162; ibid. 5747, vol. 4, p. 103; ibid. 5749, vol. 4, pp. 48 and 126; ibid. 5750, vol. 1, p. 135; ibid. 5751, vol. 4, pp. 83 and 99; ibid. 5752, vol. 2, p. 86; Sichot Kodesh, Balak 5731, chap. 1; ibid. Voeschanan 5737, chap. 4 and 8; ibid. Devorim 5741, chap. 1.

# ימים חשובים בחב"ד

# Notable Days in Chabad

The special days below are customarily commemorated with a *farbrengen* (Chassidic gathering), at which the associated events are recalled and positive resolutions in areas of Torah study and religious observance are made. On the 10th of Shevat, 3rd of Tammuz, and before Rosh Hashana, it is customary to visit and pray at the Rebbe's *Ohel* (resting place) at the old Montefiore Cemetery, in New York.

| | |
|---|---|
| **6 Tishrei** | Yartzeit of the Rebbe's mother, Rebbetzin Chana Schneerson |
| **13 Tishrei** | Yartzeit of the Rebbe Maharash |
| **20 Cheshvan** | Birthday of the Rebbe Rashab |
| **1 Kislev** | The Rebbe recovers from a serious illness |
| **9 Kislev** | Birthday and Yartzeit of the Mitteler Rebbe |
| **10 Kislev** | Liberation of the Rebbe Maharash |
| **14 Kislev** | Marriage of Rebbe and Rebbetzin |
| **19–20 Kislev** | Liberation of the Alter Rebbe; Yartzeit of the Maggid of Mezeritch |
| **5 Tevet** | Victory in respect to the ownership of the library of the Rebbe Rayatz |
| **24 Tevet** | Yartzeit of the Alter Rebbe |
| **10 Shevat** | Yartzeit of the Rebbe Rayatz; Start of the Rebbe's Leadership |
| **22 Shevat** | Yartzeit of the Rebbe's wife, Rebbetzin Chaya Mushka Schneerson |
| **25 Adar** | Birthday of the Rebbe's wife, Rebbetzin Chaya Mushka Schneerson |
| **2 Nissan** | Yartzeit of the Rebbe Rashab |
| **11 Nissan** | Birthday of the Rebbe |
| **13 Nissan** | Yahrtzeit of the Tzemach Tzedek |
| **2 Iyar** | Birthday of the Rebbe Maharash |
| **6 Sivan** | Yartzeit of the Baal Shem Tov |
| **3 Tammuz** | Yartzeit of the Rebbe |
| **12–13 Tammuz** | Birthday and liberation of the Rebbe Rayatz |
| **20 Av** | Yartzeit of the Rebbe's father, Rabbi Levi Yitzchak Schneerson |
| **18 Elul** | Birthdays of the Baal Shem Tov and the Alter Rebbe |
| **29 Elul** | Birthday of the Tzemach Tzedek |

# Resources

# Glossary

| | |
|---|---|
| *Achron; Acharonim* | (lit. "the latter ones"), also known as *poskim* or adjudicators of Halacha. |
| *Alter Rebbe* | Rabbi Schneur Zalman of Liadi, founder of Chabad Chassidut |
| *AriZal* | Rabbi Isaac Luria, author of the Zohar, a foundational work of Kabbalah. |
| *Aron Kodesh* | Holy Ark |
| *B'hidur* | In the most beautiful manner |
| *B'rachot* | Blessings |
| *Baal Shem Tov* | Rabbi Yisrael Baal Shem Tov, founder of the Chassidic movement. |
| *Beit Hamikdash* | The Holy Temple in Jerusalem |
| *Bimah* | Reading table |
| *Bina* | Understanding |
| *Birkat Hamazon* | Grace after meals |
| *Bitachon* | Trust; assurance; confidence |
| *Brit Milah* | Circumcision |
| *Chakira* | Jewish philosophical doctrine |
| *Chassidut* | The teachings of Chassidic Rebbes that explore the inner dimension of Torah based upon the tradition of Kabbalah. |
| *Chinuch* | Jewish education |
| *Chochma* | Wisdom |
| *Chumash* | The five books of the Torah |
| *Daat* | Knowledge |
| *Emunah* | Faith |
| *Eretz Yisrael* | The Land of Israel |
| *Galut* | Exile; diaspora |
| *Gan Eden* | Garden of Eden; paradise |
| *Halacha* | Torah law; lit. "the path" |
| *Korban* | Offering; sacrifice |
| *Limud Torah* | Torah study |
| *Maharash* | Rabbi Shmuel of Lubavitch, fourth Rebbe of Chabad |
| *Maggid of Mezeritch* | Rabbi DovBer, chief disciple of the Baal Shem Tov |
| *Mesirut Nefesh* | Self-sacrifice |
| *Mesorah* | Tradition; the Oral Torah |

| | |
|---|---|
| *Mikva* | Ritual pool |
| *Minhag/Minhagim* | Jewish customs |
| *Mitteler* Rebbe | Rabbi DovBer, the second Rebbe of Chabad |
| *Mishnah* | Records the oral tradition given to Moses on Mount Sinai. Compiled by Rebbe Yehuda HaNasi around the year 200 CE. |
| *Mitzvot* | Commandments of the Torah |
| *Moshe Rabbeinu* | Moses; faithful leader of the Jewish people at the time of the exodus from Egypt and the giving of the Torah. |
| *Moshiach* | The Jewish Messiah |
| *Nigleh* | The "revealed" part of Torah |
| *Niggun* | Chassidic melody |
| *Nistar* | The "concealed" part of Torah |
| *Neshama* | The Jewish soul; lit. "breath" (i.e., the breath of God) |
| *Pnimiut HaTorah* | Literally interpreted, "the inner [mystical] part" |
| *Rashab* | Rabbi Sholom DovBer Schneersohn, fifth Rebbe of Chabad |
| *Rayatz* | Rabbi Yosef Yitzchok Schneersohn, sixth Rebbe of Chabad |
| *Rambam* | Rabbi Moses ben Maimon; Maimonides |
| *Rishon; Rishonim* | Early scholar/scholars; literally interpreted, "first ones" |
| *Ruach Hakodesh* | Divine inspiration |
| *Sefer/Seforim* | Sacred books |
| *Sefira/Sefirot* | Spiritual "vessels" which reflect divinity |
| *Shulchan Aruch* | Code of Jewish law |
| *Taharat Hamishpacha* | Laws of family purity |
| *Tefillah* | Prayer |
| *Tefillin* | Phylacteries, wrapped on the arm and head of adult men during weekday morning prayers. |
| *Teshuvah* | Repentance; return |
| *Torah* | The five books of Moses |
| *Talmud* | Fundamental compendium of Jewish law and thought comprising the Mishnah and Gemara. |
| *Tanya* | The foundational work of Chabad Chassidic philosophy |
| *Tehillim* | The Book of Psalms |
| *The Rebbe* | Rabbi Menachem Mendel Schneerson, seventh Rebbe of Chabad |
| *Tzaddik/Tzaddikim* | Extraordinarily righteous individual; holy person |
| *Tzedakah* | Charity |
| *Tzemach Tzedek* | Rabbi Menachem Mendel of Lubavitch; third Rebbe of Chabad |
| *Tzitzit* | Ritual Fringed four-cornered garment |

# The Rebbes

## THE FOUNDING LEADERS OF CHASSIDISM AND THE REBBES OF CHABAD

**Rabbi Yisrael ben Eliezer, the "Baal Shem Tov"** (1698–1760)
Founder of the Chassidic movement, the Baal Shem Tov ("Master of the Good Name") transformed and invigorated Jewish life and the service of God by emphasizing the unity of God, Torah, and every Jew; by promoting the value of Torah study and mitzvah observance among ordinary Jews; and by stressing the need to serve God through joy.

**Rabbi DovBer, the "Maggid of Mezeritch"** (1704–1772)
A chief disciple of the Baal Shem Tov, the Maggid ("preacher") continued and amplified his master's approach to serving God, anchoring it firmly in Jewish thought and practice.

**Rabbi Schneur Zalman of Liadi, the "Alter Rebbe"** (1745–1812)
Student of the Maggid of Mezeritch, the Alter Rebbe ("old/elder Rebbe"), also known as "The Rav" and the "Baal HaTanya" ("author of the work *Tanya*"), founded Chabad Chassidut. His works encompass the entire spectrum of Jewish thought, including mysticism, ethics, and Torah law. He also supported the Jews in the Land of Israel.

**Rabbi DovBer, the "Mitteler Rebbe"** (1773–1827)
Son and successor of the Alter Rebbe, the Mitteler Rebbe ("Middle Rebbe") was renowned for the breadth and depth of his Chassidic teachings and his incredible love and concern for every Jew. He worked tirelessly to better the lives of Jews, both materially and spiritually.

**Rabbi Menachem Mendel, the "Tzemach Tzedek"** (1789–1866)
Grandson of the Alter Rebbe and nephew and son-in-law of the Mitteler Rebbe, Rabbi Menachem Mendel became known by the title of his book of *Halachic* responsa, the "Tzemach Tzedek." He also wrote other works, as well as glosses to his grandfather's works. He dedicated his life to the Jewish people, intervening on their behalf politically, economically, and spiritually.

**Rabbi Shmuel, the "Rebbe Maharash"** (1834–1882)
Youngest son of the Tzemach Tzedek, the Maharash (an acronym for the words, Moreinu Ha-Rav Shmuel; "Our Teacher Rabbi Shmuel"), strengthened Chassidut, combatted anti-Semitism, and prepared the groundwork for Chabad's global reach during his short leadership.

**Rabbi Sholom DovBer, the "Rebbe Rashab"** (1860–1920)
Second son of the Rebbe *Maharash*, the Rashab (an acronym for Rabbi Sholom [Dov] Ber), strengthened the education of Jewish children near and far and spoke out against

the anti-religious trends threatening the Jewish people. He also founded the Lubavitch Yeshiva Tomchei T'Mimim, which emphasized the in-depth study of Torah, Talmud, and Jewish law, along with Chassidut. He is known as "the Rambam of Chassidut" for his profound explanations of deep Chassidic concepts.

**Rabbi Yosef Yitzchok Schneersohn, the "Rebbe Rayatz"** (1880–1950)
Only son of the Rebbe Rashab, the Rayatz ("Rabbi Yosef Yitzchak"), also known in Yiddish as "der Frierdiker Rebbe" ("the Previous Rebbe"), continued his father's lifework. He risked his life under Communist rule to ensure the survival of Jews and Judaism in Russia and Europe. After he immigrated to America in 1940, he continued his soul-saving work in the West.

**Rabbi Menachem Mendel Schneerson, the "Rebbe"** (1902–1994)
Eldest son of the saintly Kabbalist Rabbi Levi Yitzchak Schneerson, chief rabbi of the city of Dnipropetrovsk (then Yekaterinoslav), Ukraine, fifth in direct patrilineal line from the *Tzemach Tzedek*, and son-in-law of the *Rayatz*, the seventh Rebbe of Chabad; is considered to be the most phenomenal Jewish personality of modern times to his hundreds of thousands of followers, as well as to his millions of admirers around the world. Called simply "The Rebbe," he was singularly responsible for awakening and promoting the spiritual growth of Jewish people around the globe. He was a prolific author and correspondent. Thousands of his letters have been published and continue to give strength to those who seek his advice.

# Recommended Reading

## BASICS

**Lessons In Tanya**, authoritative guide to the Alter Rebbe's classic work; compiled by Rabbi Yosef Wineberg; Kehot Publication Society, Brooklyn, N.Y.

**Chasidic Heritage Series**, elucidated discourses of Chabad Rebbes; translated by various authors; Kehot Publication Society, Brooklyn, N.Y.

**Mind Over Matter**, the Rebbe on science, technology and medicine; by Herman Branover (Author), Joseph Ginsburg (Author), Arnie Gotfryd (Translator); Shamir, Jerusalem

**My Prayer**, a commentary on the daily, Shabbat and Festival Prayers; Translated by Nissan Mindel; Kehot Publication Society, Brooklyn, N.Y.

**On the Essence of Chassidus**, by The Rebbe; Translated by Rabbi Y. H. Greenberg & S. S. Handelman; Kehot Publication Society, Brooklyn, N.Y.

**Philosophy of Chabad**, by Rabbi Dr. Nissan Mindel; Kehot Publication Society, Brooklyn, N.Y.

**The Divine Commandments**, the philosophical and mystical significance of the Mitzvot; by Rabbi Dr. Nissan Mindel; Kehot Publication Society, Brooklyn, N.Y.

**Think Jewish**, essays on contemporary Judaism; by Rabbi Zalman Posner; Kehot Publication Society, Brooklyn, N.Y.

**Torah Studies**, based on the Rebbe's talks on the weekly Torah readings and Jewish holidays; adapted by Rabbi Jonathan Sacks; Kehot Publication Society, Brooklyn, N.Y.

**Toward a Meaningful Life**, based on the works of the Rebbe; adapted by Simon Jacobson; William Morrow, New York, N.Y.

## BIOGRAPHIES & HISTORY

**Days in Chabad**, historic events in the dynasty of Chabad-Lubavitch; compiled by Rabbi Yosef Y. Kaminetzky; Kehot Publication Society, Brooklyn, N.Y.

**Lubavitcher Rabbi's Memoirs**, by the Rebbe Rayatz; by Rabbi Dr. Nissan Mindel; Kehot Publication Society, Brooklyn, N.Y.

**Rabbi Schneur Zalman of Liadi - Biography**, by Rabbi Dr. Nissan Mindel; Kehot Publication Society, Brooklyn, N.Y.

**The Great Mission, the Story of the Baal Shem Tov**; compiled by Rabbi Eli Friedman; Kehot Publication Society, Brooklyn, N.Y.

## CLASSIC WORKS

**Beyond the Letter of the Law**, essays based on the teachings of the Rebbe; adapted by Yanki Tauber; The Meaningful Life Center, Brooklyn, N.Y.

**Chasidic Perspectives**, a festival anthology; based on discourses of the Rebbe; translated and adapted by Rabbi Dr. Alter B. Metzger; Kehot Publication Society, Brooklyn, N.Y.

**Derech Mitzvosecha**, reasons behind key mitzvot; based on discourses of the Tzemach Tzedek; translated by Rabbi Eliyahu Touger; Kehot Publication Society, Brooklyn, N.Y.

**Hayom Yom**, classic work by the Rebbe following each day of the year; translated by Rabbi Yitzchak M Kagan; Kehot Publication Society, Brooklyn, N.Y.

**Holiday Maamarim**, based on discourses of the Chabad Rebbes; translated by Rabbi David Rothschild; Kehot Publication Society, Brooklyn, N.Y.

**Inside Time**, based on the works of the Rebbe; adapted by Yanki Tauber; The Meaningful Life Center, Brooklyn, N.Y.

**I Will Write It In Their Hearts**, collection of personal letters by the Rebbe; translated by Rabbi Eliyahu Touger; Sichos in English, Brooklyn, N.Y.

**Led By God's Hand**, on Divine providence; based on the works of the Baal Shem Tov; adapted by Rabbi Eliyahu Touger; Kehot Publication Society, Brooklyn, N.Y.

**Likkutei Dibburim**, collection of talks delivered by the Rebbe Rayatz; translated and adapted by Rabbi Uri Kaploun; Kehot Publication Society, Brooklyn, N.Y.

**Sefer HaSichos**, talks delivered by the Rebbe Rayatz; translated by Rabbi Uri Kaploun; Sichos in English, Brooklyn, N.Y.

**Selections from Torah Ohr & Likkutei Torah**, selected discourses by the Alter Rebbe; translated by Rabbi Eliyahu Touger; Kehot Publication Society, Brooklyn, N.Y.

**Shulchan Aruch**, classic Halachic work by the Alter Rebbe; translated by Rabbis Eliyahu Touger and Uri Kaploun; Kehot Publication Society, Brooklyn, N.Y.

**The Chassidic Dimension**, themes in Chassidic thought and practice; by Jacob Immanuel Schochet; Kehot Publication Society, Brooklyn, N.Y.

**Timeless Patterns In Time**, insights into the cycle of the Jewish year; adapted from the works of the Rebbe; by Rabbi Eliyahu Touger; Kehot Publication Society, Brooklyn, N.Y.

# Study Guide

The following study guide, compiled by Chassidic teacher and mentor Rabbi Michoel Seligson, provides a launching point for those wishing to further their study of Chabad Chassidut. While it is a solidly comprehensive guide, beginning with foundational works and progressing to the most advanced and esoteric, it is neither exhaustive nor meant to take the place of classes with an experienced teacher.

All of the primary works are in Hebrew or Yiddish (the English translations of titles are included for clarity). Nevertheless, many of the original sources have been translated into several languages over the past few decades. Additionally, an ever-growing library of books by gifted Chassidic teachers illuminates esoterically complex areas of Chassidut, as well as provide annotated guides to many of the classic works. These and more can be found in the English section of www.Kehot.com.

## LEVEL ONE

**The Tanya - Part 1: Sefer Shel Beinonim** (The Book of the Average Man); Rabbi Schneur Zalman of Liadi (the Alter Rebbe); Published in 1796. —*Understanding and refining one's drives and character traits, and guidance on fulfilling one's potential.*

**The Tanya - Part 2: Sha'ar Ha-Yichud Ve'ha'Emunah** (The Gateway of Unity and Belief); Rabbi Schneur Zalman of Liadi (the Alter Rebbe); Published in 1796. —*Examines the meaning of God's Unity versus creation, and explores how all of creation exists "within God."*

**Kuntres Umaayon**; Rabbi Sholom DovBer of Lubavitch (the Rashab); Published in 1943. —*Written in response to the challenges of secularism and non-Jewish ideologies in the early part of the 20th-century, it addresses free will, selfish drives, curbing physical inclinations, and man's role in this world.*

**Derech Mitzvosecha** (Path of Your Mitzvot); Rabbi Menachem Mendel Schneerson (the Tzemach Tzedek); Published in 1807. —*Detailed study on core mitzvot in the light of Chabad Chassidut.*

**Likkutei Torah** (Collected Teachings); Rabbi Schneur Zalman of Liadi (the Alter Rebbe); Published in 1848. —*Chassidic discourses on the Torah.*

**Likkutei Sichot** (Collected Talks), Volumes 1–4; Rabbi Menachem Mendel Schneerson (the Rebbe); Published from 1962 to 1992. —*Part of a monumental 39-volume set of public talks given by the* Rebbe, *who also edited them for publication. Primarily on the weekly Torah portion, but also addressing many contemporary issues* *affecting the Jewish people, they are brimming with practical lessons for elevating one's service of God.*

**Torat Menachem** (The Rebbe's Teachings); Rabbi Menachem Mendel Schneerson (the Rebbe); Published from 1951–1970 and 1982–1992. —*Transcripts of the* Rebbe*'s talks, spanning four decades. Primarily on the weekly Torah portion, but also addressing many contemporary issues affecting the Jewish people, they are brimming with practical lessons for elevating one's service of God.*

**Sichot Kodesh** (The Rebbe's Teachings); Rabbi Menachem Mendel Schneerson (the Rebbe); Published from 1951 to 1981. —*Transcripts of the* Rebbe*'s talks, spanning four decades. Primarily on the weekly Torah portion, but also addressing many contemporary issues affecting the Jewish people, they are brimming with practical lessons for elevating one's service of God.* (*In Yiddish; mostly unedited by the* Rebbe).

## LEVEL TWO

**Sefer HaSichot** (Book of Talks); Rabbi Yosef Yitzchok Schneerson (the Rayatz); Published in the early 1960's. —*Transcripts of the* Rebbe*'s talks during this time period, edited by the Previous* Rebbe.

**Likutei Diburim,** volumes 1–4 (Collected Sayings); Rabbi Yosef Yitzchok Schneerson (the Rayatz); Published from the 1930's through 1943. —*Transcripts of the Previous Rebbe's talks during this time period.*

**Sefer HaMaamorim, Kuntreisim** (Collected Discourses), volumes 1–3; Rabbi Yosef Yitzchok Schneerson (the Rayatz); Published from 1928 to 1931. —*Chassidic discourses of the Previous Rebbe on various Chassidic themes, distinguished by their detailed logic and easy-to-grasp style.*

**Sefer HaMaamorim,** (Book of Discourses), 5701–2; Rabbi Yosef Yitzchok Schneerson (the Rayatz); Published in 1941 and 1942. —*Chassidic discourses of the Previous Rebbe on various concepts, including explanations of certain prayers.*

**Torah Ohr** (Torah of Light); Rabbi Schneur Zalman of Liadi (the Alter Rebbe); Published in 1837. —*Chassidic discourses on the first two books of the Torah, as well as on the holidays of Chanuka and Purim.*

**Sefer Hamaamorim** (Book of Discourses), 5727–5749; Rabbi Menachem Mendel Schneerson (the Rebbe); Published from 1967 to 1989. —*Chassidic discourses on many areas of Torah, including Jewish festivals, with an emphasis on practical Divine service.*

**Sefer Hamaamorim** (Book of Discourses), 5654–56; Rabbi Sholom DovBer of Lubavitch (the Rashab); Published in 1983–1984. —*Chassidic discourses on the Torah and Jewish festivals.*

**Sefer Hamaamorim** (Book of Discourses), 5679–5680; Rabbi Sholom DovBer of Lubavitch (the Rashab); Published in 1979. *—Chassidic discourses on the Torah and Jewish festivals.*

**Torat Chaim** (Living Torah), *Breishit/Shemot*; Rabbi DovBer of Lubavitch (the Mitteler Rebbe); Published 1826 (*Breishit*); 1947 (*Shemot*). *—Chassidic discourses on the Torah and Jewish festivals.*

**Ateres Rosh** (Crown); Rabbi DovBer of Lubavitch (the Mitteler Rebbe); Published in 1821. *—Chassidic discourses on Rosh Hashana and Yom Kippur.*

**Shaarei Orah** (Gates of Light); Rabbi DovBer of Lubavitch (the Mitteler Rebbe); Published in 1822. *—Chassidic discourses on Chanuka and Purim.*

**Shaar Ho-Emuna** (Gate of Faith); Rabbi DovBer of Lubavitch (the Mitteler Rebbe); Published in 1822. *—Chassidic discourses on Pesach.*

**Likkutei Torah/Torat Shmuel**; Rabbi Shmuel Schneerson (Maharash); Published in 1945. *—Chassidic discourses on the Torah and Jewish festivals.*

## LEVEL THREE

**Sefer HaMaamorim** (Book of Discourses), 5680–5710; Rabbi Yosef Yitzchok Schneerson (the Rayatz); Published between 1920 and 1950. *—Chassidic discourses of the Previous* Rebbe *on various concepts.*

**Sefer HaMaamorim** (Book of Discourses), 5711–5725; Rabbi Menachem Mendel Schneerson (the Rebbe); Published from 1951 to 1965. *—Chassidic discourses on many areas of Torah, including Jewish festivals, with an emphasis on practical Divine service.*

**Sefer HaMaamorim Mlukat** (Book of Selected Discourses), 6 vols.; Rabbi Menachem Mendel Schneerson (the Rebbe); Published from 1951 to 1981. *—Chassidic discourses on many areas of Torah, including Jewish festivals, with an emphasis on practical Divine service. Edited by the Rebbe.*

**Sefer HaMaamorim 5659**; Rabbi Sholom DovBer of Lubavitch (the Rashab); Published in 1976. *—Chassidic discourses on the Torah and Jewish festivals.*

**Sefer HaMaamorim 5660–5665**; Rabbi Sholom DovBer of Lubavitch (the Rashab); Published in 1982. *—Chassidic discourses on the Torah and Jewish festivals.*

**Sefer HaMaamorim 5666** (Samach Vov); Rabbi Sholom DovBer of Lubavitch (the Rashab); Published in 1970. *—Chassidic discourses on the Torah and Jewish festivals.*

**Sefer HaMaamorim 5672** (Ayin Beit); Rabbi Sholom DovBer of Lubavitch (the Rashab); Published from 1912 to 1915. *—Chassidic discourses on the Torah and Jewish festivals.*

**Sefer HaMaamorim - Maamorei Admur Hazoken** (Book of Discourses of the Alter Rebbe); Rabbi Schneur Zalman of Liadi (the Alter Rebbe); Published from 1791 to 1812. *—Chassidic discourses on the Torah and Jewish festivals.*

**Shaar Ha-Yichud** (Gate of Unity); Rabbi DovBer of Lubavitch (the Mitteler Rebbe); Published in 1820. *—Explaining the chain of creation as one expression of the Almighty.*

**Ohr Hatorah** (Light of Torah), 45 volumes; Rabbi Menachem Mendel Schneerson (the Tzemach Tzedek); Published between 1805 and 1866. *—Chassidic discourses on the Torah portion,* Talmud, *prayer, and Jewish festivals.*

# Listing of Works Cited

**WORKS IN HEBREW**

Album HaRebbe
Aspaklaria
Bach on Shulchan Aruch
Ben Ish Chai
Biurei HaZohar
Biurim L'Pirkei Avot
Breishit Rabba
Chida Lev Dovid
Derech Mitzvosecha
Gevurto Shel Torah
Ginze Yosef
Hamelech Bemisibo
Hayom Yom
Heichal Menachem
Hilchot Talmud Torah (Alter Rebbe)
Hiskashrus (weekly)
Ibn Ezra
Igrot Kodesh of the Rayatz
Igrot Kodesh of the Rebbe
Kfar Chabad (weekly)
Kuntres HaTefilla
Kuntres U'Mayon
Likkutei Dibburim
Likkutei Sichot
Likkutei Torah
Maamorim of the Alter Rebbe
Maamorim of the Mitteler Rebbe
Maharsho
Menachem Tzion
Midrash Pesikta Rabbati
Midrash Rabbah
Midrash Sechel Tov
Midrash Vayikra Rabbah
Midrash Tanchuma
Mishne Torah
Mishvochei HaRebbe
Nelcho B'orchosov
Ohr Hachaim on the Torah
Ohr HaTorah
Pirkei Avot
Pirkei D'Rebbe Eliezer
Prophets
Rabbeinu Nissim (Aggada)
Rama on Choshen Mishpat
Rambam, Mishne Torah
Ramban on Torah
Reshimos of the Rebbe
Responsa Minchas Elazar
Sefer Hachinuch
Sefer HaLikutim of the Tzemach Tzedek
Sefer HaMaamorim of the Rebbe
Sefer HaMaftechos L'Sichot Kodesh
Sefer HaMinhagim Chabad
Sefer Hamitzvot
Sefer HaSichot of the Rayatz
Sefer Pirush Hamilos
Sh'mot Rabba
Shaar Habchira by the Mitteler Rebbe
Shaar HoEmuna
Shaarei Ohra
Shaarei Teshuvah by the Mitteler Rebbe

Shir Hashirim
Shomer Emunim
Shulchan Aruch
Shulchan Aruch Harav
Sichot Kodesh
Siddur Tefilos Mikol Hashana
Talmud Bavli
Talmud Yerushalmi
Tanya
The Ramban
The Torah
Toldos Reb Yitzchok Eizik of Homil
Torah Ohr
Torat Chaim
Torat Menachem
Torat Shmuel
Torat Sholom
Tzemach Tzedek Responsa
Y'Mei Breishit
Yagdil Torah (periodical)
Yom Malkeinu (kovetz)
Ziv HaShemot
Zohar
Zohar Chodosh

**WORKS IN ENGLISH**

Going Kosher in 30 Days
Jewish Mourner's Companion
Mind Over Matter
On the Essence of Chassidus
The Chassidic Approach to Joy
The Letter and the Spirit (vol 1.)
The Philosophy of Chabad
The Thought for the Week